C000174136

From the River to the Sea:

Aquitaine, A Place for Me.

From the River to the Sea:

Aquitaine, A Place for Me.

Basia Gordon

Matador
9 Priory Business Park,
Wistow Road, Kibworth Beauchamp,
Leicestershire. LE8 0RX
Tel: 0116 279 2299
Email: books@troubador.co.uk
Web: www.troubador.co.uk/matador
Twitter: @matadorbooks

ISBN 978 1800461 352

British Library Cataloguing in Publication Data.
A catalogue record for this book is available from the British Library.

Printed and bound in the UK by TJ Books Limited, Padstow, Cornwall
Typeset in 11pt Minion Pro by Troubador Publishing Ltd, Leicester, UK

Matador is an imprint of Troubador Publishing Ltd

For Gerry
fellow terroir-ist

In Memoriam.
Sharon Lancaster
22/12/61 – 3/10/20
What larks we had.

'A rat race is for rats. We're not rats. We're human beings. Reject the insidious pressures in society that would blunt your critical faculties to all that is happening around you, that would caution silence in the face of injustice lest you jeopardise your chances of promotion and self-advancement. This is how it starts and before you know where you are, you're a fully paid-up member of the rat-pack. The price is too high. It entails the loss of your dignity and human spirit.'

Excerpt from Jimmy Reid's inaugural speech as Rector
of Glasgow University, 28th April 1972.

Laissez votre rêve s'emparer de votre vie avant que
votre vie ne s'empare de votre rêve.

Let your dream take over your life rather than
your life take over your dream.

CONTENTS

SUMMER 2018

AUTUMN 2018

One

THERE IS ALWAYS A BEGINNING

Half-island house: that's really what Coutal should have been called. This charming wreck in a field in a *bled perdu* – a godforsaken place, lost to the world. We would never quite belong there, half-marooned, half-anchored to it as we were. We would always be regarded as foreigners, invariably referred to locally by the misnomer *Les Anglais*.

The estate agent, the round-faced Mr Applebee from Eymet, had shown my father around several houses in various states of disrepair, pointing out helpfully if a British or Dutch community lived nearby, at which my father had always baulked and refused to proceed any further. He had wanted to live in a place where only French people lived, where he would be able to work the land and rebuild the house himself, far from the madding crowd, far from any airport. A place to which no tourist would flock. Aloof and not given to small talk, my father did not wish to be part of any club. What better time to realise his dream than in 1973, the year when Britain would at last join the EEC, the European Economic Community? Property could be bought for a song. No young locals wanted to be burdened by these crumbling money pits that littered the landscape. And many an expat, full of happy expectation, who took the risk and invested in one of these semi-ruins, watched as their money disappeared into a black hole and their hopes morphed into disappointment.

In the ensuing years since that purchase by my father, Coutal has come to be my *point de repère* – my point of reference – where I have experienced unbridled joy and the depths of despair. I have known seriousness and silliness there, both in equal measure. It is more than a house; it is a presence, a backdrop which charts all the varying stages of my life: from happy child to truculent teenager, from anxious young adult to married mother and grounded woman, happier as I age and mature. I am like wine and cheese.

Who would have thought, all these years later, that I would regard this stone house as the start of a new adventure with my new partner, Gerry? It has proved to be our ultimate *défi* – challenge – which will test our relationship, resourcefulness – and resources.

Up to the age of twelve, and before the fall of the Iron Curtain, I spent my summer holidays in a communist country. My two sisters and I would be bundled into a Hillman Imp, with our legs dangling out of the back windows (in the days before seatbelts), and be driven by my parents for days on end, through France, Germany and Austria, munching *szynka* sandwiches, until we reached a campsite in the Eastern Bloc where our extended family was already waiting to welcome us.

Both my parents were Polish, although a generation apart: my father born in 1924 and my mother in 1939. My father (whom I called *Tatuś*) enjoyed his youth in a hiatus when Poland was at last independent, but my mother's early years were scarred by war and trauma. This in itself created a gulf between them. They were dissimilar in many other ways: my father quiet, analytical and self-contained and my mother fiery, mercurial, adventurous and sociable. This rootless, unlikely couple found each other in Glasgow.

My father had made his way through ravaged Poland as a soldier, to Italy, and then arrived as a refugee in Britain. Like many exiled Poles, he was reluctant to go back to an uncertain future in Soviet-held Poland, especially later when he was working in scientific research. He was deemed an 'enemy of the state' and never saw his homeland again. Years later I discovered he was working on the secret nuclear Poseidon project in Britain; no doubt the radiation he encountered in his work contributed to his early death.

My mother – or *Moosh* as I affectionately call her – is still alive and kicking and only now does she give talks to the public about her early life. I am aware that if I say anything contentious about her I will be more dead than alive. She was born in Warsaw, a capital city that was razed to the ground by the Germans as the Russians watched from the other side of the Vistula River. Only about 1,000 people – wraiths – were left in the city at the end of the war, wandering around the devastation.

Miraculously, my mother managed to survive many near-death experiences in Warsaw and Krakow. Maybe this is why she is unsentimental, resourceful, and tenacious. She rarely harks back to the past and is completely focused on the future. My mother witnessed the survivors of Auschwitz, in their tattered clothing, being helped out of lorries and brought to the central marketplace in Krakow. Towards the end of the war, this lice-ridden, emaciated child, who had lost both her parents in the chaos, would crawl through a window into Gestapo headquarters in Krakow to steal envelopes. She managed to survive by selling them in the street.

The Red Cross gathered these children together at the end of the war. One old lady who had bought envelopes from her recognised her as her nephew's daughter and took her into her own home. My mother instinctively knew as a child that to ask about her own parents was a taboo subject (the Soviet reprisals before Stalin's death were in full swing), but eventually, as an adult, she discovered that her father was alive and living in Scotland. He had been a Polish officer, arrested by the Soviets in the early days of the war. He was one of the very few to survive Siberia, by walking across the Steppes to Tashkent with General Anders' Polish Army in exile. After he crossed the Caspian Sea, his odyssey took him to South Africa, where he joined the British Forces and travelled to Palestine before coorying down in the safe harbour of Scotland. He met my father, a fellow Polish soldier in exile, who had arrived there via Italy.

And so it was in the late 1950s that this young woman, my mother – full of trepidation – travelled from the East to the West to meet her own father in Scotland for the first time. Three years later she was married to his friend (my father); she heard Édith Piaf sing at the Olympia in Paris on their honeymoon and had two children by the time she was twenty-two. My grandfather had remarried, to a Scottish lady, whom we called our Auntie Margaret. She had been a nurse from Perthshire and delivered me on the kitchen floor in a Glasgow tenement flat across from the River Kelvin. She often said that hers was the first face I ever saw.

My mother was anxious to leave the tenement flat because she was frightened that we children would run across the road and tumble into the river and drown. They moved when I was two years old.

My grandfather and Auntie Margaret had two children, around the same age as me and my elder sister, so we all lived as an extended family, living next door to each other in a Glasgow suburb where, apart from the recently arrived Ugandan Asians, we were the only foreigners around.

Indeed, we lived in a foreign bubble; all my parents' friends were Polish and played endless games of bridge together. Polish was spoken at home. My mother cooked the most delicious Polish food and every Saturday morning we were dragged to Polish school, moaning about the fact that we had to go to school six days a week.

My grandfather recounted bedtime stories of Siberia (no fairytales for us) and told us the happiest time for him had been the inter-war period in Poland (1918 till 1939) when Poland was free after 123 years of partition and oppression.

In the autumn, our family would compete with the Italians for the best mushroom sites in the Scottish forests and the sea of bottoms sticking out from the undergrowth would always be a tell-tale sign of good fungi pickings.

My mother was very glamorous and I can see her in my mind's eye in a pink leather mini-skirt with matching jacket, a slick of pink lipstick on her mouth, eliciting stares of admiration as she strode past. She had once won an Ingrid Bergman lookalike contest. She was also possessed of a fiery temper and you could never predict the psychic weather in our home. Once my father had inadvertently taken a few grapes from a dish put out for guests and the next moment my mother had clattered a frying-pan over his head for his audacity!

As an extremely intelligent woman who had gone to Jagiellonian University in Krakow at the age of fifteen to study physics and found herself instead at the age of twenty-five with three small children living in Glasgow with a smattering of English, she was understandably frustrated. It was certainly not *la vie en rose*. It didn't help that we children were constantly up to mischief and once poured all her favourite perfumes (Guerlain's Mitsouko, Dior and Chanel) into one big bowl, mixed them up with a wooden spoon and offered her the contents as a birthday present, in the belief that she would be overjoyed by this perfume made in Paradise. I think we were thoroughly skelpt for our efforts. My mother is a superb cook but nevertheless we fussy children didn't always want to eat everything she prepared. Possibly as a result of her childhood deprivations, she insisted that we were not allowed to leave the table if any food remained on our plates. In a cunning sleight of hand we would tip our leftovers into the drawers of the dining-room table and scrape out the mouldy mess at the end of each month. My mother was horrified when she found out and no doubt we were skelpt for this as well. My mother redid her physics degree – this time in English – and graduated from Glasgow University at the age of twenty-eight. Only now am I full of admiration for all she has accomplished.

We didn't know that my mother's Polish was full of expletives until relatives came over in a steady stream over the years (since my father could not go to Poland) and recoiled in horror at the slang language innocently uttered by her children – learnt at their mother's knee! Once I told my prim Aunt Lula from Warsaw that I loved her 'claws' instead of her immaculately painted nails and earned myself a reprimand. When my mother swore, we thought these words (*cholera jasna* – bugger, *szlag trafi* – damn) simply meant 'bad children'.

When I was about eight years old, my mother took her three daughters alone on a train journey from Glasgow to Poland for the first time. The journey took three days in deepest winter. We crossed over by boat from Harwich in swirling seas. It was even snowing in the Hook of Holland. I loved the starched, white linen tablecloth in the dining car of the train. Every evening I enthusiastically ordered up steak tartare or trout and felt I was on the brink of adulthood. The thrill of being able to choose my own food, when up to this point I had not been allowed to choose the clothes I was going to wear each day. I even had some money of my own. My grandfather had given me a five-guinea note which I carefully folded and put under the pillow. The border guards, dressed in heavy military overcoats, checked our belongings in the carriage as we travelled from one Eastern Bloc country to the next. I was impressed that no one touched my money.

Once in Poland, we had rapturous reunions, mostly with my father's family. The telephone clicked as the Security Service listened in to our phone conversations, which were obviously of crucial intelligence as I asked for a new doll with red lace-up boots. We were definitely in Eastern European territory in the Cold War era with the low wattage lights of Warsaw and Krakow and the evocative smell of the diesel derivative in the streets full of trams.

I know that it is ridiculous to have nostalgia for the Cepelia shops, with their distinctive wrapping paper, so closely resembling Orla Kiely's designs today. Cepelia shops sold Western goods and upmarket Polish souvenirs for foreign currency, usually dollars or pounds sterling. It was difficult for Poles to obtain foreign currency at that time and I became adept at illegally changing the much-needed dollars into złotys in shady venues. Only a spoilt Westerner like me could feel a thrill doing an illicit act like this. I never had to endure the reality of living under oppression in a communist state, as my family had.

My great-aunt Helena lived alone in a small house in Szczawnica in the Tatra Mountains and she recounted stories of her time in Auschwitz. Nearly six million Poles died in the German death camps. Three million were Jewish; three million were not, but they were all Polish citizens and deemed *Untermenschen* – sub-human – and part of the ethnic cleansing called *Lebensraum*, the settler-colonialist policy pursued by the Germans to clear the land of indigenous natives in order to make way for the German people. After the war, my great-aunt and her husband, my great-uncle Ergo, who had also survived Auschwitz, made their way to Britain and set up a rehabilitation centre for concentration camp survivors in the outskirts of Manchester. 'There was no help at all. We were just supposed to get on with it,' she told me with anger in her voice. Aunt Helena and her husband witnessed the murder of my father's eldest brother, Ryszard, in Auschwitz. Their own son, Bolek, had been killed as a partisan at the age of twenty. My father eventually came over to England from Italy to help them at the centre.

My great-aunt and I listened to the banned Radio Free Europe broadcasts under the table. Although, why under the table? Who would have known? The airwaves would often be jammed and the words would come and go. I still have all the photo albums of my aunt's privileged pre-war life and, as I gaze into the densely filled salon of bibelots and beautiful pictures on the wall, I wonder, where are they now? All the questions I would have asked her but it is now too late.

Strangely enough, we watched a lot of the Glasgow-based crime series *Taggart* on television, where all the characters, male and female, were dubbed into Polish by the same man with the most monotonous voice imaginable. When Czechoslovakia split in two (forming the separate countries of Slovakia and the Czech Republic) I thought the shooting I could hear from the nearby border was part of *Taggart*.

My mother managed to go to Poland fairly often with my sisters and me after that first winter train journey. Once she arranged that my elder sister and I go on a communist trip which was heavily subsidised by the Polish government. It was a covert way of encouraging the offspring of dissidents to return to the homeland once they had tasted her many delights. My mother had different ideas. She thought that it would be a cheap way of getting us to Poland and that after a few days we would be liberated by my relatives. However, the Polish authorities would not give up on us so easily and we had to spend a few weeks banged up in a borstal-type establishment in a drab town in the south near the Czechoslovakian border, where we were holed up with other inmates from London. The town, Wadowice, became famous in later years as the birthplace of the Polish pope, John Paul II. To call the town drab in the 1970s would be to imbue the word with some colour. The only result of the incessant propaganda, the early morning marches, and the singing of communist songs was to render our behaviour truly appalling. One morning I hid in the toilets to get out of the gruelling 7am session of *gymnastyka* in the courtyard outside. Ania, a girl from London, whispered from the next cubicle, 'Is that you, Basia?'

'Yes, it's me,' I whispered back.

'Come here and have a look at this,' said Ania. She pointed in the toilet bowl at the biggest 'jobbie' I had ever seen; the specimen curled in the porcelain looked like a fossilised *pain aux raisins*. It was much bigger than any my Labrador, Rocco, has ever produced. 'What do you think about that then?' she asked, her voice full of satisfaction. 'It's a beauty, isn't it?' I nodded dumbly. The Polish carbohydrate overload of potatoes and cabbage washed down with sweet tea had made its indelible mark. The time had come to get out of that hell-hole. Drastic action was required.

One day our camp commandant asked my sister and me to stand up and sing the Scottish version of 'Happy Birthday'. We stood up and sang loudly:

Hippy birthday, you moo
Hippy birthday, you moo
Hippy birthday, you cunt you
Hippy birthday, you moo.

Clearly, all the re-education and brainwashing had not worked. My mother's foul language had transcended into English. Someone must have tipped them off that we were highly undesirable. The motherland could manage without us. The next day my Uncle Wojtek (my father's brother) and his wife, our Aunt Kazia, were waiting at the gates, ready to whisk us off the premises. We waddled towards them, arms outstretched, rejoicing in our freedom.

My father came from a very large family and he was closest to his dynamic, handsome brother, Wojtek. My father was tall and thin and quietly spoken while Wojtek was stocky, muscular and full of energy. Every year we would meet up with Wojtek's family, usually in Yugoslavia, since they could easily travel to a nearby communist country. My Aunt Kazia once asked me, 'But what will the West do once Tito dies?' What did I know about what the West would do once Tito died? Adults have weird ways of communicating. I looked at her blankly.

'What do you mean?'

'Well,' she answered, 'the whole thing will fall apart.'

'What will fall apart?' I persisted.

'Yugoslavia,' she answered.

I imagined Yugoslavia deflating like a soggy meringue, a failed pavlova.

I didn't know that twenty years later the Balkans would explode and fragment into ethnic, genocidal rubble. Our last holiday all together was in Bulgaria, just before my parents bought Coutal.

In the early 1970s, my father decided that if he could not go to Poland in the foreseeable future, then the best way to see his family would be in a halfway house, his own half-island house, in a warm climate. He was a keen gardener and we only ate organic produce from his garden. In the greenhouse in Glasgow there was an abundance of melons, tomatoes and peaches. An engineer by trade, he loved fixing and making things and so why not buy a house in the south-west of France with a lot of land to grow fruit and vegetables? An added bonus would be if it were a complete wreck so that he could patch it up himself. And so it came to pass he bought his heart's desire with no running water, toilet or electricity.

At that time, there were few British people who lived outside of the Dordogne; abandoned, dilapidated stone houses proliferated. Many of these farmhouses – *gîtes* – were built in the 1830s, dotted around Aquitaine and the rest of France as a direct result of the French Revolution. Once the initial upheaval had died down and law and order was restored, citizens, who were third generation after 1789, benefitted by being given their own parcel of land on which they could build their home.

The last descendant of the original family who had built our house, Coutal, died without children. Monsieur Delmas had fallen off his tractor in front of the barn and died of his injuries. The gravestone of Pierre Delmas and family is still in the graveyard in the village cemetery. Coutal was left to their neighbours as thanks for caring for them in their old age. No one lived in the house from 1954 and soon parts of the roof caved in and the rodents took ownership.

Farmers in the 1970s were encouraged to grow tobacco and so money was needed to build a tobacco barn. This prompted the neighbouring farmer who had inherited Coutal to sell on the house and land to my father in 1972 for the princely sum of £3,000, on the eve of Great Britain at last being reunited with the European family.

Once again, we children popped into a car and stuck our legs out of the windows, but now we were driven for two days south, not east. By the time we reached Harwich and spent the night in the tiny cabin of the Townsend Thoresen ferry, we were truly scunnered.

My father's mother was driven over from Poland in a Polski Fiat, really a home-made bomb since there were cans of petrol in the boot, with the rest of the family squashed together in the tiny car. My deeply religious grandmother was overjoyed that she at last could make a pilgrimage to Lourdes and for years we had a least ten bottles of holy water languishing underneath the sink. Many other Polish relatives came to visit as well as *Dziadzia*, my maternal grandfather, who came over from Glasgow. There were many reunions and tears shed over the years. Somehow, being foreign, not quite fitting in, was very familiar to us all.

As children, we were feral and relished our freedom, playing in the ruined Château de Scandaillac and the abandoned village of Gigouzac, only coming home late in the evening when we were hungry. An old neighbour showed me her wedding photographs taken in Scandaillac before the château was abandoned. Many years later it was bought and restored by an English couple called the Grayling-Salmons. I once told them that I had played in the castle as a child. 'Did you ever play in the tyre?' (pronounced *tyah*) enquired Mrs Grayling-Salmon. I looked puzzled. 'The tyre?' I answered, uncomprehendingly. 'Yes, the tyre,' enunciated Mrs Grayling-

Salmon, slowly, with her cut-glass vowels. I thought it was odd that she would be asking me about swinging from a tree in a Dunlop tyre. It slowly dawned that she was asking about the tower. It was time to flatten my vowels.

Our local mayor remembers seeing me running through the fields unkempt, blonde hair flying, a Rubenesque Manon de Sources, dressed in some Laura Ashley flowing creation, with many spare tyres around my middle. We never wore shorts, just cheesecloth smock tops and long skirts mostly scavenged from a cheap high-street chain called What Every Woman Wants. Sophisticated we were not.

When I was fourteen years old, I was convinced that there was a Roman track at the back of the house and in full archaeologist mode I donned my overalls, wielded my trusty trowel and carefully uncovered slabs of stone. I was ecstatic but my delight was short-lived. Although it did look like a rough track (if you squinted your eyes) it was actually bedrock. I immediately threw down the trowel and reverted to being a sulky teenager. I now realise that we are fortunate that Coutal will never fall prey to subsidence.

In the absence of a television, we would improvise and write our own scripts to compete with *The Generation Game* and *Morecombe & Wise*. Composite sketches like *The Singing, Ringing Tree* mixed with *Vision On* were a particular favourite, and a bit more edgy to the bland offerings of 1970s television. Polystyrene packaging in the rectangular shape of a screen became our voice to the world. Our talking heads uttered sound bites in funny accents: 'Give us a twirl, Anthea', 'Give me sunshine, with your smile, give me laughter all the while, In this world where we live there should be more happiness', and then seamlessly switch into the solemn Morningside voice of the news-presenter, Mary Marquis, coolness personified, introducing *Reporting Scotland*. I longed to look like the BBC2 test card girl with her long brown hair, red dress and hair-band. I envied her air of self-assurance. There was something that puzzled me, though: I understood the blackboard in the background, but what was the point of the mad clown?

From time to time, we all played Scrabble in Polish and English. The letter 'z' was highly coveted because the Polish language is notorious for its lack of vowels. Suffice to say the one with the most 'z's usually won.

One favourite game was skipping, using an old rusty scythe as the substitute for a rope. 'Higher, higher!' we egged each other on, narrowly missing our feet. I recently found the scythe in the barn, lying abandoned for all these years, waiting for Gerry and me to resurrect it for our own private games.

All great fun for children but glorified camping for the adults. The house had two big rooms downstairs and two attic bedrooms (the latter not high enough to stand up in) and three barns. The only furnishings that had survived the twenty-year hiatus between families was an enormous oak sideboard, called the *crédence* (with one side propped up by books where one of its legs had completely rotted away), rusty pots and pans, farming implements and a picture of the Madonna over the fireplace. Red quarry tiles covered the floor. An enormous palm tree stood right outside the middle of the house and I often woke up to the swishing of the palm fronds against the stone. Sadly, most of the palm trees in the area died in a freakishly cold winter in the 1980s. My father had built an extension and porch to the house in Glasgow. He planted a grapevine that travelled inside the porch, producing small but sweet grapes. We would have breakfast there under the canopy of fruit. He brought a cutting over to Coutal so that the vine covering the outside of the house is a profusion of Scottish grapes!

One of the barns was converted into the kitchen and I was dismayed to find that my father had concreted up the wine and cheese cellar and destroyed the giant wine barrel as my mother zealously covered the ancient timbers with pine to resemble a 1970s bungalow. With the building of the kitchen came the joy of an indoor water tap, although to this day we still have a well with a natural spring.

The first year was disastrous as it rained incessantly and there was a plague of flies. But this did not deter us, the children, as we made small pots out of the rich clay soil and composed a story called 'Memo to Flies', an apocalyptic, graphic tale of flies taking over the world. Farmers did not use harmful pesticides at that time and so at night we were entertained by luminous, shimmering displays by fireflies in the surrounding fields like currents of electricity. Then, as now, there is no light pollution; the stars appear cushioned in black velvet in an uncontaminated sky in sweeping constellations. The shooting stars flitting by entertained us for many a happy hour.

No one could speak proper French, so my Aunt Magda and Uncle Zygmunt would be commandeered from Paris to translate the guttural Occitan language spoken at the massive meals we would be invited to at neighbouring farms. Afterwards we would all repair to a barn to relieve ourselves. Few farmers had bathrooms at that time. Indeed, we had no modern toilet in Coutal in the beginning and had to make do with a bucket in the barn with a curtain draped in front, where my siblings and I would sell tickets to desperate people with crossed legs. We made colourful signs saying *occupé* and *libre* that hung from a stick and handed out the French version of Izal toilet paper. A 'sahara' shower (a bucket with holes in it filled with lukewarm water) served to keep us clean.

My poor aunt and uncle struggled to make sense of the local dialect, but without their translation skills we would have been totally isolated. They came with their young family for the first few summers, driving nine hours down from Paris, and joining in with the indoor camping – a gaggle of expat Poles. Many years later I still communicate with my aunt and uncle in *françki*, a homespun, playful mix of French and Polish, as in *Basiu, gdzie są les couverts*? (Basia, where are the plates/cutlery/glasses?)

The open fire in the living room was initially on the ground. It had been lit all day in an unusually cold spell and must have become so hot that a stone exploded from the back wall and ricocheted to the back of the room, missing baby Antoś's face by inches. From then on, the fireplace was built up and a large wood-burning stove installed. It was less romantic but much safer.

This was a time when you would still see farmers out in the fields in their workers' *bleus*, the thick blue smock. We were truly in the *La France Profonde*, at least thirty years behind the cities.

Occasionally we would be taken out to the Vietnamese restaurant, quaintly called the Phuc Long, in the hilltop village of Monflanquin. The Vietnamese grandmother sat on the terrace all day long, flicking the ash nonchalantly from the cigarette she held at the end of a silver holder.

The circus, inspirationally called 'le Cirque de Provence', rolled into the village at least once a year. It was a true family affair; the daughter took the money, the father showed us in and the mother was the master of ceremonies. The father performed the first act, the daughter the second act, the mother the third act; while the ladies sold the popcorn and candyfloss at half-time, the father came out as the clown. I even loved the performing dogs, pony, cat, birds and spitting llama.

As I grew into a sulky teenager, I graduated from reading my stash of *Bunty*, *Mandy* and *June and School Friend* comics to devouring the wrist-cutting tomes of Solzhenitsyn and Anatoly Kuznetsov's *Babi Yar*. Occasionally I would dip into the light relief of the teen bible *Jackie* girls' magazine, especially the agony aunts 'Cathy and Claire' on the last page, where I would glean advice on understanding recalcitrant parents and how far necking should go. Answer: only above the waist. I had an image in my head of swan-like necks wrapped around each other; we called it 'winching' at school, a rather more rough and ready approach. *Cosmopolitan* was far more sophisticated and scarier, with articles by Shere Hite (I kid you not) on multi-orgasms and hitting the G-spot and Irma Kurtz's problem page. I would cast a censorious eye at the letters and answer them before I read wise Irma's response. 'Just walk out and leave him'; 'I think you are being too self-indulgent, get a grip on yourself.' I would advise – harshly – only to find that Irma's solution to the problem was completely different from my own.

It was obviously not good for the soul and I would cycle back from the dairy farm in the evening with a pail of milk clinking on the handle-bars thinking, 'What's the point? What on earth is the point? Why go on? We are all going to die one day...' I was surrounded by the futility of existence.

There was nothing to do for a teenager – nothing, nada, niente. We were stuck in the middle of the countryside, in a time warp, no friends nearby, reliant on an adult to drive us anywhere. The longueurs of being trapped in the countryside grew ever longer. We teenagers were lugubrious, resentful presences, totally self-absorbed, brought into this world to torture our parents. I made lists of things I would do in the future – my escape plan – and places I would travel to, thereby starting a lifetime of to-do lists and procrastination.

The highlight of the day was to cycle to the tiny shop next to the church in the village where a gnarled old woman with a dowager's hump in a blue housecoat would sell us sweeties. There were about twenty items for sale and we were probably her only customers. Carambar, a chewy caramel toffee, was our favourite sweet.

The attic bedrooms were stiflingly hot in the summer and initially there was no glass in the windows, which let all the bugs float in. After a successful bout of nagging, an adult would drive us to the open-air public swimming-pool in Castillonnès so we could cool down. I felt particularly jealous of the luxurious holidays my schoolmates enjoyed in some exotic places like Blackpool, Majorca and Arran.

My father started the renovations, installed electricity and running indoor water. He planted an orchard with various varieties of plum trees (*prunelle* and *mirabelle*) and apple, pear, fig and walnut trees. He planted the orchard twice; during the first winter the saplings were munched by the farmer's goats. My father was apoplectic with rage.

Graduating from the sulky stage, I soon became a fat and obnoxious teenager, constantly arguing with my mother and making huge pots of ratatouille. My signature dish was cheese soufflé, washed down with copious amounts of the beautifully named *Pschitt!*, a popular fizzy drink. Perhaps teenagers should be locked up for a fixed term to empty themselves of narcissism and existential angst. Parents are simply boring people who provide for your needs and stop you doing the things you want to do. They only become interesting when you yourself are older, and then it is usually too late.

When I was seventeen my mother announced that she had something to tell us. My sisters and I were excited and fully believed that she was going to reveal that a dishwasher was on its way. It was a baby on its way instead – a boy – and our noisy family merged with our family from Paris, with the addition of terry towelling on the clothesline.

Ah, the clothesline. Many an argument raged over the clothesline right in front of the house with a long line of washing forever hanging on it. My mother insisted it should be there despite the fact that the washing machine is located in the kitchen at the back of the house where the door opens directly onto an open field. It seemed completely irrational for this logical woman with the forensically sharp scientific mind to categorically refuse to move the clothesline to the back of the house, a far more practical – and now I think more aesthetic – proposition. Despite our protestations, she carried on trudging through the whole house with the laundry. It was an argument that grew out of all proportion. And now I realise we are all full of inconsistencies, unexplained acts of stubbornness. After thirty-five years my mother eventually capitulated. But we did get one of the first dishwashers, a complete lifesaver.

My father did his best to escape the family mayhem, working on the house and on the land. He grew thinner and more taciturn. We saw him visibly slipping away from us before he died of prostate cancer a few years later.

It was difficult for my mother to hold on to the place after my father died, with little money and four children, the youngest a toddler; yet somehow she did. My mother, tenacious and resourceful as ever, kept the house ticking over, repaired the roof, covered the well in case of accidents, continued to cook the scrumptious Polish meals and built a better, functioning indoor toilet.

It was far from easy and the brambles took over the back of the house, the fruit trees were left untended and grew so tall we couldn't gather the fruit and, most alarmingly, the tiled floor in the living room seemed to develop a small hill in the middle giving one the impression of being mildly inebriated when walking up and down. The root of the fig tree outside had thickened and snaked underneath the house, displacing the tiles and only when the fig had been chopped down, poison administered to the root, did the growth stop.

The cycle goes on; my own children love this place and I have fallen back in love with it, surrounded as I am by brilliant frozen moments of childhood and happy memories of those alive and gone. I know the geography of this house, the bare bones of it and the shadows that live within its walls. Some of the farmers I knew when I was young are still there, albeit in their nineties.

After coming to an amicable arrangement with my mother and siblings, I plunged once more into the breach of debt. The local estate agent gave an evaluation of the property and immediately deducted €10k from the price because of the duck farm at the back of the property and €10k for the septic tank being in the wrong spot.

My partner, Gerry, and I decided to come out in 2018 to upgrade and redevelop the barns in order to have proper bedrooms at last. We had tried to build from afar, but it proved too problematic, so we made the big decision to take a year's sabbatical from our teaching jobs to renovate Coutal. 'What about a great escape, joogle the finances somehow?' suggested Gerry. I re-mortgaged the house in Glasgow, cashed in my pension, took out another loan and somehow it came to pass. However, a sabbatical it had to be as we need to go back and replenish the coffers afterwards. I know how lucky I am; I cannot complain.

I have come to appreciate all the quirky things about Coutal – the low doors, the thick stone walls with spaces hewn out of them for storage. Proustian memories abound: the furniture my father made, the dining-table, the armchair; my Aunt Teresa's colourful folkloric Polish cut-outs hanging on the walls; and my great-uncle Ergo's delicately drawn patterns on blown-out hens' eggs – a therapy for patients to overcome trauma.

Then there is the realisation: the house is raw and unfinished, like me. I am surrounded by my familiars and, oddly, this is my home.

EN ROUTE

We have no choice but to go now, since Gerry packed up my underwear in the trailer a few days prior to leaving. I have cancelled the council tax from July 1ˢᵗ and my cousin and his wife are about to move into our home in Glasgow.

So from Ruchill to rural France, a mere twenty-nine-hour hop door to door with our trusty beast of a car and a trailer stuffed with three armchairs and two wood-burning stoves from an Easterhouse pub as well as enough junk to furnish an empty barn or two.

We attempt to leave on time but the car refuses to budge. 'Look at it this way,' says Gerry. 'We are in a hot air balloon and we are going down. Some things have just got to go!'

A whole unloading operation ensues; church pews, a bicycle and bric-à-brac are dragged back into the house. Gerry is ruthless; I am in begging mode, clinging onto the Philippe

Starck cheese-grater and a copy of Shir Hever's book *The Privatisation of Israel's Security* (I like to keep it light). Both are abandoned.

We take turns driving slowly for two-hour shifts and make the 11pm Dover-Calais ferry just in time. The crossing is the most rest we have had in weeks. Initially we booked the shortest crossing, because Rocco, my son's Labrador, cannot go too long without a toilet stop. As the ferry sign with a dog hangs from our car window I realise how much I will miss the old hound. Ziggy has just returned from eighteen months in Poland playing Premier League football and has reclaimed his doggy rights, so there is nowt we can do. Doggone!

Coutal, our house, will not be the same without Rocco. He gave us excuses to go for long walks in the countryside and find new haunts. I will miss seeing him trying to pull off the lizards' tails, but I won't miss him trying to join in a game of tennis. Our neighbours will probably not miss him diving into their pools and leaving a fug of black fur in his wake.

In the event, it is just as well. We left Scotland in scorchio weather and it gets greyer and wetter as we travel south. The old car puffs and pants up hill and down dale (and France sure is hilly) through torrential rain, thunder and lightning. In an attempt to curb the almost ubiquitous speeding on the roads, President Macron has changed the limit on A roads from ninety to eighty kilometres per hour. This doesn't stop bad-tempered cars from clinging onto our trailer's bahookie, urging us to get off the road or drive faster. I doubt if this initiative will stop drivers from getting stotious after lunch and careering over roundabouts.

Just two hours from the house in France, the car radiator explodes. Boiling water drips down the windscreen. We manage to get off the motorway near Périgueux but, being so tired and spaced-out, we are not too stressed. Five hours later we are en route again in a hired car, having abandoned our car and trailer at a garage. The garage owner is aghast. 'What? No breakdown insurance?' No salary for a year focuses the mind and, in the planning, full all-star European breakdown cover had seemed like a dispensable luxury. We had breakdown cover all the way down through England, so that is where, by rights, we should have broken down. A whole month's allowance has now been spent in one day, so we will be living off the fruits of the land. Other people's land.

In the early evening we pop into the local town to pick up some milk and pizza and discover that the whole town is out in the thirteenth-century town square for dinner. With horror I realise that I recognise some people. I hide my face behind the pizza and sprint back to the car. Meeting our friends, stinky and exhausted, after being on the road with no sleep day and night is not going to happen. 'Drive!' I order Gerry, Monsieur le chauffeur.

The world seems a better place the next morning. The grass has been cut, the walnut tree that had threatened to tumble onto the house has been removed and there is a neat pile of wood there in its place. Monsieur Menuet, the stonemason, has done exactly what he promised to do. The openings for the windows and doors have been cut in the thick barn walls. There is still an eye-watering amount to do before this place is ship-shape. '*Vouloir, c'est pouvoir*,' I say to Gerry. 'Where there is a will there is a way.' While Scotland has been basking in unusual Mediterranean temperatures, it has been raining a lot in France. My shoes have mushrooms in them and everything smells foosty, so airing is required.

Gerry manages to get the thirty-three-year-old Nissan Micra started and we zip to Villeneuve town to put it in for its two-yearly *contrôle technique* (MOT). The Micra cost two bottles of wine a couple of years back and I am very attached to it. It has been lying outside the house for the last year. We now have two cars in two garages in two towns, two hours apart. I feel I am in a perfect mathematical equation.

What happens when you get rid of a hired car and old banger and replace it with an old workhorse and trailer? Answer=*relief* and *ecstasy*. Wednesday's storm has taken its toll and we see a few trees lying on top of roofs as we skitter from one end of the region to the other visiting our cars, avoiding the debris on the road.

The mathematical equation has now changed. I have always found maths difficult to master.

The old Nissan Micra is not going lightly to the scrap heap. My love for it is slowly turning sour. For the first time ever it refuses to start. When Gerry opens the bonnet he finds a wasps' nest in full angry gyrations. After a few yelps he manages to jump start the car and, spluttering and stalling (car, not Gerry), the old banger limps to the car cemetery (again, the car, not Gerry). We only have a few drops of petrol left and this time we have forgotten to bring the petrol can with us.

During the paperwork stage the jobsworth shakes his head and informs us that he cannot accept the car because the registration number on the car and the insurance number do not match. 'Why haven't you changed the numbers?' he asks, shaking his head. 'Have you really been driving this car like this for two years?' At this point the only thing to do is emulate Penelope Pitstop. No, I do not speak French. No, I do not know what he is talking about. What is this legal thing? By this time, we are desperate enough to do a runner. Then, another miracle happens, saving us from this impasse. The jobsworth checks the chassis and finds that it corresponds with the insurance number. What larks! This reprieve calls for one last sprint to the office to finish the paperwork. 'That will be €19.40,' says the lady at the desk. '*Pas de problème*,' I answer and fish out the cash with alacrity. '*Non.*' She smiles. And she gives me a cheque for said amount. I look at the cheque with incredulity. Money so far has been a one-way conduit for us, not in our favour. Miracle indeed. Adieu, Nissan Micra.

Back in Coutal the sun has come out and we feel ridiculously happy to be here: the start of a new adventure. After lunch, some wine and a nap, we discover that the phone is working. The internet is working too, but at the speed of an arthritic donkey. Brexit will happen soon: a completely unknown territory for us all.

At first, I think that the French flags waving all over the place signify a rise in nationalism, but of course I have forgotten that the World Cup is on!

Football has gripped the nation. We manage to catch the end of the France v Uruguay match. France wins 2-0 and a sigh of contentment spreads across the valley.

NEUTRINOS AND THE MERDE

We are slowly emptying the trailer and there is a mountain of stuff lying in the hallway, or throughroom as we call it, because it is all purpose and no purpose at the same time. I cannot believe I have brought such an array of worthless objects: thirty T-shirts, a book on '750 delicious cocktails' (but no cocktail shaker), a book on yoga for the face, two boxes that were destined for the attic and managed to escape and sneak into the trailer without being caught. The detritus of almost fifty years surrounds me, from childhood letters in drawers to my daughter's baby bath.

Somehow this does not deter me from searching out my first *vide maison* (house contents sale) and *vide-grenier* (car boot sale) in the hope of acquiring more junk. The first is unsuccessful; clearly an old couple have snuffed it and the son is selling off their bath chairs, walking sticks and cracked pots.

The *vide-grenier* is better. I promise Gerry I definitely will not buy anything, but after five minutes I give in to temptation and buy two 1950s side tables which will eventually go into a bedroom yet to be built. There is nowhere to store them, but we manage to squeeze them into the bathroom. The good news is that we find folded publicity posters of rugby and football matches in Casteljaloux in 1952 and 1961 – good enough to display! Another treasure is a batch of old letters tied up in string hidden underneath newspapers. I will wait till I feel sufficiently nosy to read them.

More *vide-greniers* follow, with more bargains: a 'block and tackle', perfect for slinging a hammock between the trees. Gerry is delighted to find a stash of 1960s *Lui* magazines. These are the French equivalent of the *Playboy* and *Penthouse* of the day. However, they are so innocent in comparison to the raunchy titles on offer today: no nudity, no nipples, just coy and suggestive looks. A young Raquel Welch gives a tantalising 'come hither' look from a front cover. Gerry was a photographer for seventeen years in a previous life and tries to convince me that the style of photography is ahead of its time, which is why the magazines appeal to his latent photographer's antennae. Aye right, as they say in Glasgow.

Our first real leisure activity is to go to the annual village meal, which is a four-hour booze and food extravaganza. A surfeit of chickens is usually encountered on arrival, stacked on the overburdened outdoor rotisserie. Vats of soup containing yet more copious chicken parts are usually bubbling away. Sadly, the introduction of new health and safety guidelines means this is no longer the case; the village committee who organised this event for years has been disbanded and a catering company has stepped in. Maybe it is more hygienic, but the colourful atmosphere has gone. Also, there are hardly any Brits; have they packed up and slunk home already?

We have a good chat with a couple who lost nearly everything in the earthquake in Aquila in Italy a few years back. They spoke about the science research station under the mountain which was attached to CERN in Switzerland. Gerry and I visited CERN some time ago and he remembers that the original purpose was to get all European countries united in scientific collaboration and thus deter them from waging war against each other. (Perhaps this is something to remember in our Brexit moment.) The Large Hadron Collider is the product of this collaboration. When protons collide, they break down into particles which in turn produce neutrinos and the scientific superbrains somehow direct them to Italy under the mountain in Aquila. It was believed briefly that these neutrinos were travelling faster than the speed of light which Einstein theories said was impossible. That is my layman's understanding of it, which is stretching my science-resistant brain cells to the limit. The conversation comes about because the lady was involved in visits to the research station. Then a complete light-bulb moment for Gerry: he remembers his CERN joke. 'We don't serve neutrinos here. Then the neutrino walked into the bar. The Italians had got it wrong and in fact mistimed the neutrinos. So the bar went back to refusing neutrinos after they arrived.'

Maybe we had a lot to drink, but it seemed very funny at the time.

The septic tank is in the barn and has not been emptied for twenty-five years. All last year we went through the saga of obtaining permissions from the wonderfully named water organisations, SPANC and SAUR, in order to move our *fosse septique* outside into the field so we can renovate the barns. It proves to be an expensive operation, €12k and counting, because it requires the blasting of bedrock. On Monday morning, Monsieur Pajot's shit-sucking lorry trundles up our lane and promptly breaks our telephone and internet lines.

'Ah,' explains Monsieur Pajot's representative, 'the lines are not five metres high (the minimum level), so you will have to phone France Telecom to get them to repair the damage.'

I am now shit-hot at dealing with French bureaucracy and find the number for him to phone them. An hour later they are still haranguing each other, but today I am waiting for France Telecom to turn up and do the necessary repairs.

I am fully prepared for a fartomania of smells to erupt once the lid is taken off the tank but *non*, the microbes have done a fine job and the whiff is bearable. I set to work on the job of the day, shovelling rubble into the void so it can be sealed before the concrete floor is eventually laid on top. Shovelling rubble into the shit-hole is far less unpleasant than I thought it would be in thirty-three degrees heat and I happily sing along to the lines of one of my favourite Johnny Cash songs, 'Hurt' – 'and you can have it all, my empire of dirt, and you can have it all, I can make you hurt.' This segues clumsily into Sinead O'Connor's hit, 'Nothing Compares 2 U'. I am referring to the duck farm at the back of the property. It has always been there for as far back as I can remember, but four years ago the ducks moved nearer to us. Now the *bouquet* of guano is overpowering. In addition, the farmer has installed a scarecrow gun that goes off every five minutes to deter other animals from stealing the ducks' food. Last summer was memorable when our friends Vicky and Charlie were staying with us and the noise and smells were horrendous. The rock-blaster man was there making a hole for the new tank; his dogs and our dog were taking part in a howling competition; military jets zoomed dangerously low; the scarecrow gun regularly went off with a bang and the gagging aroma of eau de canard permeated the air. My nerves were frayed. Welcome to the tranquillity of the countryside.

In the winter, hunters pass by and use the end barn as a 'relieving area'. The year before, Gerry and I did a long shift shovelling human excrement and I left a cardboard sign,

'*Monsieur le chasseur, Laissez-moi tranquille, Ne faites pas le caca ici, Je vous en prie, Merci!*' (Mr Hunter, please leave me alone and please don't do your poos here.)

The wind of change is in the air. One winter's evening, back in Scotland, I could hear the sound of Gerry whooping with joy. I came into the living room to find the boy doing an Indian dance around the furniture. 'Guess what! Avian flu!'

And so it came to pass this summer that the ducks have been culled somewhat, moved to the back of the farm, the gun-blasts are heard no more and tolerable country smells have returned.

It is still full football season. France wins 1-0 over Belgium. More whoops of joy can be heard over the valley. A good result overall.

In the last forty-eight hours our local radio station has reported that Boris Johnson and David Davis have *claqué la porte* (slammed the door). Brexit has imploded. Not long ago, Nigel Lawson (ex-chancellor of the Exchequer and Brexiteer Extraordinaire) applied for French residency. Do even the die-hard Brexiteers want to escape? It has all gone pear-shaped.

Four

FLYPAPER, FOOTBALL AND POLITICS

For the last three years we have asked the mayor to reinstate our house sign. If you don't know where we are, it is very difficult to find us: off the second lane, off another track, off a side road, in the middle of nowhere. Maybe this is a good thing. The house was built in 1833 of white limestone and stands on its own land halfway up a hill, looking up at the château above.

The second generation after the revolution started a flurry of housebuilding on their wee bit of homestead after the mayhem of complete change had died down. In the last thirty years five more houses have been built, all calling themselves Coutal, the same as ours, the original Coutal. I suppose Coutal could now be construed as a hamlet. The Coutal sign hangs outside their properties and I suspect one of the neighbours nicked our sign.

The mayor suggests as conflict resolution that we change our name. 'But we were here first!' I pipe up with the strop of a five-year-old. Ron and Janet, our neighbours who live in '*Les Voisins*' a few kilometres away, give us a copy of a seventeenth-century map where Coutal is clearly marked. When my father bought the house, a mass of earth was wedged quarter way up and he hired a digger to excavate a large area all around. My Uncle Zygmunt spent many summers building a wall to hold back the rest of the hill from collapsing on top of the house. The excavation reveals clear evidence of previous foundations dating back to Roman times. This 'new' wall is now crumbling as the earth inexorably pushes the hill towards the house.

In one's absence, things happen. Our argument (we were here first!) falls on deaf ears and we concede defeat. We are now known to the world as 'Coutal Haut' (High Coutal) which sounds like a soothing lullaby. In any case, in the next few years all the houses will be given a number so that GPS can track them down. Maybe now deliveries will come to the right place.

Work is progressing well; a terrace is now hewn out of the earth at the back, and I spend a day raking out pebbles and sand over it. Gerry has built a deck out of disused barn doors at the top of the field so we can have a view of the valley, now that one of the massive walnut trees has been cut down. We persevere to have our lunch there, even though there is no shade and it is far too hot. Sweat drips down our red faces as we munch our *tartines. No pain, no tartine.*

Colourful plants are bought to decorate the front terrace.

The latest football score is Belgium 2-0 England.

The fireworks for Bastille Day from the hilltop village of Monflanquin are dazzling and the next day, the *cerise* on the *gâteau*, the cherry on the cake, is the French team winning the World Cup 2018. *Allez les bleus!* We cheer on the victors and watch the TV highlights with friends at their house, and on the way back home a wild boar runs in front of the car, narrowly missing us.

In Paris, the Metro stations have been temporarily renamed with French football connotations: *Bercy les Bleus, Victor Hugo Lloris* and my favourite *Nous Avron gagné*. The whole country is pumped up with pride; merriment and celebrations abound. The *tricolore* flag flutters from cars and houses.

Here at Coutal we are getting into a rhythm: up early, work, break for lunch, siesta, down time or work again. Work consists, in the last few days, of cutting the grass in the field, helping Gerry thread wires through electric cables (an extremely monotonous job), sorting and washing mosquito nets (although thankfully there have been very few of the wee buggers) and general cleaning and scrubbing.

I catch a reflection of myself in the mirror: my hair is covered in cobwebs and grass and tangled in flypaper in the kitchen. Outside the mosquito nets are hanging like tired, discarded wedding dresses from the clothesline. My legs are covered in bruises. *Allez les bleus!*

We are in the full flurry of activity here since our first guests, Ann and David, are due to arrive any minute. From that point, until the final guests depart a month later on the 19th August, Gerry's birthday, we too will be on holiday, sort of, but manning the hotel, our home, at the same time.

David (a professor of physics) arranged to meet a former PhD student of his in the town of Casseneuil (twenty minutes' drive from us) and we tag along as his entourage. I pop into the town occasionally to the secondhand shop to pick up some bargains. Three rivers converge in Casseneuil which makes it a perfect spot for kayaking and canoeing, but nevertheless it is still off the tourist trail. I don't understand why since it has so much charm.

We happen upon a tour guide with only two tourists in tow and he is desperate that we join in a tour of the church. I dare say he doesn't get much business. The guide is overflowing with information, pointing out the Occitan inscriptions in the church, explaining that this was a huge political move since the king at the time was making a statement that the language of Latin was now redundant. It is difficult to get away for our next appointment.

When we arrived earlier in the month, we followed the 'Quentin Crisp School of Housekeeping' since there was so much to do in the barns. Our presence can be detected by gaps in the dust. 'There was no need to do any housework at all. After four years the dirt doesn't get any worse,' wrote Quentin Crisp in his memoir *The Naked Civil Servant*. He became a gay icon in the 1970s after publication of this memoir and an eponymous film followed, starring John Hurt. It brought to the attention of the general public his defiant exhibitionism and longstanding refusal to conceal his homosexuality. He was obviously a wee bit on the clatty side. As far as I am concerned his witticisms surpass those of Oscar Wilde. Anything to digress and procrastinate.

Time is marching on and I have still not emptied everything out of the trailer. This morning I count seventeen cookbooks on the shelf – was I planning a full-scale banquet? Was I completely, barking mad?

We have bought a garage online to store some of the things that used to be in the barn. The kit duly arrives in large blocks of metal, after the driver has visited all the other Coutals. Before the garage can be assembled, we have to clear the land to install it and then lay down concrete slabs. Two steps back for one step forwards as they say: *reculer pour mieux sauter*. There are so many jobs to do; it is difficult to know where to start. The barns are full of electrical cable, but we will have to avoid looking at them for a bit.

I receive a red letter for non-payment of tax for Coutal. A reminder had been sent to a house where I used to live in Glasgow ten years ago. Quite incredibly it has managed to reach me. I have been trying to sort out the tax in France for two years now. We keep trudging up to the tax office and being told that we need not worry, everything has been sorted. Until the next cock-up. Our tax office in Monflanquin always blames the bigger tax office in Villeneuve for the mistake. The two tax offices clearly don't communicate. The bureaucracy can drive you mad. Even in the smallest way. I recently went into the bank with bag loads of small change and asked if they could give me notes in their place. The bank clerk (dressed casually in a I AM A FEMINIST T-shirt) shrugged, raised an eyebrow and said she didn't know where one could change the money, but Crédit Agricole was 'not that sort of bank.'

A few months ago, I went to see the comedian Alexei Sayle performing in the Citizen's Theatre in Glasgow. He let rip about those who opposed Brexit because 'house prices will fall in Nouvelle-Aquitaine.' That will be me. Not really since I am not going anywhere. But I do like this definition of Brexit:

BREXIT. (noun)
'The undefined being negotiated by the unprepared in order to get the unspecified for the uninformed.'

How do you continue being a political activist in La France Profonde? This is a question we have been mulling over since we arrived.

We suspect that there will be few people who share our political leanings – on the left and advocating for Palestinian human rights – in such a sparsely populated place, and certainly we doubt that our beliefs would be the expats' cup of tea. I can just imagine that very cup of tea spluttered out the mouth, the digestive biscuit crumbled in the hand. A preliminary search shows an active pro-Palestinian group in Bordeaux, which is too far for us to travel on a regular basis, but we will keep on looking. Perhaps we will stay under the radar for a year, although Gerry has decided to carry on with running the Twitter feed for the Palestinian Campaign. Every morning he is up early and reporting on the daily shenanigans in the Middle East. The internet is truly a wonderful thing.

People talk about the need for objectivity. Objectivity doesn't mean treating all sides equally; it simply means giving each side a hearing.

We buy *Le Monde* and *L'Observateur* newspapers to see the news through a different prism. I will really need to clue up about local politics. But the derision about Trump is the same as in Britain. I wish I could join friends at the anti-Trump march back in Scotland.

Gerry brought this tweet by Craig Murray (a freelance journalist) to my attention. He was forwarding a tweet by Nicola Sturgeon that nearly made me fall off my perch. Who is twiddling with Nicola's puppet strings? The gem is this:

'If you want something non-party political to get your intellectual juices flowing this Monday morning, I recommend this by Henry Kissinger on the philosophical questions that Artificial Intelligence poses for the human race.' Henry Kissinger! The US Secretary of State under Richard Nixon and Gerald Ford in the 1970s involved in murky dealings with

Asia, the Chilean coup and Argentina's dirty war at the time. I love Craig Murray's retort: 'The only conceivable excuse for this – and I shudder to say it – is that Nicola Sturgeon does not know who Henry Kissinger is. What next – Peter Sutcliffe's thoughts on market gardening?'

This starts me on a Google hunt for Henry Kissinger. I was unaware the old fart was still alive. It was interesting to hear about the controversy that ensued after he was awarded the Nobel Peace Prize. Two of the Nobel Peace Prize committee resigned; his fellow nominee also refused to take his prize since he did not want to be associated with Kissinger and the human rights violations in Vietnam, Laos and Cambodia... the list goes on. Someone commented that it made political satire obsolete. And now we have Trump coveting the self-same prize. If you look at what happened to Kissinger, then all is possible. Maybe Kim Jong Un's sister, Kim Yo Jong, as head of the department of agitation and propaganda in North Korea, might put in a good word somewhere.

We can still be politically aware in La France Profonde.

Five

TALES FROM THE HOOD

As the rest of the world fragments and pulls itself asunder with conflicts and wars, life in Lot-et-Garonne gently ebbs and flows, more clip-clop than zoom-zoom.

Our nonagenarian neighbours are still in good spirits. They are proud to call themselves 'peasants'. Their smallholding still has enough vegetables to feed them and though the cows have now gone, the chickens still cluck by the door and the two ageing dogs, Coco and Bibi, still go truffle-hunting.

Étienne is a skelf: sprightly and rake thin. He is up early every morning to tend his vegetables, cutting away any weeds with a scythe. Suzanne's garden is a glorious profusion of flowers. They feel so safe where they live that they leave the keys of the car in the ignition, for, as Suzanne points out, that way it's so much easier to find them.

As children we used to wander over to their farm and cuddle the rabbits. We were given presents of home-made *eau-de-vie* that would blow your brains out and tins of their own *pâté de lapin* – rabbit pâté.

Étienne is now as deaf as his dogs and can't hear us approaching but he pops his head round the barn and is startled when he sees us. He is holding a chicken with its neck just wrung. Carnage is strewn all around the farmyard; he has wrung all the other chickens' necks. He shrugs. 'I told them that all I had to feed them was potatoes and if they didn't eat potatoes, I would have to kill them.'

He makes a gesture with his hands open, palms heavenward. 'You see, I had no choice. They didn't, so I did what I said I would do.'

It seems that every time we pop in, the chickens are being butchered. A few months before it had been a similar scene when the recently strangled chickens were lying on the kitchen table and his wife, Suzanne, holding a plucked chicken by the neck, blow-torched its body with the other hand, nearly setting her pinny on fire.

Suzanne gives us eggs when we pass by. 'They are a day old,' she explains apologetically, 'and we only eat eggs laid this morning.'

We have had the tastiest meals, the envy of any Michelin-starred restaurants, in their kitchen. The living room and the kitchen merge together forming one big rectangular room, simply furnished with one long table in the middle and a few armchairs around the television. It is always stiflingly warm as the Gougets keep the wood-burning cooker on the go day and night. It is a dark room, illuminated only by a strip of fluorescent lighting which casts a grey tinge on the walls. The austerity of the surroundings is in direct contrast with the deliciousness of the food. Truly *impeccable*. Inevitably the meal would start with an *amuse-gueule,* a taste-tickler, that would have something to do with *foie gras.* When we just can't eat any more, Suzanne proffers a *digestif* which helps push down the food and miraculously makes room for more. Sometimes, when we bring a shop-bought pizza home and eat in front of the TV, we evoke Suzanne's culinary delights.

'Do you remember when she served us up turkey as the *plat de résistance* and we didn't recognise what it was?' I remind Gerry. It had no resemblance to the rather dried and bland meat we knew. Instead, the turkeys had been reared on the farm and in the last weeks had been fed with grains and fruit and the end result produced the most succulent, mouth-watering meat we had ever tasted. I once served them sweetcorn as a starter when they came to Coutal Haut for lunch. They ate the sweetcorn dutifully but with a noted absence of enthusiasm. Only later did we discover that sweetcorn is regarded as fit for animal, not human, consumption. Our *faux pas* was forgiven.

Étienne's mother had died washing clothes in the pond of the local mill across the road from us, Moulin de Labique, when he was four. His father, a house painter, died when Étienne was twelve. Etienne was brought up by his aunt in nearby Beauregard, and eventually went back to the family farm when he was twenty-one and married Suzanne. Their lives have followed the rhythms of the earth and the seasons ever since.

Our other neighbour, Blanche, is ninety-nine years old and lives in her parents' house, having lovingly 'restored' it to cover up all traces of ancient oak beams and past history. The outside of the house is covered in *crépi* (rendered) to get rid of the appearance of an old limestone house. In an effort to modernise, this was the fate of many an old house in the 1960s and 1970s. Blanche calls ninety-four-year-old Étienne 'young Étienne' and remembers when he and his father painted the interior of her house.

Blanche's real name is Bianca Goloti. She was born in 1920 in the North of Italy and arrived in this neck of the woods in 1932. Her mother came from Venice, her father from Naples and they met during WWI. There was high unemployment in Italy after the war, especially in the south of Italy, and Bianca's father found work in the mines in Alsace for three years, although he was a stonemason. When a more stable job as a mason came his way, building the theatre in Villeneuve, he brought his wife and children over to Lot-et-Garonne.

At first, they rented and then bought the house at the hamlet of Lagardonne, two kilometres from us. Bianca walked to the school in Born, one kilometre up the road, with her brother and sister. Everyone around spoke Occitan at the time and the Goloti children were nicknamed the *Macaronis*. Occitan is a Romance language spoken mainly in southern France, and also in Monaco, in northern Spain and in northern Italy. The road to Born was just a track then; there was no tarmac and it was muddy in the winter. Blanche recalls that there were only two cars in the whole of Lot-et-Garonne.

Until 1935, trains stopped in the morning and evening in Born, St Vivien, Beauregard and Villeréal, all the hamlets and villages around here. How wonderful not to be so totally reliant on a car as we are now. Eventually, Bianca's name was changed to Blanche and she worked in Agen before retiring to her family home with her late husband. She is still a fount of information.

I hadn't realised that the whole of the surrounding area was covered in vines, not sunflowers, which explains the sign *Vignoble de Coutal* (Coutal vineyard) at the foot of our track.

The abandoned rail tracks were dismantled and used for the construction of the 'Maginot line' built in the 1930s to deter a possible German invasion. Then buses took over. Now there is no public transport at all.

One sunny August afternoon, we invite Blanche and her youthful seventy-year-old son, Bernard, and his wife to come over to Coutal Haut and meet up with Étienne and Suzanne for a trip down memory lane and indulge in some local gossip and some of their own eye-popping *eau-de-vie*. They talk about a friend who has recently gone into an old folks' home. She is a tad older than them and they disapprove of how she has decided to ditch them at the age of 104! 'I've got new friends,' she informs them haughtily. 'I just don't have time for you now.'

She has moved on – at the age of 104!

The smell of chocolate from the plum factory in St Vivien is a pervasive, olfactory memory. I cannot remember when the factory closed down, maybe in the 1980s. The *pruneaux* were stuffed with chocolate and sold in the local shops. I dream of chocolate.

The secretary in the mayor's office keeps appearing in different places. One morning we turn up at the *Mairie* on business and later, when I go to the library in Born – there she is again! Apparently, she has a third job in holiday rentals. It reminds me of the film *Local Hero*, when one character pops up in various work guises. The secretary/librarian recommends three books which reveal different angles to the same story of the enslavement of a whole family.

Two kilometres from here lies the small Château Martel, hidden away among the trees. For eight years, until 2009, eleven members of an aristocratic family were brainwashed

43

(*le lavage de cerveau*) by Thierry Tilly, a confidence trickster who convinced them that he was a secret agent from NATO. The family believed him when he said he was helping them to hide away from the dangerous outside world. He physically and mentally abused them, stole their entire fortune and made them his slaves before he was found out and jailed. Tilly learnt many of his techniques from studying the CIA. At the end of their ordeal, the family received financial help from the ANF (Association d'Entraide de la Noblesse Française), which is an association which helps the French nobility who have fallen on hard times. This strikes me as somewhat anachronistic in post-Revolution France.

As I scavenge through our *sac à dough* (phonetically backpack, but our pet-name for purse: dough as in cash) I realise that it's time to plunder 'The Indigent Gentlewomen's Fund', if one should exist.

The château has since been sold, but this does not stop me prowling around, peeking through the gates. It is difficult to believe that while I was immersed in the domestic front, just a stone's throw away, a family was being destroyed.

I only have one slave here, Gerry, and he is showing signs of insurgency.

Robert Maxwell, otherwise known as Cap'n Bob, was a larger-than-life character. Originally from Czechoslovakia, he made his home in England and became a newspaper tycoon. He gained notoriety by stealing his employees' pension fund and drowned when an investigation was about to take place. No one knows if he fell or was pushed off his yacht. His helicopter used to sweep over our house and land nearby. Maxwell's wife, Elisabeth, came from the next town and my mother knew her. They met up occasionally. It seems unbelievable that Elisabeth didn't know her husband was a crook. 'I only feel safe when I am behind the electric gates of my property,' she said to my mother. Conversely, Elisabeth Maxwell was terrorised by her bully of her husband and probably just as psychologically damaged as the inhabitants of Château Martel.

When I was a teenager, I met an Irishman called Seamus who lived in a barn in the nearby ruined village, called Gigouzac, with his Mexican girlfriend, Yolanda. They had a baby called Maurice. I visited them in their biblical setting: Seamus looked like Joseph with his long hair and beard, and Yolanda, a serene Madonna, with long black hair, sat on the straw floor with the baby in the middle of the barn. Sand was raked round about them. I wouldn't be surprised if a shaft of golden light lit the scene, but I think my mind is playing tricks on me.

Aptly enough, Seamus was a dab hand at carpentry and built a log-burning stove. I would often see this New Age family cycling into Villeréal, five kilometres away, with the baby in the basket at the front of the bike. I am not quite sure how Seamus and Yolanda met, but I know that he had gone to the Isle of Wight music festival in 1969 or 1970 and then somehow found himself in rural France, met Yolanda and settled down. He had a very thick Irish accent and most people found it difficult to decipher what he said. But I suppose as I came from the North, he and I could make each other understood.

'At first they were all wary of us,' said Seamus, as he pointed out the houses around him that had been recently been sold and redeveloped. 'Now they trust us and I have all their keys and they tell me I can use their bathrooms. But you know,' said Seamus, tossing his mane of matted hair and laughing, 'I never use their toilets, I still like to piss outside.'

Their idyll would be shattered one day, in a set of bizarre circumstances. Seamus had decided to go on a cycling holiday (maybe enticed by some music event). He cycled alone all the way through the whole of Spain until he reached Gibraltar. He was a complete innocent, but he got caught up with the IRA killings in Gibraltar in 1988. The authorities couldn't believe that this fey Irishman was just there by chance and had nothing to do with these events and promptly deported him back to Ireland, in his too tight shorts. Seamus hadn't been back to Ireland for about twenty years. He got back on his bike and cycled home to Gigouzac to his precious family. But the French authorities were catching up with people living outwith the system and although Seamus, being Irish, could stay, Yolanda was deported back to Mexico with their child, Maurice, and of course, Seamus went with them. We heard that he died in a motor accident there a few years later. My neighbour, Janet, tells me that Yolanda made a 'pilgrimage' back to Gigouzac a few years ago, bringing Maurice to see where he was born and spent the first years of his life. I think he was shocked at the ocular proof of his humble beginnings and they soon headed back to the more comfortable trappings of their Mexican home.

Most of the empty and abandoned houses in the area have now been bought up, mostly by foreigners. The villages that were deserted when I was a child have now been revivified. We used to keep clear of Montaut up the road since a mad old woman had murdered a school child there in the 1970s and no one would talk about it, and the spectre of the Gestapo headquarters haunted Issigeac for many years. These memories have faded over the passage of time.

Each *commune* (micro local council) is very much a part of French life, especially in the country. Our *Monsieur le*

Maire, who knew me as a child, is pleased that I have returned as an adult and have decided to renovate Coutal Haut. In France there is a clear separation between state and religion. In the wall in our local mayor's office is clearly displayed *la Déclaration Universelle des Droits de l'Homme* (the Universal Declaration of Human Rights) and we should all be reminded of this on a frequent basis. Nowadays we have the *Animal Farm* version of human rights for some, but not for others. There is a list of all the mayors since the revolution on the wall. The only gap is the period between 1940 and 1945, which is self-explanatory.

Now that our friends, Ann and David, have arrived we decide to open up the yellowing envelope I had found originally in the cabinet drawer from the first *vide-grenier*. There is a number on the front: 3.4.72r – we do not understand the significance of this at first but then it becomes clear. All eight letters are written between 24th August 1954 and 12th November 1954 from women who had applied to a marriage agency, 'CMF', to a farmer here who was looking for a wife. It is not long after the end of the war and France is still recovering from the German occupation. All the letters are written in the same cursive, copper-plate writing. Most of the women are in their thirties, getting desperate at the prospect of being left on the shelf. All definitely lonely hearts.

The first candidate, from Paris, writes that she had 'her confidence abused by a man' and was now a single parent of a three-year-old boy. The next is more persuasive: 'if you are looking for a pin-up, I'm not it, but I'm not a goose either!' And she too has a child but widowed when very young. All describe themselves as *catholique et sérieuse* with womanly traits. One writes 'I appreciate the comfort and quietness of home.' None of them sets the town alight but I guess they address the desires of a lonely farmer stuck in the sticks. Given that he kept all the letters under lock and key, the probability is that he didn't choose any of the hopeful ladies in the end. I wonder what happened to them all.

Pentimento is the name given to the process where a picture fades or cracks, revealing a previous image painted by the artist. As is the case in all rural settings, scratch the surface and there is so much more going on underneath.

$\mathcal{S}ix$

FANNY COIFFURE: MIXTE

'I've been based in Paris for four years and I still find it exotic. I haven't learnt French – I don't need it for my work, and it would spoil the excitement of my alienation if I understood everything that was said.'

Susac's Syndrome.

Louise Clarke of Bristol, England, is one of 200 people suffering from a bizarre brain disorder called Susac's Syndrome. Her symptoms include migraines, hallucinations, and thinking that she's French. Ms Clarke started speaking French at all times, inviting friends to stay with her in Paris, and even asking for croissants. As she reports: 'It might sound funny to others, but suddenly thinking you are French is terrifying.'

Squirreled away in one of the boxes I keep full of newspaper cuttings that tickle my fancy, I found these two newspaper articles that are pure gold. Unfortunately, both are without reference to author, date or publication.

I was worried about feeling isolated, but so far that hasn't happened. We are gradually getting to know more people. There is definitely a motley crew here in the Lot-et-Garonne, the haves and have-nots. There are some who are totally integrated into French society and those who only stick with their own language group/fellow compatriots. The latter group stick out like a sore *pouce*. I have heard of one English couple who have lived here permanently for 35 years and don't speak any French at all. It seems so disrespectful not to make any attempt to learn the language. Surely just a wee effort shows a modicum of respect. There is a brilliant expression which means to speak French badly: *parler français comme une vache espagnole* (literally: to speak French like a Spanish cow). Although I have taught French for many years, I nevertheless must admit I have not been up to speed with new linguistic developments. Gerry has been assiduous and does a few grammar lessons every morning and we try to watch the French news on France 24 to keep *au fait* with what's going on in the world and hone our linguistic skills.

My area of expertise at the moment is the vocabulary of building and DIY. I now know that *l'équerre* means set square, *la dalle* means slab (and not *le pavé*, which I had mistakenly ordered from the building yard and means cobblestone – not what was required), *le gond* is a hinge, *le bardage* is old wood used for decoration, and to uplift all these things I need a *crochet de remorque* – a tow-hook – to attach onto my *remorque* – trailer. I am ready for a job at *Monsieur Bricolage*, the local French DIY emporium. Some words are not easily translatable, like *riverain*, people who have dwellings on the side of a river or road. The word *le poutre* (beam) is what we probably discuss most, usually in the plural. Our house and barns are awash with *les poutres*, and I am always anxious to ensure that there is no woodworm in them.

I still smile when I see the house names round here: *l'Arse*, *Sexteree*, *Jalousie*, *Le Chavie*, *La Ruine à Quatre Vents* (Ruin of the Four Winds) and my all-time favourite *Gratte Lapin* (Scratch bunny? Even French people do not know how to translate this). On one of our walks I notice a tumbledown wreck called *Le Défi* (The Challenge). Maybe in a few years' time it will be named *La Réussite* (The Success). *Ce n'est pas le Pérou* is a saying which means there is nothing to celebrate. It is therefore heartening to see a house named *Le Pérou*. There's no doubt that the owners love their home.

Nearby local vineyards are called *Château de Planques* and *Buzet*, pronounced 'plonk' and 'boozy' respectively. We have been to the Buzet vineyard so many times we have been given the honorary title of 'Friends of Buzet' and blessed with a magnum of wine.

There are also some choice place names. Just down the road is the hamlet of *Piis*. When we drive by the village of *Tourette* to go to the lake for a swim it is understood everyone has to shout in unison 'Fuck! It's Tourette!' We are easily amused.

When I asked my Aunt Yvonne, my mother's half-sister (although she is only a couple of years older than me), what she would like as a special birthday present, she replied with no hesitation. 'Please give me Fanny Coiffure: Mixte!' This was one of my most coveted possessions: a sepia-coloured framed photograph with the words 'Fanny Coiffure: Mixte.' emblazoned in huge letters.

I had no choice but to hand it over to Yvonne. But it isn't the original Fanny. Let me explain. Three years ago, Gerry, Fran (a visiting friend) and I were driving through the town of Le Buisson in the Dordogne, when Gerry spotted the old lit-up sign, 'Fanny Coiffure: Mixte.' hanging outside a hairdresser's salon. We screeched to a halt so that Gerry could take a photo of it and eventually had Fanny, the photo, mounted on the wall (you do know what I mean).

Ever since handing over the Fanny sign to Yvonne I have nagged Gerry to make another one. It so happened that recently we were driving with friends past Le Buisson again and noticed that the sign had been replaced by an innocuous modern job. I was inconsolable. In my dreams I had thought that I could go to the shop and offer to replace the original one. My prayers were answered when I phoned the hairdresser's the next day and I was told that the old sign might have been put away in the attic and could I phone back in a couple of days? Two hand-wringing days ensued. I phoned the hairdresser's salon and they had found the sign! We hot-footed over to the shop and now Fanny is home in her rightful place in our barn.

'It's strange,' said the hairdresser (named Fanny?), shaking her head, 'but people were always stopping their cars to take photos of my shop.'

Last year we bought a massive 1950s original 'TABAC' sign which needs to be rewired and hung opposite Fanny.

August brings a spate of guests in full holiday mode – sixteen in all. This calls for a military operation to ensure everyone is fed, watered (well, actually wined) and catered for. The usual French transport summer strikes and cancellations (a favourite French pastime) ensure that few arrive at the specified time. After such a hot summer, a few dreich and bogging days arrive in time for the guests. Scottish weather!

Nevertheless, the sun always seems to muster up the energy to make a sporadic welcome appearance.

In between arrivals and departures, Gerry and I resemble speeded up silent movie characters dressed in rags, in a state of frenetic activity, trying to get all the work done to a very tight schedule. I thought I was clapped-oot working in the school, but now I am constantly whirling around.

At one point the house is so full we retire to our dilapidated caravan at the bottom of the garden. As soon as this happens the mercury hits forty-two degrees and we are roasted in our oven. The torpor induced by the hot weather is like cutting through warm butter; only the cool interior of the house brings any relief.

Ann and David, our first guests, are quickly followed by Sharon who has been here on and off since she was nineteen years old. Sharon says, 'I don't think I have met anyone as clever as David.' It's true, he might be a professor of physics, but he is an all-round brainbox, although he never makes us feel inadequate about our lack of grey cells. Sharon has been here so often we don't have to take her anywhere, and she is just happy to enjoy chewing the fat with us.

Jo and Grant then appear, and we have a gourmet and sight-seeing time in Périgueux. We take them to the opening of the artist Armando Bergallo's show and nearly expire from the heat.

While Jo and I enjoy a manicure and pedicure in the local town, Grant sets to work with the chainsaw to ensure our old view of the surrounding countryside is restored to its full glory. There is a certain satisfaction to be had from cutting down your own trees (originally planted by your father) to feed the two log-burning stoves, one in the kitchen and the other in the living room. We are preparing for winter, even though it is a long way off.

The boys are a bit miffed when Jo and I arrange for a Mexican masseuse to come to the house. Her magic fingers set to work and much sighing is heard from the living room. 'Got a sore back!' 'My leg hurts!' 'Twisted my hand!' The boys feebly protest from the orchard, but the female committee decide that our needs are greater than theirs, thus massaging requests are refused. Order is restored in the house.

It is a joy to see the place I have known since a child through new eyes since Jo and Grant have never been here before. Jo remarks how clean and spotless everything is – not a speck of rubbish left on the streets, even after a night market. A highlight for us all is sitting on the viewing platform watching the beautiful, uncontaminated night sky with Mars and the Milky Way shining brightly. A chocolatey delight.

One Monday evening, Jo and I are chatting to two Englishmen at the Villeréal night market. One tells us that he has spent the last six months travelling around France in his campervan and how wonderful he finds France. He explains that he has bought land nearby and intends to build a house, but with all the uncertainty about Brexit he is delaying his project. We both commiserate. Then he pipes up, 'But of course, I voted for Brexit. Do you know we don't even elect our own commissionaires?' At this point the conversation dries up and Jo and I tuck into our *canards et frites*.

I don't understand British people living in France and voting for Brexit, and there are a few of them around here. I lived in Paris as a teenager and it was so hard to get a *Carte de Séjour* – a resident's permit, which would allow you to work in France. It was a catch-22: you couldn't get a job if you didn't have one and you couldn't get a *Carte de Séjour* without a job. I was lucky to get one but many of my friends had to work illegally and it was tough for them. I was happy that the young people today could enjoy being European without all these bureaucratic problems, and now what had been promised to them at birth is just being snatched away from them. And by people who had enjoyed all these advantages all their adult lives. Now I read an article in the local English magazine, 'Have you applied for your *Carte de Séjour*?' which describes the long wait involved in obtaining one. We have gone full circle.

The looming spectre of Brexit has already cost us a lot more money than we had anticipated. The pound has plummeted like a concrete bollard into the English Channel. We were due to send a large sum of money over to France to pay the stonemason and the septic-tank man just before the Brexit referendum three years ago. The rate of the pound against the euro was going down as we approached B-Day, and the bank manager advised us to wait until after the referendum result, as he was sure the exchange rates would perk up. In Scotland none of us were prepared for the UK YES vote for Brexit; the markets went into freefall because the computer systems could not cope with all the erratic exchange systems, so all transactions were halted. It was mayhem! We were about to leave without the necessary cash! When order was eventually restored the exchange rate was at an all-time low. So right from the outset, for us, Brexit has been Brekshit.

We watch a programme on television about the discrimination that black artists faced in Britain. I still marvel at how Theresa May managed to wriggle out of her overtly racist Windrush scheme (it was she what signed the papers, guv) and it makes me realise just how many politicians become slippery, slimy creatures once they manage to climb up the greasy pole. As a greasy Pole talking to other Eastern Europeans in Britain I realise just how vulnerable our situation is, in a country that tells you, in no uncertain terms, thanks for the plastering, building and service industry contribution but you can just *bugger off* now.

Cristina and Peter from Barcelona arrive with their children, Nina and Alex, in their campervan. We are their last stop before going home to Spain. They have just completed a massive twenty-one-country tour and it is interesting to hear that it costs €60 to park the van overnight in a park in Denmark, compared to €16 in France. Both Cristina and Peter have packed in their regular jobs, sold their country house and decided to start a company together, running bespoke tours in the Costa Brava, making use of their linguistic skills. They both speak Spanish, Catalan, English and Swedish, with a smattering of others. We are all in pastures new (i.e. currently 'jobless' with no money coming in) and on the first day back at school in Scotland, Monday 13th August 2018, we celebrate our liberation in style.

Irena, my daughter (known also by her immediate family by her childhood nickname, Katy) arrives with her boyfriend, Ant(ony) from London. They invite their friends, Catriona and Adam from Glasgow, who promptly cancel their return flights to enjoy the party for a few extra days. At the same time, David (Irena's father) arrives, but wisely stays in the plush hotel, Le Moulin de Labique, a ten-minute walk away. We have always remained close and respectful of each other's privacy. David has always said – in jest, I hasten to add – that 'when I am good, I am very, very good, but when I am bad, I am horrid'. In the end, David and I want the best for each other and our children.

After an eleven-year gap, I think David has enjoyed revisiting old haunts and friends. The area is certainly more thriving and tarted up. Full tourist mode ensues: canoeing down the Dordogne (and Catriona can't swim), swimming, sunbathing, cycling, day and night markets, visiting the holy site Rocamadour (Ant reported back it was the third most visited tourist spot in France after Paris and Mont-St-Michel), tennis, table tennis evolving into Prosecco pingpong, laughter, gastronomic overkill, BBQs and visiting the medieval fair in Monflanquin, which was a first for me since I am usually never here when it is on. Imagine wearing all that armour in this heat. We head straight into the ice-cream parlour and sample the ecstasy of Bounty and Caramac cones.

Irena attended the kindergarten in Monflanquin and it is heartening that she still wants to come back here and loves the area enough to show it off to her friends. She is a lark whilst I am an owl; she can sew and draw and I can do none of these things, but in other respects it is strange to see glimpses of your daughter in yourself; the driven and sociable side as well as the occasional crisis of confidence. She too is a lover of food and wine and stickers pop out of the pages of her favourite cookery books. Her fridge is neatly stacked with healthy snacks. I admire her sensual and meticulous nature; her attention to detail. Smells, music and beautiful fabrics are important to her. But she is elegant whilst I am elephantine. I am not as organised, self-disciplined or as generous-spirited as Irena – I can nurse a grudge for far longer and my tongue can cut and wound – and I can see her getting exasperated by something I have said or done. Or worn. 'Mum, you just can't wear that, take it off immediately. I really need to style you.' I really wish she would. I need some of her fashionista flair.

The boys are not let off the hook. They all toil to build the garage (more a hangar) which we need to house all the stuff from the barns before the concrete is poured on the floors.

Who needs to go to the gym? Ant proudly pats his biceps and says in his Ozzie way, 'Look at these cannons, getting bigger every day.' The progress report so far in August:

- Garage and carport erected.
- Electrical cables through barns.
- Big stones emptied from barn (manually) and rubble put in barn, ready for concrete.
- Outdoor sitting area created in front of house.

The hotter it is the bigger the critters.

A giant wasps' nest is discovered lodged in the fireplace. It is forty-two degrees and Gerry and Grant light a fire but fail to open the windows. Immediately a gush of incandescent, gargantuan wasps plaster themselves onto the glass and day turns into night. The living room is unlivable for a few days, until we can dispose of all the corpses.

At the same time, *les fuines*, the pine martens, decide to make a comeback after a four-year break. Gerry and I are sleeping upstairs when I suddenly hear the *clomp clomp* noise, like 'rats with clogs on' as Ron, one of our neighbours, memorably described them. 'Gerry, they're back!' I squeal. Action is required. The radio plays outside all night, powerful torches like air raid beams sweep over the roof. We can see the big eyes of the pine martens swivel towards the light. After three days they disappear again, but when will they be back?

Luckily, Jo and Grant leave before the bat is trapped in the house for three days. But what can one expect living in a house in the middle of a field? Occasionally mice pop their heads around the corner but there is plenty to eat outside so mercifully they keep out of our way.

Another critter stalwart is the *punaise*, a flying green bug that is inoffensive but smelly when squashed (and could be mistaken for a pistachio), and its friend the *gendarme* (policeman), so called because of the red stripes on its back. Their favourite pastime is to cosy up at the bottom of shoes and windowpanes.

Gerry is cutting back on the undergrowth and suddenly stops in his tracks when he hears an unmistakable hissing sound. Snakes ahoy! He slowly backs off. Mosquitoes have been strangely absent this year. No need for the nets to hang suspended from metal hooks over the beds.

I have yet to see a fox here in Coutal Haut, while urban foxes are a common sight in Glasgow, especially where we live on the canal. Rocco, our dog, is forever growling, his nose pressed against the window, desperate to join in the foxy carousing below. One day I was walking home in Glasgow and noticed a fox walking by my side! He/she walked in such a jaunty fashion he/she could have had a shoulder-bag swinging by his/her side. Our neighbours here in France, Simon and Jill, have occasionally woken up to chicken massacres pulled off by wily foxes.

The worst possible culprits, as far as I am concerned, are the *aoûtats* aka harvest mites, which usually appear in August (hence the name) but can hang around until October. I first encountered them in the autumn two years ago. I woke up one morning in agony, my body covered in red, angry blotches, especially in the moist bits. We rushed to the chemist and the pharmacist confirmed that I didn't have shingles as I thought, but had I been in a wood lately? *Non*, I shook my head vehemently, *absolument pas*. But then we realised, of course, we effectively lived in a wood! The orchard was so overgrown then, brambles everywhere; it was impossible to walk through it. The sun had difficulty in piercing through the green canopy. The day before, I had been carrying firewood into the house. The pharmacist nodded her head sagely. *Ah, oui, les aoûtats.* We were handed a bottle of pungent liquid to dab on all the itchy bits at frequent intervals. Midges (the scourge of Scotland) move over; the crown of agony has been snatched from you.

As a teacher, I should really learn my lessons. I have been too cocky. August arrives and I have the liquid ammunition at the ready. I am well-protected from the enemy. Madame Gouget, our neighbour, had advised us not to cut the grass after August 15th but I ignore her advice because everything grows with tropical enthusiasm here. I am determined that the long grass will be cut before our September visitors arrive. Latterly, our offensive against the foliage has been partially successful, but, as I say to Gerry, we must be vigilant and ruthless. In a fit of madness, I whip out the lawnmower.

Today my body is on fire, but not in a good way. It is midday and I am in my pyjamas. The thought of putting clothes on is anathema. I am trying hard not to rip my skin off.

As I write this, I am listening to the lyrics of one of Runrig's songs: 'There must be a place, under the sun' and I feel nostalgic for Scotland. We live in two wonderful places under the sun.

As soon as the latest visitors leave, we do a smash and grab at the local supermarket to get supplies for Gerry's birthday party. Gerry's birthday usually coincides with the return to work, so this is a real break from the norm. No disco or strobe lights. We decide on a more sedate affair, a *fête champêtre* in the garden.

It isn't quite Manet's *Le Déjeuner sur l'herbe* – no nudes – but there is a timeless quality of the dappled sunlight through the trees, the clink of glasses, laughter and banter, the luxury of hours swimming by, unhurried. As the evening comes the last of the guests sway down the track.

I promised Gerry he could have a special *gîte* to himself as a present. His own private space. I have dressed up the caravan, with an outside toilet and BONNE ANNIVERSAIRE stuck in big letters on the side, and of course the FANNY COIFFURE: MIXTE sign lying jauntily against one of the caravan wheels.

A TALE OF TWO TOWNS:
CANCON AND CASTILLONNÈS

There is a surfeit of prettiness here; no wonder it is so popular as a tourist destination, as the rolling hills and bucolic charm have something of the Cotswolds about them. The region has also been dubbed the 'Tuscany of France'. Within a twenty-minute drive of Coutal we can visit five medieval *grands villages* and numerous wisteria-clad, smaller ones.

However, one of our favourite villages, Cancon, is not a *bastide* nor is it touristy or even particularly pretty. It sounds like a Chinese high kick; especially pronounced in the local dialect, *cangcong*. Gerry comments that you don't realise how hilly it is around here until you have cycled to Cancon, seven kilometres from the house. I used to cycle in the direction of Cancon, just before the hamlet of Beauregard, to collect milk in pails many moons ago. It is the direction we go in to visit Judith and Peter, who live in a house on a hill.

Cancon is much as it always was, a bit down at heel, with the same houses for sale off the main street for the last twenty years. It is a passing place to Monflanquin and Villeneuve to the west and Marmande and Bordeaux to the south. The *route nationale*, the main road, cuts through it with a constant stream of lorries.

Uncle Zygmunt and Aunt Magda loved going to the church in Cancon on Sundays. Every summer they would religiously go for their mud 'cure' in Dax for three weeks (it couldn't be shorter than that, they asserted, or the cure wouldn't work), something generously subsidised by the state. On the way back to Paris they would break their journey to see us in Coutal and go to church in Cancon. Gerry and I go religiously to the small, covered market every Monday for our vegetables and *steak haché* from the butcher's van. The market is where the locals meet, mingle and gossip. It is timeless, like a Brueghel painting: children playing, a dog cocking its leg, a carrot dropped on a cobblestone. The market is the only place I still hear Occitan being spoken by the elders of the community. It is only in the last few years that we have discovered the medieval backstreets leading up to the (now destroyed) castle on a hill. In the 1960s these higgledy-piggledy streets were home to migrant Portuguese workers. It was only realised recently that these houses were recognised to be an asset, not an eyesore, and a sprucing-up operation was set in motion. The old houses were restored and the cobblestones polished up. A signposted pathway led to the top of the hill. There the vista is sublime, soaring over the valley to the Pyrenees.

In August, our guided visit around Casseneuil gave us the impetus to discover more about local history. I have never gone on an organised walk round the *bastide* villages here until this month. The fabulously named Dick Bogg (air commodore, retired) takes us round Castillonnès at breakneck speed. The interesting things that stuck in my head: the profusion of the new *bastide* (large villages, not quite towns) are laid out in straight lines to deter the invader, with a market square in the middle rather than the meandering mess of the medieval towns. The church is always built just off the market square. The *bastides* were all built around 1269 and spanned the Hundred Years' War (116 years, but that does not trip off the tongue easily) and the towns went back and forth from French to English allegiance.

The charter for Castillonnès was signed after the battle of Castillon, hence the name Castillonnès – new Castillon. The town planners had catered for a population of about 1,200, given that there are 100 wells, and today the population has remained mostly the same. What planning! For the local population who spoke the Occitan language, regardless of the rulers, the only change to their circumstances was that their taxes just switched from the English to the French masters. *Pruneaux* or prunes, yummily succulent, not dried up and turd-like as in British supermarkets, are still the staple produce.

The covered square in the centre of the *bastide* was burnt down during the 1789 revolution, but the town has remained remarkably intact. The church bells ring twice every hour with a two-minute gap, originally to alert the peasants in the field of the time. If they missed the first chimes they would just listen out for the next series of dongs. Horse racing is a very popular pursuit in these country parts and the hippodrome is located, as in most other *bastides*, just outside the town walls.

Castillonnès, like many other *bastides* around here, is on the route for Santiago de Compostela. The pilgrims' lodgings attached to the church are still free if you can prove you are a pilgrim; but what does this entail? A show of bunions? Tattered

Jesus sandals? The latest occupant left Belgium on January 1st, so he had truly hot-footed it here.

The main feisty dame in town is, of course, Eleanor of Aquitaine (circa 1122–1204), a true bunny if there ever was one. Aquitaine at the time was bigger than England and she was sole heiress to a vast fortune and estate. She was fifteen when her father died and immediately she was betrothed to the King of France, her first husband. Eleanor was a clever, manipulative, ruthless woman who was both Queen of France and England, as well as mother of Richard the Lionheart – who didn't speak English. She gave birth to ten children and married a man eleven years younger than herself, but nevertheless had time for a few lovers, one being her uncle. She was also a shrewd political player who led a crusade to the Holy Land and influenced political decisions at the time.

Bordeaux is the most famous wine in the world thanks to Eleanor. She ensured that only Bordeaux wine was traded to England and her other trading partners and this went on for the 300 years Bordeaux was an English possession.

But more interesting in Castillonnès are the snippets about the locals. On the grande-rue is a hairdresser's shop which is now all boarded up. I often noticed the big photo of a nineteenth-century bicycle in the window, but I didn't know why it was there. The shop had been owned by a diminutive hairdresser called Théodore Joyeux who had a big dream which became reality: The Tour de France. In 1895 he cycled 5,500 kilometres in nineteen days without a brake (and nearly without a break). Sadly, fame eluded him since his feat coincided with the Dreyfus affair, the big political scandal at the time in France, so poor Joyeux slipped down the headlines and went back to hair-snipping. At the same time, there were two other hairdressers with shops on the same street called 'Content' and 'Gai', so all happy bunnies in the end.

I always enjoy visiting the cinema in Castillonnès which was established in 1955 and is still running. I am looking forward to the winter, ready for the flicks with Gerry. The cinema is now run by volunteers and projects all the latest films in both English and French. No one bothered about age guidelines when we took our children to the cinema; it was up to the parents. Ziggy and Irena were happy to watch *Erin Brockovich*, the Julia Roberts blockbuster, when they were ten and eight years old with Susan and the Belkacemi children. It was only recently I discovered that it was rated a '15'. Why, I don't know.

After the tour of Castillonnès, we take our visitors to the recently opened 'La Maréchalerie'. Gerry and I know the premises well, since it used to be the old haberdashery shop. We got to know the old lady who owned the shop along with her husband. They had run the business for over fifty years as had her father and grandfather before her. But now was the time to retire to Bordeaux. They were just going to turn the key in the lock and let their children do what they wished with the premises. On the outside remained the faded old blinds with the original lettering; inside was a treasure trove, completely frozen in time, which delighted Gerry's photographer's eye (he does actually have two).

In the shop's tiny office hung original Paris Olympics posters from 1926. The *pièces de résistance* were the old *bleus de travail*, the farmers' overalls for working in the fields still in their packaging with old franc pricing from the 1950s. When I was a girl all the farmers wore them. Gerry and I bought a couple, waiting for the right time to wear them. Maybe the time is now.

On the 'Jour de Patrimoine' on September 15th (Doors Open Day), we visit the grandest house in the town, 'Hôtel de Cours de Thomazeau'. It was bought by an English couple, Ron and Jennie Whetton, in 2009. The house had been sold at auction because no bills had been paid for years and the building was in a parlous state. It had been owned by an alcoholic doctor who drank away all his money and left himself severely in debt. Needles and bottles littered the place. It was a complete dive. The transformation has been amazing and Jennie's keen eye for restoration and collecting (she owned antique shops in London) has been put to good use. Particularly interesting is her fan collection, demonstrating how women would covertly wield their influence in difficult times. Two of the fans had maps of France imprinted on them and had been used during World War II when the Germans made it illegal to own maps. This was a perfect way to help the resistance.

In 2014 the Whettons had a massive stroke of luck. While they were renovating the walls, fifty-five gold coins from the sixteenth and seventeenth centuries tumbled out. Possibly someone had left them there on the pilgrimage route for safe keeping, with the intention of picking them up at some later stage. Then, another sweet moment: the Whettons were allowed to keep the coins. They promptly sold them for a cool sum. What a lottery win; if only we could have the same luck…

Eight

COUNTRY BUMPKINS (LES PLOUCS)
HIT THE BIG CITY

We decide to take advantage of the fact that friends are arriving in Bordeaux (it's a hike away) and explore the city with them.

People, cars, streets, traffic lights, shops, noise: complete sensory overload! I mistakenly open the door of our wardrobe in the IBIS hotel and discover it is the adjoining door into our friends' room; we all look comically shell-shocked as we face each other late in the evening. After a sleepless night due to Keith's snoring, Bridget insists he book another room for the next night. There are a few IBIS hotels around the train station, which is confusing, and he has booked another room in another IBIS, but manages to sort it out so that he isn't completely ostracised.

In the last few years, Bordeaux has completely shaken off its stuffy image and reinvented itself, even to the extent of having UNESCO status since 2007. Trams; contemporary buildings which remind me of Copenhagen; wide spaces; river views; classic architecture; a thriving arts scene; the longest shopping street in Europe, Rue Ste Catherine, all lit up by the sun. Bridget and I frolic in the 'miroir d'eau' – the water fountains outside the Place de la Bourse. We meander down the ultra-expensive Rue Notre Dame with bric-à-brac and antique shops. I am really taken by a super compact metal staircase that looks like a propeller; only a cool €12k!

An exhausting day trying to pack in as much as possible culminates in a visit to the futuristic 'La Cité du Vin'. It is worth a visit for the building alone, as well as learning such nuggets as wine was cheaper than water in 1907, instigating riots. Ironically, we had understood that we would imbibe a proper slug of the nectar and grumbled at the dribble served up in our glasses in the roof-top bar. Wine, not water.

The next day we drive down to the Atlantic coast to the 'Dune du Pyla' (or Dune du Pilat), the highest sand dune in Europe. I used to go camping in the pine forests that surround the area with my family when I was a child. People used to call me 'Brigitte Bardot' (I was four years old) and now I hope no one can point out a resemblance. I remember the wooden steps going up the top of the dune. The wood eroded long ago and now has been replaced by stone steps which make it slightly easier, but certainly our calves were sore after slogging over the sand to get to the sea and back. While the Mediterranean Sea is calm and docile, the Atlantic Ocean by contrast is wild, vast and breath-taking. The breakers start far out, and the smudge of intrepid surfers dot the waves, like seagulls from a distance. We did not venture past the shallows because of the treacherous, strong undercurrents which have claimed many lives. The Ancient Greeks believed the Atlantic to be the gigantic river that encircled the world and it feels like that, knowing that America is directly opposite.

And then another mix-up. I had booked a visit to 'Château Smith Haut Lafitte' months ago and we are really looking forward to visiting one of the best vineyards in the world. Some of the Bordelais vineyards have been bought up by Chinese consortiums, but Château Smith Haut Lafitte is still owned and run by a French family.

We roll up at the château with thirty minutes to go, to find we are the only ones there, apart from workers setting up for a wedding. Something smells fishy not winy. We enquire if this is 'Château Lafitte' and the workers reassure us with a resounding *oui* and go on to say that Madame has just nipped out to run some errands but will be back shortly, and *oui*, the château does do tours. We are not totally convinced but decide to hang around for a while. Just in the nick of time we realise our error and I phone the number I have for the initial reservation. They are waiting for us! Or as a sultry voice says on the phone line, '*ah av bin wetting fer yew*'; the last tour of the day is about to start. Lafitte means a 'hill' and there are a few 'Château Lafittes' in the area. The 'Smith' and 'Haut' distinguish it from the others. Our car screeches to a halt outside the château and steam rises from us and the bonnet. The lovely tour guide, Agathe (she of the dulcet tones), calms us down, takes a shine to us – or is it pity? – and spends hours showing us around.

It transpires that the vineyard dates back to 1365 and was bought by a Scottish merchant called George Smith in the eighteenth century, hence the unusual 'Smith' addition to the name. The vineyard and its traditional way of working was revolutionised by Florence and Daniel Cathiard, two French former Olympic ski champions, who bought the estate in 1970 and decided to embark on the 'circular economy' to ensure an organic approach and that every part of the grape was used (including for beauty products) and that the *terroir*, the beloved land, is cherished. I joke with Gerry that we could be mistaken for *terroir-ists*.

The wood for the barrels in the cooperage come from French oak forests and they are infused with spices. The smell of vanilla and cinnamon is overpowering, as are the cellars full of barrels of wine. Most of the wine has already been ear-marked and is ready to be shipped overseas. My nose twitches with olfactory overload. I wonder why it is all so *nickel* – pristine – and free of cobwebs. Spiders don't like hazel and therefore brooms of hazel switches are hung around the walls. Sculptures are woven around the vines. The sculpture by Anthony Caro is to remind us that the word 'agriculture' encompasses 'culture', the word 'artisan' has art in it, and 'aesthetic' has the word 'ethic' in it. If you are ridiculously wealthy then you can be utterly pretentious. It goes with the territory. *Pardon, le terroir.*

The big James Bond drum roll moment comes when Agathe takes us down to the owners' personal wine cellar. The wooden floor slowly opens up and stairs appear, a stairway down to heaven. And then, of course, the mind-blowing wine-tasting finale sends us to celestial heights. Wine, Agathe reminds us, is the source of longevity, good health and happiness.

The sound of satiated purring fills the car as I drive to Coutal in the evening, pooped. Gerry and I are back in the caravan – our oven – so that our guests can enjoy personal space. Our mutual friend, Norma, was supposed to join us but couldn't park her pooch in Glasgow. In the event, it was just as well, as there is no room at the inn.

The next three days are spent touring all the *bastide* villages and chilling by the lake. We are joined by another friend from Glasgow, Kate, who attended her nephew's wedding at a nearby château. These days couples tend to marry in a British registry office and then splash out on a wedding in an exotic, stately setting. Kate brings leftover cheeses and bottles of whisky with her. She last visited Coutal twenty-five years ago (as did Norma) and nothing much has changed in the area since that time; everything is suspended in aspic.

'You know, Gerry, why didn't you make a path going all the way up the top terrace?' Keith suggests. Gerry looks at him with astonishment. 'Have you any idea of what we have had to do?' And he shows Keith one photo after another of the impenetrable jungle with eight-foot brambles, bushes, trees, thorny undergrowth. We had to hire a machine to do the major work. The end result was to reveal some of the view. 'Okay, the path can wait,' acknowledges Keith.

Ron and Janet come round and we spend an evening swapping funny stories about tortoises (Bridget and Keith's tortoise, Albert, has had a recent stay in a tortoise hospital in Cumbernauld) and we listen to my favourite Ron joke about 'Morag and her hielan' hospitality.' I have heard this joke for the last thirty-five years and always end up laughing my head off. Ron is a born raconteur, or ronconteur, and can spin out the teeniest story until it is a polished nugget. An oft-told tale is when Irena was about four years and Ron read her a bedtime story, *Katie Morag*, by Mairi Hedderwick, about a wee red-haired girl who lived on a Scottish island. Ron put on his best Scottish accent, and when he finished reading, he smiled at Irena who looked at him disapprovingly with pursed lips. 'Now read it again in a *proper* voice,' she ordered.

Ron and Janet first came to this area in the 1980s, cycling on their bikes with their two girls, and now their grandchildren enjoy the same childhood.

And then the rain appears for the day, *pfft*, as they say. The guests leave and we are alone again.

It is an Indian summer, soft sunlight, high twenties, chilly at night but beautiful. We can sit on the lookout platform at midday and feel the sun in our bones. We pick the walnuts, a bumper harvest, and our hands and nails are stained dark brown no matter how hard we scrub. Harvest is in full swing everywhere. The plums are sweet and succulent. The plum-picking machines grab the tree trunks, shake the trees and the massive umbrella poles swing out to catch the fruit.

I am listening to Alain Bachung's song, '*La nuit je mens*'. The lyrics are enigmatic but there is something thrilling about his voice.

Still no Brexit deal. We watch the news item about Rotterdam. It takes five hours from picking and packing tomatoes in the Netherlands to land them on UK supermarket shelves. Once all the custom checks kick in, this will no longer be the case.

A good analogy is to think of the EU as having Premier Gym membership. You pay for access to the equipment and pool; if membership includes free classes, childcare, coffee, food, etc. then you make good use of these extras. But if you leave the gym you lose them all.

It has been the warmest September since 1990. Our daily standard attire is T-shirts and shorts. I am not Under the Weather, rather basking in it, so most afternoons after a day's slog, we go to the Cramptons' swimming-pool (they have kindly let us use it while they are back in London) for a swim or chill out in the heat. There is nothing so refreshing as waiting until your body is at boiling point then plunging it into blissful cold, cold water. We are so glad we have met up with the Crampton family; they are on the same wavelength as us and Robert and Nicola went through a similar, bureaucratic process to secure their farmhouse, a mere five minutes' drive from Coutal Haut. It is an added bonus to have friends at the same stage in life.

Not being in regular employment in the re-education facility on a daily basis means that my life is a doddle with all the head space. Although we are busy every day doing up the house, the freedom to think, to let thoughts flit lazily in and out without being drowned by huge waves of stress, has been quite alien to me for such a long time. I recall that Stephen King compared his energy levels after a morning teaching to a boa constrictor that had just swallowed a goat. I know exactly what he means.

I also realise I have regained my old, odd sense of humour. And I have been smiling a lot more.

Just now I am listening to a radio interview with Rick Wakeman, who speaks of his love for an audience coming from the days he was signed up for various piano competitions by his parents. He recounts the host saying, 'And now we have Richard Wakeman, aged five, who is going to play "Monkey on a Stick".' When he heard the applause, he kept on playing the tune over and over so he could hear the applause again and again! I couldn't help but laugh. Meantime, Gerry is bizarrely watching a programme on TV about crannogs on the Clyde estuary outside Glasgow.

Gerry's brother, Douglas, lives in Lossiemouth in the north of Scotland. Opposite where he lives is the house of 1930s prime minister Ramsay MacDonald. Despite his high office he was looked down upon by the local worthies as he was the illegitimate son of a farm labourer. Even the local golf club cancelled his membership when he became prime minister. It was such an upheaval for the Tories to have this new-fangled Labour government with their outlandish ideas of social order. They played a lot of nasty tricks on him; for example, having his house built facing the wrong way, far from the beach that he loved, and not in the desirable part of town. Douglas went to visit the house recently (Doors Open Day) and told us that there were three photos on the mantelpiece: MacDonald with Gandhi, MacDonald with Einstein and MacDonald with Mussolini. What an incongruous juxtaposition. He is now regarded as an embarrassment, selling out his socialist principles and having a penchant for the good life.

Friends come to dinner and recount their experiences of house-sitting around France. In one property there are seven cats to be fed, three of which are outdoor cats. It was an impossibility to work out which cats were allowed in the house and which were to be parked outside since all the cats did exactly as they pleased! They were felinely exhausted by the experience.

It is still autumn, despite the balmy weather and the sun slinks slowly and lazily into view in the morning. It is time to take the lipsticks and face-cream out of the fridge and dig out the dressing gown. The summer visitors are slowly disappearing and there are far fewer people around; the town squares are quiet at lunchtimes with just local people in the cafés. The sunflowers have changed from being pretty young things to darkened crones. The farmers are busy chopping off their heads. We hear the grim reaper of the tractor getting ever nearer.

Now that we are alone at last we are getting into a routine. Every day I promise myself that I will dig out my Spanish course books, but then something urgent turns up and they lie on the desk unopened. I have started a Zumba class followed by Pilates class on Monday mornings and my hips are decaying not swaying as I follow the moves of the sinewy Crevette, our flexible teacher, as she yells:

Levez les fesses! Baissez les fesses! (Lift/lower your bottom!) Breathlessly, Jen whispers: 'When I lived in Sweden the teacher was always shouting "Kick the rumpa!"'

Every Friday morning, I walk about ten kilometres with a ladies-only walking group. Each person takes a turn to plan the walk and we all end up at the planner's house where cakes and tea are consumed. The group is a mixture – French, Dutch and British – so I am enjoying chatting in French and listening to the political disagreements. I have recently found out that there are quite a few expats from Hong Kong in the area. They are all British and preferred to come to France rather than return to Britain in 1997 after Hong Kong ceased to be a British possession and became part of China once again. All the women have led interesting lives in the past and are very welcoming. One tells me she sold her house in Bordeaux on *Le Bon Coin* (Gumtree) within twelve hours, simply because Parisians are flocking to buy in the south of Aquitaine due to the fact that the new high-speed train from Paris takes only 2h 10m. I tell her of the stream of visitors we have had and she informs me that they are commonly known as *Les Chicoufs*. What this means is that when people initially arrive you are full of joy, *Chic!* but when they leave you wipe your brow in mock exhaustion and exclaim *Ouf!*

I am learning idioms like *Je n'ai plus de nyac!* (I don't have any energy left!) But I doubt that these things are actually written down, like a 'squoosh' of ketchup.

My own walk takes us around the bridlepaths and tracks that surround Coutal. There used to be a riding centre near here, run by the handsome François. I loved the freedom of riding through the woods, but what I remember is that François always made a point of riding through the hamlet of Gigouzac to emphasise that this is a public right of way and a bridleway. This is the deserted place where I used to play in the ruins with my siblings as children and where Seamus and Yolanda lived in one of the ruined barns with their baby. It has been gentrified and rebuilt for some time now, but I am still incensed to see the sign at the bottom of the track declaring it to be a private road. Piffle and tosh! I am tempted to come out at night with a can of aerosol and give it a good old proper graffitiing. I lead the ladies through the hamlet to the path on the other side through the trees. Hardly an act of any significance or defiance, but I was pleased when a few said that they did not know this place existed.

On one of our walks we pass the memorial to 118 young men and boys who were gathered together on 21st May 1944 in Lacapelle-Biron and deported by the Germans to Dachau and Mauthausen concentration camps. They comprised all the males in the village between the ages of sixteen and sixty. The local lawyer had denounced them for being members of the Resistance.

At Coutal, Gerry has begun pointing the walls and I am his zero-hours contract assistant. But as he says, I have done zero work so far (except for the pointing finger) so I should not complain. Gerry describes himself as someone *qui touche à tout* because he can turn his hand to anything.

Gerry comes from a poor background with little encouragement to go on to higher education. He became an electrician in the Clyde shipyards at the age of fifteen, travelled the world for a few years, became a photographer before eventually going to university to study computing later in life, and is now a teacher, like me. I think he gets annoyed when I say to him, 'I see you brought your inheritance with you, an ironing board and a Stanley knife.' However, the other day he was quite triumphant as he was cracking the walnuts on the table. 'See, I knew my father's carpet hammer would come in handy!'

We meet young farmers who speak about making a living in the countryside. Although they find Brexit incomprehensible, they agree that the Common Agricultural Policy is a complete mess since it doesn't take into account the various earning powers of Spanish, Polish and other farmers.

$\mathcal{N}ine$

A TALE OF TWO TOWNS: VILLERÉAL AND MONFLANQUIN

These two *bastides* are less than ten minutes' drive either way from us. Both Villeréal and Monflanquin were noticeably run down when I was young; tourism had not yet made its mark. The old shops remained: haberdashers, grocers, chemists, butchers; supermarkets simply did not exist. On the ground were mostly cobblestones with a few patches of tarmac needing repair. Sepia-tinted photos, taken when photography was in its infancy, are nailed to the side of many streets, depicting what they looked like in these far-off days. The buildings are instantly recognisable, save for fresh licks of paint and repairs made to the *torchis*, a mix of mud and urine with superglue qualities holding the medieval beams and structure intact. Most of the people in the photos are wearing the *sabots*, wooden clogs, and I can just about remember old villagers dressed in black sitting in wicker chairs outside their homes wearing sabots on the feet and berets on their heads. It would be surreal if it were the other way round.

Both *bastides* are recipients of the accolade *les plus beaux villages de France*, the most beautiful villages in France. This is an independent association, created in 1982, for the promotion of the tourist appeal of small rural villages with a rich cultural heritage. Only about 160 villages have won the award, and most of them are in Aquitaine.

Villeréal and Monflanquin are thirteenth-century *bastides* like Castillonnès: planned, fortified, large villages that went back and forth from being English and French. Our pal Bernard says that *les plus beaux villages de France* accolade brings in at least 100,000 more visitors a year in coach tours – those who want to bag all the towns/villages with the award in France. Villeréal is the new kid on the block, and as a result, the place has been noticeably tarted up: new flagstones and baskets of flowers hanging over doorways. There are some interesting street names: *Rue des Abeilles* (the Street of the Bees), *Rue du Canard* (Duck Street) and *Rue des Amours* (Lovers Street). In the three *boulangeries* they sell cakes called *religieuse*, *pet-de-nonne* (a dessert called a nun's fart) and the risqué *divorcée*.

In the summer, the two nearby camp sites, Château de Fonrives and Les Ormes swell to 3,000 tourists. It all has a knock-on effect. The night markets have three sittings under the still-standing thirteenth-century covered market: an early 6pm sitting for the Dutch, then the British then the French late late late!

The 'Bodega' – the annual party that labyrinths in and out of the medieval streets – takes place at the beginning of August in Villeréal. Every year it becomes bigger and more colourful with street theatre, clowns, dancers, jugglers and musicians. It also lasts longer than twenty-four hours. 'I've had enough of this. The noise is driving me bananas,' complains Carol, who lives just off the town square. Carol is one of the most tolerant people I have ever met, so this is unheard of: 'Early this morning, I looked out the window and counted thirty-three men peeing in my lane. What a stink!' Paradoxically, the lane is just behind Rue des Amours, where love and piss intertwine.

Next year is the 750th anniversary of Villeréal and in preparation a small exhibition is being held in 'Salle de François Mitterrand' in the centre of the *bastide*. As soon as she hears of the exhibition my friend Christine drives over for the weekend from her home in Geneva to happily read up on the intricacies of the Occitan language. Christine and I met as teenagers when we studied languages together at university. She has lived in Milan and Geneva (working for the United Nations) for most of her adult life with occasional forays back to Glasgow to meet up with family. I suddenly realise that our most animated conversations have been about the complexities of language and yet we have never, ever spoken about maths and science. It may well be precisely because my knowledge of both is pitiful.

We now know that there are around 450,000 words in the Occitan vocabulary, nearly the same number as in English. Sometimes we hear old people speaking in Occitan, but it is fast dying out. Our old neighbours, the Gougets, remember the language and laugh when I say *Fai cailou*! (It's hot.)

There are a few well-known Occitan writers and poets who came from these parts like Victor Delbergé, Paul Froment and Noé Vaylet. (I know, me neither.) There is a strong folk tradition and out of curiosity I look out a few Occitan songs, for example, one by Félicien Beauvier called '*Si io sabiei volar*' (which I guess means 'If I knew how to fly'). A little bit goes a long way, but it is sad to see that there are only eight views in YouTube.

There were at least seven drinking dens in Villeréal, *cabarets*, in 1778, and these illegal bars were closed down by the order of the king. What I find odd in these *bastide* villages is that there are few green areas and no parks. Where do the children play? Then again, we are surrounded by glorious, accessible countryside.

Nine million died in the trenches in France during World War I and many of the young men from the countryside were used as cannon fodder. Many of the names on the numerous boards are familiar: Gouget, Birot, etc. from these parts. It is no surprise that the French had little appetite for war in 1939 after the carnage wreaked in World War I.

Our appetite is whetted for more local history, so we decide to go on a tour round the hilltop town of Monflanquin, which is organised by the local jester 'Janouille' who has bells on his toes, but no rings on his fingers. He is taking round a group of teenagers from the local school and we tag along at the end. He sings in Occitan, addresses us as *gueux/gueuse* (paupers) and dresses the kids up as historical figures and locals. He refrains from asking the adulterers to strip off as they are whipped and run through the square. I discover that the famous *pruneaux d'Agen* plums were originally from Damascus (damson plums) and brought back from the Crusades.

Given that Monflanquin is built on a hill there are few gardens, but a jaunty selection of flowers outside front doors make it so colourful. Eight new businesses have popped up in the last year, so the town has had a revival in fortune. But the best thing ever is the new ice-cream parlour. I can talk about my love of ice cream forever. Forever and a day. Oh, for a '99'!

The Labour Conference in Liverpool seems to have gone well and Corbyn's popularity is on the rise. In contrast, Theresa May's weird dancing to Abba in the Conservative ding-dong is cringeworthy. Where are her advisors? Guffawing behind their papers?

Here in France there is no end to Charles Aznavour tributes. Pavements are covered in photos and candles; there is a national outpouring of grief. He is (was) a famous, diminutive French crooner of Armenian descent. I thought he had already died some time back.

Beyond the grave, Johnny Hallyday is still selling albums and his unearthed material is being released this year. Known as simply 'Johnny' to the adoring French public, his career spanned fifty-seven years, making him one of the best-selling artists in France and in the world. He remains largely unknown in the English-speaking world, where he is dubbed 'the biggest rock star you've never heard of.' Nothing can beat Johnny blasting out '*J'oublierai ton nom*'.

Je t'aime, Johnny.

FROM CHAMPOLLION TO CHOPIN
VIA GRAVES

We have decided to make the most of the opportunity of not being officially at work for the year to go travelling when we can as we are no longer limited by teaching holiday dates when travel is at its most expensive. We reason that we are already broke so it makes little difference, and besides, we will be working furiously next year to pay off our debts. 'Time is precious and life is short,' I justify our decision.

My mother and her partner Douglas come with us to the Champollion museum in Figeac. 'But why are we going to a mushroom (champignon) museum?' enquires my mother. Secretly, I think she is pleased, as a connoisseur of fungi, and is slightly amused when I explain that it is nothing to do with them.

The museum is not only about the life and times of Jean-François Champollion (1790–1832), the famous French

Egyptologist who helped decode the Rosetta Stone, but it is also about *Les écritures du monde*, detailing the birth of writing to the present day. Dedicating himself to the study of various languages – including Persian, Ethiopian, Sanskrit, Zend, Pahlavi and Arabic – Champollion also began work on a dictionary and a book of grammar for the Coptic language. Not a shirker, Champollion said that after his Hebrew and Aramaic homework, he would do some 'light Latin reading', as you do. Examining texts brought from Egypt, he began to identify a relationship between hieroglyphic and non-hieroglyphic scripts, thereby turning the key to the translation of Egyptian hieroglyphics. We could easily spend the whole day in the museum, and in fact, we never got round all of it. It is quite engrossing, beautifully laid out with a very hands-on approach, showing the evolution of writing and language and how writing is used not only for communication but propaganda too.

On show was also Champollion's French internal passport. I hadn't realised that movement was so restricted in post-revolutionary France. I think it was Balzac, in the earlier part of the nineteenth century, who supported the introduction of passports for servants, so they wouldn't presume to aspire to rise above their station.

In keeping with the Champollion's Egyptian connection, two of the cafés in Figeac are called Café Giza and Café des Pyramides.

I am starting a mug collection, mainly because most of our mugs are chipped, so it gives me an excuse to buy new ones. I have two new mugs: one with hieroglyphics on it and the other with musical notation.

Back in Coutal my mother is just as hooked on *vide-greniers*, car boot sales, as I am. She buys a chamber pot and a huge steam iron. I dissuade her from buying a breadmaker. Why would you need such a thing here when the bread in *boulangeries* is so good? My mother is worried that I will chop down her favourite tree: the massive lime tree in front of the house. She wraps her arms around it. 'Please, Basia, I love this tree, leave it alone!'

For a change of scene and to maintain our well-defined calves, Gerry and I decided to go on a week-long hiking holiday to Majorca in the middle of October. We arrive on the tail-end of storms, hurricanes and tornadoes (Michael? Lesley?) and while we are blithely tramping the tracks, the village of Sant Llorenç on the other side of the Tramuntana Mountains from us is swept away while twelve people die in the floods in South West France. We are oblivious to all of this.

Despite the beautiful surroundings, I can't help feeling anxious and low; I am not in my *assiette*, I am out of sorts. Only by exhausting myself by hiking do I manage to somehow quell, or at least minimise, the internal clamour. I have no idea why I am feeling this way. My New Year's resolution of the previous year was to stop taking the high dose of anti-depressant pills I had been prescribed for the last ten years. Surely I can live without them?

We walk through ancient olive groves, through citrus orchards, but it is very difficult to veer from the paths, and everywhere we go there are '*Pelligroso, caza mayor*' signs: Dangerous, big game. What big game, I wonder? Lions, elephants, hippos, leopards, buffaloes? Don't see any here.

We stay in a very chic hotel called 'Ca's Xorc', a brilliant excuse to embellish their tourist literature with 'Welcome to the land of Orcs!' They just need to add 'Humans of ferocious nature also accepted!' No such luck. The view over Soller to the Mediterranean is magnificent.

Last April, we stayed in Banksy's hotel in Bethlehem and I loved the hotel's two-fingered approach to advertising. 'Come to stay in the hotel with the worst view in the world' and the booking letter quotes the hotelier extraordinaire Basil Fawlty, 'You ponce in here expecting to be waited on hand and foot while I'm trying to run a hotel.'

We didn't meet a single Spanish tourist while hiking; it's far too expensive a place for them. This is the playground for mainly German tourists. Even the smallest *finca*, farmhouse, is snapped up for at least €1million. An expat Brit married to a Spanish tradesman explained: 'If you are a woman in your fifties looking for a job, you can forget it. Best not be over forty years old. Unemployment is high, or rather it is all seasonal work. If there is a chance that you will be able to acquire "workers' rights" you will soon find yourself un-hired. A good salary is €1,200 a month; a manager earns €1,500 a month.'

I buy a mug with 'Frederic Chopin' emblazoned on it. I cannot believe that for years I did not realise that his father was French, hence his name. After all, he was not called Szopenski or anything like that. Gerry and I once visited his birthplace in Żelazowa Wola in Poland. It isn't far from Warsaw but it took ages to get there by public transport. There was nothing to see. Chopin was only there for a few months and then his family moved on. We were therefore determined to find out something more substantial about the pianist.

Sadly, his *séjour* in the winter of 1838/39 in Valldemossa in Majorca also turned out to be a bit of a swizz. He had gone there with George Sand, his lover (female – it is a nom de plume), to bask in a mild climate more beneficial to his delicate health. However, when they found out that he was consumptive, no hotels would let them in, and in the end they found sanctuary in a cold cell in a Carthusian monastery. To make matters worse, the arrival of his piano was delayed by many weeks and the weather was cold and bleak, thereby weakening the poor man even more. George smoked like a chimney which aggravated his TB.

This does not stop the Majorcan tourist board from claiming that many of his famous pieces were composed there and so continues a veritable money-spinner. I would guess that in the few wretched months Chopin spent in Valldemossa all he probably did was dot and cross his notation. The clay copy of his fingers showed them to be long and slender, *quelle surprise*. As my old piano teacher, Mrs Paxton, used to say, 'Watch it, crotch it, or I'll minimise your quaver.'

One day we hiked over the mountains to Deia to visit Robert Graves' house. There is something wonderful about seeing and touching the desk where a writer you admired has once worked. I remember visiting Federico García Lorca's house in Fuente Vaqueros, not far from Madrid, and doing the same. Ten years ago, Gerry and I (and friend Fran) visited Ernest Hemingway's house, 'Finca Vigía', outside Havana in Cuba. All the windows are left wide open so tourists can peer inside and see it exactly as he had left it in 1959 with all his books and furnishings on display. There was his typewriter with his reading glasses to one side. He stood up when he wrote so that he would be fully focused on the task. No editing; no word processing. On the walls were photos of all the famous stars who came to visit and frolic in the pool. Would you believe there was a photo of Ava Gardner in both Hemingway's and Graves' houses? A gal who appeared to be a groupie for writers. It seems odd to think of all these visitors in the cramped sitting room in Graves' house with the wireless at one end and the sofa at the other.

Graves' study is at the back of the house. He insisted on complete silence, and any noise made by his lover Laura Riding, whose studio was above his, enraged him. Incidentally, Laura Riding claimed that she learnt Spanish by reading *Don Quixote* in English and Spanish simultaneously. What rot, say I.

Graves wrote prolifically, more than 100 books, mainly to keep the wolf from the door. But his wolf was different to my wolf. Throughout his life, family money propped up his own family's finances. He bought the land in front of his house, complete with olive groves, simply to prevent others from buying it and thus spoiling his view. Granted it was a sea view, so I understand. He wrote and rewrote and each page is peppered with scorings out until the laborious process reaped results and eventually the final work was typed up. He needed the money, since he had rather a large *ménage*: wives, lovers and eight children. A bit like the description of Bloomsbury: 'People in threesomes living in squares.' One of the reasons he gave for going to live in Majorca was to do with living cheaply in a sunnier clime and sloughing off the past.

I didn't buy a mug. I had read Robert Graves' book *Goodbye to All That* when I was at school and even then I was struck by the simplicity, honesty and intensity of his writing. I bought a copy for Gerry and devoured the book again as soon as he had read it.

This edition is the unexpurgated original version which hadn't been polished up for future generations and its rawness is still very powerful. Only two world wars and the Spanish Civil War disturbed Graves' productivity. At least living to the age of ninety he could enjoy the fruits of his success.

When we were at secondary school my friend Julie was besotted by George Mallory, who died during his descent from Everest in 1924. In 1999 photographs were published of his body preserved by the permafrost. I didn't know Graves had been one of George Mallory's best friends. Mallory was a school master at Charterhouse, popular with the boys, and Graves was one of his pupils, but he was not popular with the other masters. He was Graves' best man at his first wedding.

I never understood why homosexuality was illegal for so long when biographies such as Graves' suggest that it was rife in most boys' public schools. I then recalled all the homoerotic photos taken of Mallory at that time.

Graves writes that boys of the same age used each other coldly as convenient sex-instruments. He describes how he was once made to do mental arithmetic to a metronome, which made him wet his trousers. I wondered if all this repression and cruelty made him mentally resilient to endure the four years in the trenches. Unsurprisingly he suffered from neurasthenia, 'shellshock', for ten years after the war had ended.

One out of three from his generation at school was killed. Indeed, his death was announced in dispatches in 1916 during the Battle of the Somme. It was clear that big chunks of the book had formed the backdrop to the *Blackadder* TV scripts with the division of classes, the colonels and other notables holed up in quite salubrious surroundings not far from the slaughter of the front line, obsessing about buttons being shone and swords being specially sharpened by an armourer.

Ron Fairfax, who lives near us in France, wrote a book called *Corky's War: The Diary of an RAMC Stretcher-Bearer* (RAMC=Royal Army Medical Corps) which was an account of his friend Percy Cawkwell's experience in the trenches and there are excerpts of *Blackadder* behaviour in this book as well.

The author Naomi Mitchison described going on her honeymoon from Scotland in 1916 to the South of France, skirting the theatre of war. While millions were slain, others sunbathed.

Another close friend of Graves was the poet Siegfried Sassoon, who was also very openly gay. Sassoon said that he had flung his Military Cross into the sea as a gesture of disgust for the war, but this was a lie and it was found in a relative's attic in 2007. One of these odd things was that his grandfather, a Baghdadi Jewish merchant called Sassoon David Sassoon, disinherited Siegfried Sassoon's father for marrying out of the faith.

I didn't know Graves had also known T.E. Lawrence and wrote his biography. Last year I visited the Bodleian in Oxford to see Lawrence's Arabic garb out on display.

Graves describes himself as a product of his background, born into the ruling classes. He said that he could not believe that politicians or statesmen could lie. Despite himself, he could not shake off his feelings of superiority. He was dismissive about the poet Wilfred Owen because he regarded him as not being of the same class, even though he had attended Graves' wedding.

I wonder what he would have thought of his contemporary, D.H. Lawrence? When Gerry, Fran, Sharon and her son, Will, and I went to Taormina on holiday (we holiday in packs), I tried to track down where D.H. Lawrence had lived for a few years with his German wife Frieda. I had pinpointed where the house should have stood, but there was no longer any trace of it. The conclusion is that the house had been pulled down.

The Bloomsbury Group have had a certain fascination for me ever since I was at school. I knew all about their bitchiness ('she stinks like a civet cat taken to streetwalking,' a classic line by Virginia Woolf about Katherine Mansfield), petty squabbles and cavorting. Perhaps my predilection in holidaying with close family or friendship groups stems from reading about D.H. Lawrence's utopian community which he named 'Rananim'. Maybe this is what I strive for in Coutal, this close bond of community living.

Graves was also a fan of communal living, but this usually comprised a wife, a muse or mistress and a bunch of children.

In 1926 Graves wrote 'university professor' in his passport as he was taking up a teaching job in Cairo. He did not want to put down his profession as 'writer' since it attracted some suspicion in bureaucratic circles. As he explained: 'University professor wins a simple reaction – dull respect.' Everyone and anyone is a writer, I guess. And something new for me too: 'Blighty' is Hindustani for home.

I am truly at the mercy of my failing faculties. Last year I went to see a film about early onset dementia with my auntie Margaret called *Still Alice*. The following week she and I were trying to remember the film we had watched. 'Remembering Agnes?' We were both confused about the term 'fanny-pack' which I realised at the end of the film was her bum bag. Anyway, as always, I digress. Yesterday, at dinner in the hotel, I mentioned to Gerry that the waiter looks like a famous actor. 'You know, the one that was the nasty guy in *Spider-Man*. Or was it *Superman*?' Gerry looked bewildered. 'He was in *The Last Temptation of Christ*!' No joy. We ran through various other possibilities while the dinner went cold. I persuaded Gerry to google the films. 'That's him!' I squealed. 'Willem Dafoe!' I felt relieved. I am not losing my mind. It's the same thing with remembering punchlines of jokes but not the lead-up.

Walking back from Graves' house, I say to Gerry, 'Did you notice he was a friend of whassisname. You know, Martin Amis's dad? Also an author. Wrote *Lucky Jim*.' No answer. I persist. 'The person I am talking about was a friend of the poet, librarian in Hull, *really famous*, wrote *The Whitsun Weddings*.' Gerry looks askance. I offer, ever hopeful, 'They fuck you up, your mum and dad?' Eventually, after tortuous, serpentine meandering, the name of Philip Larkin, in neon lights, pops up. After a few stabs at Godley Amis, Frank Amis, etc. we eventually hit the bull's eye with Kingsley Amis. I try to tie up my story. 'So, as I was saying, did you notice that Kingsley Amis was a friend of Robert Graves and his photo is up on the wall alongside all the other famous people who visited him in Deia? Amis went all the way to Majorca to visit Graves but refused to visit one of his own best friends, Philip Larkin, because he lived oop north, in Hull?

'What Deia think of that?'

You might have noticed that my thoughts go off on a tangent with no encouragement whatsoever. I must be a nightmare to live with. When I say this to Gerry, he doesn't respond but there is a wry smile on his lips.

We get back to the hotel and dive into the infinity pool. There is a couple there; the woman is sunbathing while her husband is working. He barks into his mobile, 'I didn't hire you to be average. Don't sign it if it looks like a five-year-old has written the contract.'

In the week we have been staying in Ca's Xorc I have not heard him address a single word to his wife. She looks bored out of her head. Perhaps this is the point where not remembering and forgetting meet: total brain-death.

GLASGOW, BERLIN AND BACK AGAIN

We plan to do a whirlwind trip back to Glasgow to do the car's MOT, pick up my Polish passport, sort out tax, Chinese visas, see friends and family and get back to Coutal for the installation of the windows and our friend Jennifer's arrival. We are too ambitious and get more than we bargain for.

We sigh with relief as we drive past Périgueux, scene of the radiator blowing up on our way to Coutal in the summer. Once we let the sighs out, the clutch gives up the ghost as we slowly drive up to the motorway toll. It costs €650 for the recovery truck to take us to our local garage in Villeréal. The recovery truck breaks down in turn once we reach the garage (brilliant timing) which makes it impossible to unload the car. The 'recovery' man is furious, *et alors maintenant nous sommes dans le même bâteau*! (Now we are all in the same boat.) Our new word of the day is *l'embroyeur* – the clutch.

My mother and her partner Douglas are still at Coutal Haut – just – so luckily they can pick us up from the garage. They soon leave for other pastures; I quickly book an airline ticket for the next day for myself as I urgently need to be in Edinburgh to pick up my Polish passport. Gerry is home alone. Carless.

It takes six days for the car to be fixed so Gerry turns up the music full blast, gets back to his tree chopping and cycles around the neighbourhood.

I, meanwhile, stay in Glasgow with friends Susan and Ian in a house with central heating. Oh, these comforts – only appreciated once the weather turns frosty. Ian tells me about a certain strain of Scottish bees which are called 'Buckfast' bees and have a very amenable temperament.

I thought I would be able to pick up my Polish passport then and there in Edinburgh, and hold out my sweaty mit in anticipation, to be told to come back in four weeks' time! I beg them to send it to me. They say they will do that if I can provide an SAE. I run to the nearest post office, feet bleeding (new shoes not yet broken in), buy the appropriate envelope, rush back to the consulate and manage to hand it in just before the door closes. I nearly collapse on the stairs, tongue hanging out.

On the way back to Waverley station in Edinburgh, I stop to look at the monument to Wojtek the Soldier Bear. Dziadzia, my maternal grandfather, who had survived Siberia in World War II, told me about this bear which had accompanied his regiment to Palestine and all sorts of places. I thought he had been making it up! Apparently, Wojtek was an orphaned brown bear they had found in Iran and in order to adopt him they had him officially drafted into the army as a private. He was given his own pay packet and serial number. Wojtek enjoyed wrestling, drinking beer and smoking cigarettes. Gunfire didn't bother him and he carried ammunition in the battle for Monte Cassino. Like my grandfather and other Polish officers, Wojtek settled in Scotland. He died in Edinburgh Zoo in 1943. I could hardly believe it was a true story, but my auntie Margaret corroborated it. Unfortunately, my grandfather did not have any photos of Wojtek, but seeing the sculpture there in Princes Gardens made it all flood back and I could hear my grandfather's distinctive voice.

There was another sad event: the funeral in Greenock of Bill Lancaster, whose family I have known forever. He was such a character, and in this celebration of his life the Pentecostal Church was stowed out. Susan and I looked at each other askance when the pastor said his life was about the 5Fs. Pardon? The pastor explained: Faith, Family, Friendship, Flamboyancy and Fun.

Gerry eventually arrives in Glasgow on the Saturday morning after an epic trip from the Thursday afternoon, having faced delayed ferries, grid-locked South of England and the temporarily closed M6 motorway. He texts me en route to say that he had driven past *Orléans: au pays de George Sand.* That woman again! Stalking him all the way from Majorca!

Gerry keeps awake by accompanying songs on the radio with his own trumpet sounds. He arrives in Glasgow in the nick of time to drop the car off at the garage for the MOT and whizz to the airport to catch the flight to Berlin with me. Gerry is comatose in the plane. We have promised our friend, Christine Bovill, that we will go over and hear her sing at the beautiful Spiegeltent where she has a long-term residency.

The last time I had been in Berlin was when the children were little. It was in the summer during the Festival of Love. We were walking through the Tiergarten Park during the day and suddenly we heard rustling sounds nearby.

'What is that man doing down there?' Irena pointed at a white bottom partially obscured by bushes. 'Ah,' I replied quickly, my grey cells whirring madly in my brain, 'that man has dropped his glasses in the hedge and the other man has kindly stopped to help him retrieve them. Come on, children, no dilly-dallying!'

Apropos of nothing, the word Berlin means a dry point on swampy ground.

The high point is Christine's wonderful performance and Michael Brawley's excellent piano playing.

Christine has been a great supporter and performer at our fundraising events for Palestine and it is a pleasure to listen as an audience member and not to be the busy, stressed-out organisers behind the scenes. After the concert, we repair to a bar with the full pre-war Weimar flavour: transvestites, smoking, more singing and drinking. The conversation flits from the Irish potato famine to how Berlusconi, Michael Jackson, David Gest, Liza Minnelli and Liz Taylor all looked eerily similar because they shared the same plastic surgeon. It's all so random when you are truly blootered.

Again, we are tormented by more travel woes: I cannot find my ticket (honest, I had bought one) and I am fined €60 on the spot by the inspector in the U-Bahn (underground) and we are forced to take a taxi to the far away former Soviet airport when the train was cancelled for the day.

We pack in a full *sturmwind* tour of Berlin. Gerry grumbles. 'Surely there must be a Chopin midden we can visit?' He is chuffed to see Potsdamer Platz because of its references to David Bowie's song 'Where Are We Now?' As we wander around the Brandenburg Gate we spot the centaur iconography. Billy Connelly once said 'half-man, half-horse, licensed to shit in the street.' There were death traps on either side of the gate during the whole of the Cold War. They should have left the gate as a magnificent ruin and not the cleaned-up version we have today.

In 1940 it took twelve days to travel seamlessly from Tokyo by train to Berlin. Berlin is a stone's throw from the Polish border and perfect marching terrain. I find it galling to see so many monuments to those who suffered during the war, but none to the Poles. Over fifty million people worldwide died in the carnage unleashed by the Germans. Curiously, there are few references to Germans, just to the Nazis, as if they are some malevolent race from a place called Naziland. It is sometimes forgotten that Hitler didn't seize power. He was democratically elected by the German people, oops, Nazis.

When we visit the incredible rebuilt and architecturally magnificent Reichstag building, I sit on a bench at the viewing platform at the top of the dome and defiantly read an apposite book, Ksawery Pruszyński's *Polish Invasion*. What could be described as a work of friction. No one notices my stance. So much for defiance. The book was written in 1942 by the father of Staś, a family friend, about the Polish officers who found themselves in Scotland. They expected a more triumphant end to the war than the bittersweet exile they endured.

The view from the dome of the Reichstag is spectacular. Only one embassy survived at the end of war: the Swiss embassy, and this was probably because of the massive Red Cross emblazoned on the roof; it may have been mistaken for the eponymous charity. At that time too, the Reichstag itself was used as a hospital and many children were born there in 1945.

Interestingly (well, to me) all the Scandinavian embassies are under one roof; how very cost-efficient and egalitarian. I am impressed by Germany's green credentials, but Gerry cynically explains that the reason they are so green is because they use French nuclear energy.

The unification of East and West Berlin makes it a rather sprawling city with a population of 3.4 million. Like Villeréal it also has a 750-year history. There the comparison ends.

I look for a mug with *Ich bin ein Berliner* inscribed on it without success and make do with a 'Check-point Charlie' one instead. It was only back in Glasgow that Susan explained to us what a *faux pas* the famous quote by Kennedy is since it can also be translated as 'I am a doughnut.'

The tour around East Berlin seems eerily familiar to me since I spent so much time in my childhood in Eastern Bloc countries, waiting for the click of the phone to go so we knew we were being overheard. The tour guide points out cinemas with 'nude films with live music' but I feel that we must have misheard him. He also urges us to see Roberto Rossellini's film *Germany Year Zero*. The tour takes us around the wall which snaked through the city in large sections. There were twenty escape tunnels but only three were successful.

We fly back from Berlin to Edinburgh in time for our Chinese interviews for visas (we are set to go on a trip to China at the end of November) with what we are told is a 'high quality' invitation, but nevertheless our passports are taken from us. We didn't think we would be in the position of being *sans papiers*, or to misquote Bob Marley, 'no documents, no travel'.

Our friend Jennifer is due to arrive in Bergerac airport on Saturday afternoon and we are due to pick her up. An operation of military precision ensues. We pick up our passports and visas in Edinburgh on Friday morning at 9am, drive non-stop overnight (except for the Channel hop), and as we drive towards Bergerac airport we can see the Ryanair flight touch down on the tarmac. We saunter up to the arrival gates, smile expansively as Jen emerges and try to hide our utter exhaustion.

Jen and I have known each other since we were in Dr Taylor's Latin class in secondary school. We both loved Latin. Give us an ablative absolute to chew over and we are quite content.

As always, visits from our friends give us a perfect excuse to see things we have been dying to see. We visit the new Lascaux IV, a facsimile of the cave art painted 20,000 years ago. It is incredible to think that these people are just the same as us, homo sapiens, physically and mentally. It is a pity we cannot crack the code of squares and dots. And what paintings, the movement and perspective of the animals so beautifully executed. The paintings of the dangerous animals – bears, lions and rhinos (there in the south-west during this last ice age) – are hidden from view from the observer. It is little wonder these paintings inspired artists like Picasso.

The weather is not brilliant but the perfect thing to do in wet weather is visit the thermal baths in Casteljaloux – so blissful to be in the warm water with raindrops falling on your head. Cue for a song?

Jennifer, who is an aficionada of wild swimming, coerces me into the chilly waters of the nearest lake. I die and do not go to heaven. At last I have someone to play table tennis with. We have set up the table in the barn and have to keep moving to keep warm because of the absence of glass in the windows. It is not so much a through draught but a through whoosh of wind. Monsieur Peyrac installs the skylights in the barns and pools of light beam down, illuminating the dust, rather like the transporter in *Star Trek*.

We can hear the hunters' guns go off before we leave to go to the Armistice commemoration in our local village, St Vivien, 100 years after the end of World War I. It is chilling to hear the roll call of so many local men who died (and one in Iraq in

2018) in such a sparsely populated part of the world followed by the rousing singing of 'La Marseillaise'. 'La Marseillaise' is everything a national anthem should be: easy on the ear, easy to remember and good for marching.

The kilt-attired Gerry attracts a lot of sideways glances. Just at the end of the ceremony, as if on cue, an elderly man with lupine features (a friend of my mother's) collapses and is rushed to hospital by ambulance, with his wife, Gerry and I following behind in our car. Most of the day is spent there until he is let out; we are none the wiser about what had brought on his malaise. We had arranged to go to lunch with friends in Villeréal but have no way of contacting them, so we eventually appear at their door, hours late for a quick bite before returning to the hospital.

Now that Jennifer has left, the weather has perked up with all the russet autumnal colours and low sun. Gerry has been busy building the windows for the master bedroom and I have been planting lavender, pumpkins, rosemary and sunflowers as well as trying to declutter the house.

Our calendar is mislaid so I buy a temporary one-page replacement and discover that December 4th is St Barbara's Day and December 5th is St Gerald's Day. We didn't know a St Gerald existed, although, deep down in his heart, Gerry knew there had to be one, the saint who will bring us good fortune. I tell him he has a long way to go before beatification.

Destiny has done its level best to keep us apart. We discovered that we had the same concert tickets for the infamous Glasgow venue, the Apollo, starting with the Kraftwerk concert in 1975 when the lad was barely out of short trousers. Given the fact that there were only a handful of people at the Kraftwerk concert we must have surely noticed each other. This is the moment to mention the fantastic music scene in Glasgow in the 1970s, especially the Apollo in Renfield

Street. I have kept a few of the tickets of the acts I saw perform: Gong, The Who, Queen, Cockney Rebel, David Bowie, Black Sabbath, Tangerine Dream, Yes, Caravan, Todd Rundgren, The Sensational Alex Harvey Band, Roxy Music… I even gave my Rolling Stones ticket away because it was the night before my maths prelim! I went to the Apollo nearly every week. I lament the fact that I gave away most of my LPs and concert programmes over the years. Gerry and I also went to some of the same productions in the Citizen's Theatre, again, apart! It then transpires we were in the Himalayas at the same time and various other places too. Nope, we did not clock each other at all! We have done our best to steer clear of each other for most of our lives, so destiny is having a good laugh. What have we done to deserve this?

I am tempted by the new lottery, the lotto, called *Patrimoine*, which is about saving France's heritage as well as the chance of replenishing depleted coffers.

This morning we went to the market in Villeréal, and as well as stocking up on wood for the building requirements, we leave with wine, tomatoes and bread. What else would we need?

I am puzzled by the display of high vis jackets behind car windscreens that have suddenly appeared. On the radio we hear reports of these two ragamuffins, *Giles et Jeanne*, causing havoc and presume they are latter-day Bonnie and Clyde characters. Again, we are sceptical about what we are hearing. It takes quite a while for it to percolate that this is a mass civic protest. This is the *Gilets Jaunes* movement, a sign of protest by those in the countryside who are increasingly disgruntled by the rise of taxes (especially petrol) which affect countryside dwellers rather than those living in the city. Macron's popularity has plummeted here. One of the stallholders today has the *Chant de la Commune* attached to her vegetable stall. Roughly translated it reads: 'The bad days will come to an end and the poor will rise up and the week of blood will flow'! You go to buy some veg and get some top-notch rhetorical flourish in return.

There is going to be a big demonstration by the *Gilets Jaunes* in Paris today.

16th November 2018. Big speech by Theresa May announcing a sort of Brexit deal in sketchy form. Every time a journalist asks a question she goes into Maybot mode repeating the same, tired, worn-out statements: 'the people voted… I am here to deliver…' Four cabinet ministers resign, including Dominic Raab, Minister for Brexit. What a government, full of numpties.

Stephen Hawkins said, shortly before he died:
'Ask me anything about nuclear physics, but don't ask me anything about Brexit'.

Twelve

SHANGHAI AND BEIJING
November–December 2018

'Shanghai is a mix of *Blade Runner* and Bearsden,' (a plush Glasgow suburb) remarked Eunice, our hostess, and she is not wrong in her assessment. It is an incredible megalopolis with twenty-five million people swishing around in an ever-expanding urban zone. Since the early 1990s Shanghai has expanded by 10% every year. Forty cities in China have more than one million inhabitants and more than ten cities have more than five million. Mind-boggling numbers for country bumpkins, *les ploucs*, such as ourselves to comprehend. We can scream in Coutal, but no one will hear us.

We didn't plan to leave home so soon (I know, yet another holiday…), but our friends are about to leave their diplomatic posting after six years in the city and it would have been a shame to miss the opportunity to visit such a fascinating place. Jules is 'our man in the Pacific rim', zooming around Singapore, Japan, Indonesia and China. And he clearly thrives on the challenge. (Apparently, there is £1billion of Japanese investment in Scotland.) It so happens that their posting is yet again extended at the last minute, but too late; we have already bought the tickets and I am excited at the prospect of expanding my mug collection.

We have a few hurdles to overcome before we get there. We decided to book a hotel the night before the flight in Bordeaux and just cannot figure out why there is no availability anywhere on a Tuesday night in late November. The *Gilets Jaunes* movement has spread like wildfire and all the main roads and roundabouts are blocked with just a trickle of traffic managing to get through. The country grinds to a halt. The best chance of catching our morning flight is to leave in the early hours and spend the rest of the night in the car. Bordeaux airport is closed at night. The temperature plummets to below zero and we can feel the chill, even wrapped up in blankets.

Many hours later, we look suitably exhausted on arrival in Shanghai. The next hurdle is to actually enter the country. My visa fingerprints do not match up with my passport's and I find myself sitting in a small room with three Chinese officials looking intently at my face, comparing it with my passport and driving licence. They eventually give up after coming to the conclusion that all Westerners look the same and so, Shanghai, here we come!

It is difficult to understand the scale of the rapid expansion: shanty towns are razed to the ground on a frequent basis and gleaming skyscrapers take their place. Mature trees are brought in from the countryside and propped up by stakes, as if they had always been there. Shanghai is pancake-flat, built on a swamp, so it is full of mosquitoes, forty degrees centigrade in the summer and cold and damp in winter. The houses are badly insulated; even the palatial home of our friends could not keep the warmth within its walls. So, joy of joys, one day an electric, heated mat arrives among the daily *Taobao* (Amazon equivalent) packages that come to the house. Under the table it goes, to warm our tootsies!

In China there is no sentimentality about ditching the past and little can be done to oppose governmental decisions on urban policy. We visit an old temple that has a big shiny new temple built at the back of it, ready for the eventual demolition of the old one.

As we are taken around one migrant town ear-marked for demolition, we are told that the inhabitants would be given accommodation as owners in new replacement buildings which correspond to the exact size of their original dwelling. Clearly, this would be advantageous in a place where land values are at a premium.

Shanghainese are among the wealthiest in China. In the gated community where Eunice and Jules live, the Chinese neighbours boast Maseratis and other expensive European cars in their garages.

The surge of the country population moving to the huge urban centres looking for work and a better life comes at a price. Our friends' maid, for example, has left her family behind in the provinces, but unusually she has brought her child with her rather than leaving her with parents. The maid earns enough to send money back to her family, but she is not eligible for health insurance since she is not a native of Shanghai and has to pay for her daughter's education past middle school. Education is all; the only hope to improve one's lot. The maid's daughter is constantly studying because only the best students will get a 20% discount on university education. And there is still homelessness and poverty in stark contrast to the Chinese elite. Nevertherless, as a legacy of the communist ideals, there are plenty of jobs, although some employees are not doing a lot, like the park attendants either walking around in a desultory manner or with their feet up in the park cabin at the entrance, not bothering to issue tickets to go into the park! They, I think, are the exception to the rule. This is a city that never stops and hard work is expected with few workers' rights. *Gilets Jaunes* supporters would be horrified!

The pollution is ever-present and oppressive, and many people walk around with masks on their mouths. When I open my suitcase, I am overwhelmed by the smell of wood smoke. And then a tiny *punaise* – a French bug – tumbles out and crawls away. I have brought my own pollution.

And yet. And yet. There is so much to admire. We are looking at the future. Everything runs so smoothly compared to crumbling Europe; the trains, the digital mastery, the tidiness, the industriousness, the architectural wonders, the infrastructure, the no-nonsense approach. It is an entrepreneur's paradise. Increasingly, payments are made by mobile phone. Technology is far more advanced in China than in the West. Eunice demonstrates an app she has on her phone: she points her phone at a cup and instantly artificial intelligence picks up and displays all the information pertinent to said cup, even to the extent of comparing the suppliers of the cup.

We visit the fabric market ('same, same' as I ask for an exact copy of my dress) and the fake market for us greedy Westerners. I buy the perfect, capacious, beige carpet slippers. The sales assistant says to me, 'They are made from real carpets,' and bows her head, reverently.

The Chinese dragon is clearly on a trajectory after many years in the doldrums. Despite the enormous urban growth, there are signs of sustainability kicking in, with the expansion of electric motorbikes and cars.

I am curious to learn about the reason for China's decline in the nineteenth century, 'the moment of divergence', the time when the West superseded the East in terms of progress. There are several reasons for this; one is that the Imperial Exam civil servants had to pass, while of a certain intellectual rigour, excluded entrepreneurship and scientific advancement. Another hypothesis was that China had not discovered glass until years after the West. Glass, as it is an inert substance, is key to scientific experimentation, without which progress cannot be made, and in time this was a massive drawback to Chinese advancement. Only so much you can do with porcelain.

In modern-day Shanghai, there is something for everyone: the best shops, the best restaurants, the best floral displays. We walk down the *Bund* (the main walkway by the side of the river) in the crisp sunshine, surrounded by young couples taking their wedding pictures against a backdrop of granite buildings that hark back to a colonial past.

There is still a vestige of old colonial Shanghai in the Yuyuan Gardens and the former French Concession. The sickly smell of fried tofu pervades the alleyways. People drink hot water, not cold water. I tell Gerry that Shanghai is famous for its hairy crabs. He replies that it sounds both itchy and sore! Washing hangs out in lines across buildings. Eunice observes, 'big knickers, tiny bums'. And she is right.

We are so lucky to be taken around Shanghai by friends who know the place so well and speak Mandarin. Eunice and Jules have embraced this city. Every day is a revelation, some little gem to uncover. Somehow the ultra-modernity accommodates the traditional. We visit the marriage market located in the corner of a park in the centre of the city. Parents sit under umbrellas with details of their offspring (mainly female) written on them. If you are over thirty and unmarried it is a real worry. Many people are so busy building careers that they have missed the marriage boat, hence parents come to the rescue. Gerry raises the hopes of one lady while trying to photograph her description on the umbrella, as he said, causing mayhem as he swipes right!

There are so many differences between the East and West outlook. Little hammers pound my feet during foot massage; I am in the halfway state of laughing and crying with pain. Chinese people rarely make eye contact and it is an odd experience to try to connect with someone whose eyes are continually darting around in a bid to escape your gaze.

Some differences are insurmountable. True integration is nearly impossible, because if you have a Chinese passport you cannot join a foreign society and vice versa and similarly the schools are segregated. To limit Western influence, only twenty foreign films are shown in cinemas in Shanghai per year, although around the corner from our hotel in Beijing there is a retrospective of the Polish director, Andrzej Wajda, showing Polish films of my childhood.

I suppose the most difficult thing for a Westerner to do is to master Mandarin. The word *shi* has endless meanings (to excrete, to lick, etc.) and only the tonality and context explains exactly what is meant. Because of the small families (the one child rule has been relaxed but few couples have more than one child) there is a paranoia about a child being born with a disability, so women go into the maternity hospital a month before they are due to give birth, just to ensure nothing goes wrong.

We attend an 'Ireland and Northern Ireland dinner' and tuck into hearty fare. No talk about the backstop.

We visit an old Buddhist temple complex where money is burnt as an offering to the gods, or rather, people pay the temple to burn paper representing money and, even more impressively, they can send their temple offering straight to the cloud via QR code, where the gods are ready to receive. Progress!

The bullet train from Shanghai to Beijing takes less than five hours at the speed of 341km per hour. And there are many such bullet trains zooming around. Shanghai to Beijing is one big building site as old neighbourhoods are pulled down and gleaming skyscrapers erected in their place.

'When was the last time you were in a cable car?' asks Gerry as we approach the Great Wall. 'The Cairngorms?' I venture. 'Nope.' 'Beirut?' 'Getting warmer.' 'Jericho!' I exclaim triumphantly. We were there to find the last temptation of Christ but failed miserably.

It is sunny but freezing as we saunter along the Wall. There are robust tourists like us around, but the cold keeps the hordes at bay. It is only later that I discover what an unusual occurrence this is; it is usually jam-packed and people slowly shuffle forwards. We walk, nay, stride for about three hours, doing suitably funny walks to commemorate our visit: 'The Great Leap Forward,' 'The Giant Step Backwards,' with *pas-de-chat* poses and a bit of kung-fu thrown in for good measure. This is where West meets East. By sheer chance I am dressed in white and vaguely resemble a giant panda.

Signal beacons made from burning dried wolf dung were used to warn of attack and some naughty people had also left their dung in some outlook posts. The bricks in the wall are fixed together with glutinous rice flour. The adhesive qualities of rice are truly remarkable.

We manage to squeeze in a visit to the Forbidden City – built to impress with its sheer magnitude. One temple or pavilion gives way to an even more lavish one, as if to say, 'That's nothing, look at this!' Our eyes are dazed from the intensity of the colour red; it is rich, sumptuous and marvellous. The red colour of the buildings is punctuated with gold flecks.

'Don't talk about you know what!' hisses Gerry as we walk around heavily guarded Tiananmen Square. 'What are you talking about?' I feign ignorance. Luckily, Beijing is flat and we walk for hours on end, soaking up the atmosphere. We stay in a Hutong Hotel, one of the old-style hotels in Beijing with a clock from Bordeaux on the wall.

Speeding back to Shanghai on the bullet train, I look out of the window and notice an old man with a bicycle and cart, gathering firewood. I blink and he is gone.

In the propaganda museum in Shanghai (in the basement of someone's house) I indulge in my new passion for mugs. What has come over me? I set them off with my favourite propaganda posters of girls in ballet shoes, toting guns. The early 1920s posters are the best: 'pinkerettes, pale pills for pale people'.

Propaganda posters in the social realism style, similar to the ones during the Stalinist era in Russia, are no longer displayed in China. Notwithstanding, the veneration for Chairman Mao is still very much in evidence since he is the one who pulled China up from a quasi-medieval, agrarian society to a modern country, despite the cost to human life this entailed. His image still remains on the paper money but for how long? According to the author, Hans Rosling, Mao has a lot to answer for. In 1960, between fifteen to forty million people – nobody knows the exact number – starved to death in China, in what was the world's largest ever man-made famine. I discussed this with Jules who spoke about the positive things Mao had done. Still, it is irrefutable that the government denied that its central planning had failed and the catastrophe was kept secret by the Chinese for thirty-six years. It wasn't revealed to the outside world until 1996. How incredible – and worrying – that a government can keep the death of fifteen million-plus people a secret for such a long time.

Now I understand why the old temple we visited in Shanghai remains standing. The chief official of the area kept the grain for the local population rather than sending it on to the central office (against orders), thus averting a local famine. In a sinister move, in March 2018 the Chinese constitution was changed to theoretically allow the current president Xi Jinping to remain in the post for life.

According to official figures, only 9% of the world's population live in extreme poverty today compared to 29% just over twenty years ago. As Jules testifies, China is in many ways a success story, despite the constant barrage of negative publicity. The Chinese CO2 figures are constantly brought up as derisory, but what is not mentioned is that, per capita, Chinese emissions are half that of Canada. The West has to acknowledge its culpability in polluting the world. Changing our behaviours and stop living the way we do, would be the first step. We will never become like Bhutan, the only country in the world that removes more CO2 from the atmosphere than it produces, but we can always aspire to be like Bhutan.

Living in China is absolutely fine and dandy as long as you conform and do not criticise the powers that be. After so many years of state control the bulk of the population is acquiescent; there are few Ai Weiweis out there. A Bruce Springsteen concert was cancelled when an old photo of the singer standing alongside the Dalai Lama was unearthed.

Everyone is aware that criticism of the government leads to being completely ostracised: labelled an enemy of the state, harassed and detained by the police. We hear of Chinese prisoners being flown over to Africa to work as slave labour on the property there recently acquired by the Chinese government. One of the announcements on the bullet train: 'Dear passengers, people who travel without tickets or behave dishonourably or smoke in public areas will be punished according to regulations and their behaviour will be recorded in the individual credit information systems...'. Any failings as good citizens affect not only them (housing, career) but families too. I doubt if I would last long in this stifling, censorious atmosphere.

We are advised not to speak about the 3Ts: Tibet, Taiwan, and Tiananmen Square. Parts of the Chinese travel guide bought in Shanghai are censored, but I can still make out the references to the 3Ts under the black pen. And of course, access to the internet or YouTube is very patchy.

What I like best are the wonderful signs in English. There should be posters everywhere of them:

Menus:
- Stewed bull-frog in Sizzling Spicy Sauce
- Bean Curd Stick of Burning Flesh
- Explosion of Pork Liver
- Fat Cow
- Fleshy foam fans

In toilets: (with the appropriate picture)
- Squat Toilet
- Potty Toilet

In the street:
- No Striding
- Tips: Construction will bring Inconvenience to Your Life. Please forgive.
- Soldier First

On the underground:
- One way – no return
- No chasing
- Do not pop out of the head or other Part of the Body.

On the Great Wall:
- It is a kind of significance giving you an Everlasting Memory by virtue of tininess of life and magnificence of the Great Wall.
- Glass ladder rank, carefully slip.

There is a shampoo called 'SOD'.

In taxis: (an advert)
- Serious drinks, great music, no wankers.

We all watched the *Mamma Mia!* sequel in our pyjamas on the last day in Shanghai. It was dire but the highlight was Cher singing Abba's 'Super Trouper' and this was when I discovered the lines:

'I was sick and tired of everything
When I called you last night from Glasgow
All I do is eat and sleep and sing
Wishing every show was the last show.'

Time to head West once more. One click of the heels.

Thirteen

THERE WILL BE NO MIRACLE HERE

The soul is placed in the body like a rough diamond, and must be polished, or the lustre of it will never appear.

Daniel Defoe.

8th December 2018

Daniel Defoe reminds us that everyone is valuable and unique just like a diamond, but we need education to bring out the best of us.

An interesting piece scribbled on a wall in the Rue du Canard in Villeréal catches my eye: '*Quand l'injustice devient justice la résistance est obligatoire*' – when injustice becomes justice then resistance is mandatory.

The *Gilets Jaunes* have completely taken over France. There is such a disparity between town and country. You need a car to live in the sticks. A few years ago we had bin pickups at the end of the lane; now we have to drive to the village to get rid of our rubbish. In an effort towards sustainability, the *commune* has issued each household with a fob to open the bins and we are charged according to the amount of waste disposed. Each household is obliged to attend a talk about zero waste before we are given our fob. It's a good and noble idea, but everyone is concerned that there will be an increase in fly tipping.

Similarly, we are all forced to have a car – even the Gougets – because of the lack of public transport. It seems to be contrary to the environmental polices being put into place. Nevertheless, the French have much to be praised for in the transport department. *BlaBlaCar*, a French online marketplace for carpooling, has existed since 2006 and is extremely popular. Its website and mobile apps connect drivers and passengers willing to travel together between cities and share the cost of the journey. When we checked on the site we realised that it also gave information on cheap interdepartmental travel on buses and trains. Also popular is *co-voiturage* – car-sharing – and every village has a designated spot for *co-voiturage*. I meet up with the walking group on Fridays in Monflanquin at one of these sites. It is frowned upon to arrive in a car all by yourself at the walking rendezvous.

When Britain was busy privatising the railways and concentrating in expanding the road network in the 1970s, France was doing the opposite and investing in the state-owned railway, much to the mirth of Britain. Now the British rolling stock is the laughingstock while the TGV (the superfast trains) criss-cross France with elegance, speed and efficiency. Profit is not the name of the game and so rail travel is subsidised and affordable.

The French cling on to the rights which have now been eroded in Britain; no zero-hours contracts here, apart for me of course, as I grumble to Gerry. Prices are about 30% higher in shops than in Britain precisely because workers are paid a living wage and this is passed on to the consumer.

Around 25,000 protesters are out in Paris streets this weekend. In Bordeaux, the *Gilets Verts* – those from the ecology brigade – march side-by-side with their fellow protesters, chanting, '*Gilets Jaunes, Gilets Verts, on exprime le même colère*'(Yellow vests, green vests, we are all expressing the same anger). It's interesting the different takes on it. One of the *Gilets Jaunes* explained his stance to me:

'The petrol prices, it's the straw that broke the camel's back. We are fed up being taken for idiots; ecology is just an excuse to fill up the coffers.'

The day of the gravel arrives. A lorry trundles up and instead of tipping out the gravel gradually and spreading it evenly, the lorry gets stuck in the mud and two gravel hillocks appear. This is even more reason to have a proper driveway. I will spend months now flattening it all out. A machine could do this in a day, but where is the satisfaction in that?

Today is 10th December 2018. It is International Human Rights Day which marks the 70th anniversary of the Universal Declaration of Human Rights.

BREXIT: Delay on vote to accept Theresa May's plan.

Fourteen

ON BEAUTY AND USEFUL WORDS

In the nearby village of Villeréal there are six hairdressers and three beauty salons. Not far away, there is a five-star spa, as well as, of course, the thermal baths of Casteljaloux. Appearance matters, and yet my clothes, face and hair are usually mud-spattered. I always remember the horrifying statistic that the healthy adult human hosts microbes of between 2.5 and 3 kg, so no matter how good you look, you are carting around grotty critters that are munching away at your allure at a feverish rate, then replenishing themselves. A mud face pack would actually be beneficial.

I watch a matchmaking programme on TV for older viewers on the second round of matrimony, *le mariage plus vieux… être plus heureux* (getting married when you are older is a better recipe for success). The men seem ancient with corrugated foreheads while the women look startled but with no lines and plumped-up lips. I can't decide if that is a better look than a natural, crumpled-looking face. When I was young I would be quite happy to slather myself in olive oil and fry in the sun. Sue Castello lives nearby in St Vivien and is still a beauty at the age of eighty. Trim and blonde, with a sexy smile reminiscent of Honor Blackman's Pussy Galore, she can still do a morning shift of wood chopping. She attributes her glowing complexion and fitness to daily doses of turmeric. Now I try to remember to put sun block on my face, but invariably I forget. Turmeric is the answer.

In our local Leclerc supermarket there are rows of beauty products that I find fascinating, for example snail cream for a smooth complexion and cream for *les jambes lourdes* (heavy legs). This is an ailment common among French women but strangely alien to their British counterparts. However, the winner must be *les plug-ins (*condoms), a word that makes me giggle. It is lost in translation, since *branché* literally means 'plug in', but it is usually used to mean 'trendy', hence *les plug-ins* – condoms!

When we were in Deia in Majorca in October, I was fascinated by a five-day 'Energy Reactivation Retreat', subtitled 'Radiant Sensual Woman'. It promised to 'unleash your life-force, energy, passion and vitality'. The workshops included Breathwork, Tantric Pulsation, Movement, Kundalini Dance, Energy Work, and Sensual Awakening. I am not quite sure what all of them are; maybe one of life's sweet mysteries.

Meanwhile I spend a quiet birthday at home with a few friends. We put on silly masks and I make up a quiz about life in Lot-et-Garonne. No one this year has had the temerity to send me a birthday and Christmas card rolled into one, or even the more loathsome combined birthday and Christmas present. There has been few of either anyway. I have been checking our mailbox at the foot of the track on a daily basis. I receive a card from my friend Jennifer which reads 'Happy growing sense of inadequacy and impending mortality.' My hair is growing in grey and there is a huge, wiry hair on my chin. There is an incipient plook ready to erupt on my forehead. Spots at my age!

It seems completely unfair that my parents and siblings are long-limbed Amazons compared to my short-limbed self. How devastating to find out that I will in fact shrink as I get older. Perhaps I should pull myself together and sort out my allure before it bodyswerves me altogether. I have still to put up my wonderful 'Fanny Coiffure: Mixte' sign in the barn. But, joy of joys, I find that there is a new hairdresser opened up in Villeneuve called 'Salon Fatty'. Just the place for me. It must be written in the stars. I have noticed a big sign that says that Villeneuve is twinned with Troon. Who would have thought?

This is what life is all about at the moment:

Mortier bâtard	lime mortar used for pointing
Placo	plasterboard
Le dallage	paving
Le lambris	panelling
Le papier de verre	sandpaper
Receveur de douche	shower tray
Hors combat	cannae dae anything, bush-whacked
Le buisson	shrub, bush
Le fauchage	verge cutting
Le bluet	cornflower (worn instead of poppies for armistice)
La reprise sous-oeuvre	underpinning (what our neighbour's house needs)
Les tomettes	old quarry tiles
Le chevreuil	roe deer, venison (The joy of hunters around here).

Aï ça pique!	Ouch! (yes, of course I know this but it goes with the next word which I had forgotten))
L'ortie	nettles
Lagerstroemia	pink crepe myrtle. beautiful tree with pink blossoms in September
Gamberger	to mull over, ponder
Hora sur!	down with (I think) shouted out everywhere as in Down with Macron!
Camouflet	snub (what Teresa May got when she went off to Brussels)
Il y a d'autres chats à fouetter	there are other fish to fry (literally 'there are other cats to flail')
Moteur à deux temps	2-stroke engine. We met an old lady who didn't have a driving licence yet was allowed to tootle around the countryside in car with this.
Pinailler sur quelque-chose	to nitpick, quibble.
Elle est pénible.	
Elle pinaille sur tout	she is annoying, she quibbles about everything. The description of one of our walkers who finds fault with most things; this was on account of waiting for the Christmas meal. Well, it was Christmas time and the Portuguese restaurant was understaffed.
*Claquer la porte*to	slam the door (Description of the latest of Trump's staff to walk out).
Bonjour	the first word you must, absolutely must use, on greeting all and sundry, no matter where you are. (Even sitting in the doctor's surgery it is *de rigeur* to acknowledge

everyone who comes into the reception area).

La chaudière   boiler (The latest thing to blow up in the house in Glasgow. We will have to have it fixed pronto. This means we can't afford to install the wood-burner stove in the barn).

Back to reality.

Fifteen

P-P-PERISHING COLD

Il pleure dans mon coeur
Comme il pleut sur la ville;
Quelle est cette langueur
Qui pénètre mon coeur?

Paul Verlaine.

One day a gust of wind blew all the leaves from the trees and suddenly winter arrived. It's blowing a hooley outside; the trees are crystalline with hoarfrost.

The villages and towns are drained of colour: rain-spattered, woebegone and grey. The locals scurry around, heads bent and shoulders stooped, doing their business as quickly as possible before heading home.

We are starting to resemble grainy photos of Arctic explorers in huts – balaclavas, hats, gloves, long johns, massive slippers with thick socks on. Gerry is now sporting a grey beard which he says stops people addressing him as Madame by dint of his long hair. It reminds me a bit of Kenny Everett's bearded lady.

The heavy fog outside wraps around this stone house like a shroud. I can't help thinking of a line from Louis MacNeice's poem 'Circe': *Escutcheoned on the air with ice letters.* A cold draught coming in from the window prevents me from sleeping, so I resort to a purple, woollen bobbly hat on my head when I go to bed, a Wee Wilma Winkie with my padded nightgown.

Where has the sun gone? Not that we can see much outdoors since we have put old duvets and mattresses between windows and shutters in an attempt to keep some heat in, but the wily warm air just skips out through the gaps in the stones and unless we are right in front of the fire in the living room or the stove in the kitchen, this house is effectively a heat-free zone. All the firewood cut up in the last few months has been greedily devoured and we are forced to go to a wood merchant for supplies. I grimly keep the home fires burning.

Mr Duckman, our incorrigible neighbour, has resumed setting off the scarecrow gun and the noise of it, like the cold, goes right through us. You wouldn't believe what they say when it's bitterly cold, I say to my fellow Arctic explorer. *Il fait un froid de canard!*

A wake of buzzards has been circling around and stealing the ducklings. Luckily, though, Mr Duckman has moved the ducks to another part of the farm and the stench has disappeared for the moment, or maybe our noses are so blocked up that our sense of smell has gone.

Every morning we see deer in the field outside the kitchen door. The cold intensifies a ghostly feeling. Gerry peers out the window only to see the eyes of a stray cat staring straight back at him. He thinks a fox has been shitting in the bedroom barn, but he is puzzled to find black pellets lying on the beams below the roof. He nearly jumps out of his skin when he scales up the ladder to find himself face to face with a barn owl. Both of them screech, one flies off, the other nearly topples off his perch! I remind Gerry that it is a murder of crows, a conspiracy of ravens but a parliament of owls, so this event had an air of law and order about it, rather than massacre. He tells me to stop being so pedantic.

Gerry gets up in the pitch-black darkness at 6am, dressed like the Michelin man, and then starts work in the barns in below zero temperatures. It is so cold that it takes days for the plaster on the walls to dry.

At least the rain has abated, but we are still skeetering around in the mud outside. We basically tip through the front door as we whip our wellies off. I dream of being able to wallow in a hot bath, the water liberally sprinkled with unguents. The joy of being completely immersed in heat, rather than this piecemeal warmth.

We will not be able to buy any gravel until the second week in January when all the shops open again. If we manage to catch them in time. It is a bit cat-and-mouse to buy anything. *Hélas, oui!* We are now dab hands at catching stores open despite the two-hour lunch break and avoiding Mondays (most closed) but we are caught unawares when we drive into Villeneuve (the big town with a real industrial zone) on the 27th December to find a ghost town. We do in fact find a shop open that sells mattresses and when I ask when the sales actually start the sales assistant looks at me wide-eyed; '*Les soldes! Les soldes! Ils sont toujours en janvier!*' My neighbours tell me that the government announces the start of the sales, usually about 7th January, but this year, because of the action of the *Gilets Jaunes*, people have not been able to get to the shops. Consequently, the shops have not been able to sell their winter goods and, wait for it, *the sales might be delayed till a later date!* The opposite is true in Britain; Boxing Day is retail's busiest day. Instead, we find signs in shops in France saying *vente privée* as a promotion. I don't quite understand how shops can advertise private sales; just what is their *raison d'être*? Where is the full-blown Western commercialism? We see a whole row of wastepaper bins with the Union Jack emblazoned on the front; I wonder if they will be sold?

I also find books are sold and marketed in a completely different way. Books can only be reduced by 5% in France. It is the rule and we must not deviate from the rule. The front covers are quite simple, very pared down. I have never seen quotes on book covers – 'captivating – must read' – they are deemed as trashy. The blurb on the back must suffice; you, the discerning reader, must not have your intelligence insulted. Peruse the first few pages, if you must. The price of books in France is more or less the same everywhere: there is no competition whether you go to a bookshop (like Fnac) or even buy online with Amazon.

But in some ways this lack of commercialisation, this lack of consumerism, can be refreshing.

Shopping is not going to happen on the 27th of December. We concede defeat.

We are further stymied a few days later when we hitch up the trailer, ready for some mind-blowing retail fest when we hit the road for Bergerac. We are delivering a neighbour to the airport, so it makes sense for it to be a multipurpose visit to the big smoke. Apart from huge mileage across the globe, we don't stray much while here; every journey must count! Unfortunately I had forgotten to bring the *sac-à-dough*, the purse, so the retail splurge is averted.

Every month we receive a bulletin from the local *commune*. The mayor writes the editorial and it strikes me that something like the following would never be found in a local rag in Britain:

'2018 will be marked by the movement of "yellow vests" reflecting a malaise, a growing malaise for the last thirty years. Indeed, one has the impression of living in a two-headed country, where one has forgotten, ignored, rural and semi-urban France. Let this movement allow some to open their eyes, to understand, so that everyone can live in dignity.'

For the last two months I have been giving intensive French lessons to an English lady who has been looking after a nearby llama farm. We have long conversations about the habits and nature of llamas; I think I am becoming an expert on llamas. I am even starting to dream about llamas.

We have been hard at work trying to make the place watertight since our return from China. We have two events to aim for, which focuses the mind. We invite friends round on the 8th January 2019 to celebrate three years of being handed the keys to Coutal Haut, and the second event is a Burns Supper later in the month. Somehow in early January our friends who live here full-time manage to navigate the Somme-like driveway, abandon their cars and squelch to the door of the house. They all live within a ten-kilometre radius. Most have been here for years and carved out new lives and careers for themselves around the tourism industry. Those who live within (long) walking distance from us roll up early. Patrick and Christine run the hotel, Moulin de Labique; Simon and Jill have a garden and landscaping company; Anthea and Bill run a beautiful *gîte*, Lavinsotte, on the other side of the wood and duck farm; and Linda and Ian (an architect) have just built the house of their dreams. Those who come from further afield, Armando, Freek, Carol, Ian, Kim, Sue and Rod are either artists or retired. There is a wonderful sense of satisfaction to meet up with them in our own home in the depths of winter. We have gone through so much in three years to make our dream come true! Once all the guests have left we turn up the music full blast in the barn and dance like dervishes, singing:

> 'Daft Davy Ran
> Doon Dark Dungeons
> Daein daft dances
> Until the wee small hours.'

Gerry finds an old lampshade and pops it on his head. He looks the spitting image of Mr Boom, a children's entertainer in the 1990s, and strums his guitar. He truly is wired to the moon. Mr Boom. And Gerry. I retaliate by sticking one elbow out, bending over, inflating my stomach (admittedly easy) and squeaking in a high-pitched voice: 'Handle, spout, lid of metal, what's inside the singing kettle?' In the spirit of silly singing, we turn to the classics of the Scottish cannon: 'Ye cannae shove yer granny aff the bus' and the 'Jeelie Piece Song'. Gerry retrieves the 'big slipper', an item of footwear where two feet can snuggle up together in one warm fleecy interior, a bit like a hot water bottle for feet. Instead of hot water it is connected to an electric plug and warms up in a jiffy. Many a cold night has seen me resort to the pleasure of the hot slipper. Gerry has found another use for it. He wears it as a hat and sets it off with a pipe in his mouth. He has started a small collection of pipes. The lengths one will go in order to entertain oneself. It's either that or go round the bend. I tell him that he talks like *a pantoufle* – a slipper – that is, nonsense.

All this physical activity involved in building a home is certainly making us stronger. I couldn't lift the table we bought on the French Gumtree a few months ago, and now, not exactly lifting it with my pinkies, but *pas de problème*! It is a refectory table, so big it could be used for both birthing and mortuary purposes. One must be practical round these parts. Gerry spends a whole day putting on bright green castors so we can move it around, just to find that it is now too tall and we can barely peek over the top. We can pretend to be children at the big table. At some point we will find time to shorten the legs but for the moment a mountain of cushions are required for the chairs.

It is a welcome surprise when the windows arrive early and now Gerry has more or less built an insulated bedroom.

We have another stroke of good luck. When Gerry was stuck here without a car in October and I was in Scotland, he met Monsieur Andrieu, a retired stonemason, who was using thirteenth-century oak beams he had recovered from demolished barns and in turn was storing them in his own thirteenth-century barn in Cancon! Now that he is retired he has no use for them, and has so many that he is using them as firewood. We shake hands on a perfect deal; we will pay him for normal firewood in exchange for the beams which we are installing in our last barn. Most of the original beams were removed when the roof was redone thirty years ago. Some were taken to the Château Scandaillac up the road to repair their moat or drawbridge. 'Ha ha' the laugh is on us. I wish I could afford to buy all Monsieur Andrieu's old beams; it pains me to think that they are destined to go up in flames.

We had brought two wood-burning stoves reclaimed from pubs in Glasgow only to find that we cannot find anyone willing to install them because they somehow do not conform to current standards, which is another way of trying to sell us their products which we cannot afford. This is something we must sort before guests descend, otherwise we will have to source pelts and fur coats.

The towns and villages are all beautifully decked out in Christmas lights and trees and I have been soaking up the festive spirit, in more ways than one. I joined the carol singing at Monflanquin Square (French, Dutch and English), deftly bodyswerved by Gerry, and attended a wreath-making class in Castillonnès, as well as continuing with the walking group. Slowly we are meeting more people and are invited to a few events.

Our friend Sue told us that she had bought a birthday cake for an elderly relative with candles on it that spelt out 'Lost count' which would have been fine except the 'o's refused to light up!

Tom Leonard, the poet, died on 22nd December 2018. I had asked him if we could use his poems 'Being a Human Being' and 'Six O'Clock News' for one of our fundraising events. His respiratory illness stopped him from reciting his own poetry and he was delighted that his poetry could inspire others. He was poor – few poets make any money – but nonetheless he sent us a donation for the boys in Jenin and kind words. He was feisty and uncompromising (he championed the oppressed and I guess his poetry would be banned in China among many other places) and because of this he had found it difficult to find a sympathetic publisher.

There's nothing like belting out traditional carols at Christmas time; and now I have a big barn to *gie it laldy*, that is, to sing with gusto and unbridled joy. The look of consternation on Gerry's face is bridled joylessness.

Little donkey, little donkey
On a dusty road
Got to keep on plodding onwards
With the precious load

(Big gulp of air to fill the lungs and explode with the refrain)

Ring out those bells tonight
Bethlehem, Bethlehem.
Follow the star tonight
Bethlehem, Bethlehem.

Eric Boswell

I am going to miss my traditional Polish Christmas this year. Around this time the Christmas carols in Polish are on a loop. By November I am dreaming of the feast (*wigilia*) that will take place in my mother's house on the 24ᵗʰ of December. The festivities begin with all family members sharing *opłatek*, a thin wafer. We offer each other a piece of our *opłatek*, eat the bits of *opłatek* offered to us and wish each other *Wesołych Świąt*, Merry Christmas. There should be twelve dishes served; the number twelve represents the Apostles and all the dishes should be meatless. No one quite knows why this should be so. All I know is that each dish is a slice of heaven. My mother has narrowed down her range to about eight dishes, because there is a limit to what even we can eat.

The first dish is always *barszcz*, clear beetroot soup, usually served with *uszka*, a small dumpling filled with wild mushroom filling. Next are *pierogi* (dumplings with a savoury filling), *śledź w śmietanie* (herring with sour cream), *ryba po grecku* (fish – usually carp – prepared in the Greek style), *kutia* (poppy seeds with honey), *ciasto z bakaliami* (fruitcake), *sernik* (cheesecake) and *makowiec,* (poppy seed roll). Vodka is sipped throughout this incredible banquet. I write this licking my lips. It is now possible to buy some delicacies from the Russian shop in Villeneuve (there are a few extremely rich and secretive Russians around, hence the shop) but I feel it a tad disloyal to buy there. Besides, it would pale in comparison to my mother's feast.

Gerry and I have never spent Christmas together; instead we celebrate with our respective families. Gerry goes north to Lossiemouth and their family tradition consists of the standard British turkey and trimmings but then it transforms into something far more interesting. They build a big bonfire on the beach, strip naked and run into the freezing sea, sprint back to revive in front of the fire and turn a lobster-red colour.

We thought the children might arrive for Christmas but Irena was with her boyfriend Ant in Bethlehem ('Mum, it seems to be difficult to book a hotel here at this time of year – any suggestions?') and Ziggy had football matches as usual and then headed straight to Poland to join his fiancée, Joanna. It was just the two of us. Home Alone. We decided to eschew the French, British and Polish traditional Christmases, although I insisted on a Christmas tree and presents.

It was a bright sunny day and we walked around Lac de la Ganne, returned home, took our places at either end of the big table and tucked into *magret de canard avec frites.* A classy dish. We then proceeded to shout at each other.

'I say, Gerald, do pass le champagne, dear boy!'

'Barbara, my darling, let us imbibe the most delicious magnum from Smith Haut Lafitte!' *Joyeux Noël*! It was all very droll and satisfying.

Feeling a tad discombobulated the next morning, I checked my phone and my world turned upside down. I had been expecting the news, but I didn't anticipate the raw, unadulterated pain I would feel. Auntie Margaret had been in a hospice in Glasgow for the last month. She had refused further treatment for stomach cancer, stating that she was eighty-eight and it was time to exit this mortal coil gracefully with the minimum of fuss. I had said goodbye to her in October in the fleeting visit to Glasgow with Gerry before heading off to Berlin. As usual, she was impeccably dressed: a beautiful silk scarf wrapped artfully around her neck, a brooch pinned on her blouse. As I was leaving she said, 'Take all the copper pans now; they will look good in Coutal.' She had always wanted Irena to have them and now they hang from the mantelpiece in the living room. The last laugh is on me since she made sure Yvonne gave me a tin of Brasso, knowing full well that cleaning copper is not my forte. I like things to be clean but housework has never been at the top of my list of priorities. I am the quintessential Quentin Crisp girl.

The last message from her was in November in response to a photo I had sent her, doing silly walks on the Great Wall of China, pretending I was a panda. 'I wish I could give that panda a big hug,' it said. We had had so many adventures and fun together over the years, from clambering over Lake District Fells to visiting an exhibition of Yves St Laurent's dress collection. As an antique dealer, she had a keen eye and encyclopaedic knowledge of collectors' items through the centuries. I remember her pointing out the different facets of her netsuke collection: small, intricately carved wooden and ivory toggles for kimonos. 'Imagine,' she said, 'how impractical for kimonos not to have pockets.'

I knew she had loved me unconditionally and had faith in me. When I had been very ill some years before she phoned me every morning to ensure I was all right. She was shrewd, kind, steely and wise; a confidante to many people with the rare ability of making them feel that they were special in some way. Together with Yvonne we were co-conspirators in the absurdity of life. I am so glad I had remained in Glasgow and had spent so many happy times with her. The shock of grief is to write this in the past tense. She would have disapproved of any descent into mawkishness – pointless the tearing of hair and gnashing of teeth. 'It is time to go,' she would have said, briskly and firmly.

All our elderly neighbours have been poorly this winter. Mme Gouget phoned a few days ago to say that she and her husband Étienne were not able to go to the Monday market in Cancon and could I get her a few things? I was worried when I pulled up at the house, but I need not have worried. They were perfectly fine and handed me a list for the horses they wanted a flutter on, so I had to head down to the bookies! The most wonderful flavour-packed lunch at their farm awaited us when we came back from Cancon: broad bean soup, truffles with omelette, venison pâté; all home-made of course. It is difficult to explain how perfect and succulent everything is, straight from the earth, lovingly prepared. The Gougets have rarely bought any of their food from the shops (I doubt if they have ever tasted eggs from a shop) and their attitude towards food is very matter of fact: 'Hen stopped laying, so it had to have its head chopped off.' Suzanne gives us a jar of truffles and explains we have to put them together in a bowl with the eggs, which should never be washed, to infuse into the shell of the eggs, like osmosis. *C'est la vraie cuisine paysanne*, says Suzanne, proudly. It is true peasant cooking. A master class in the culinary arts.

We listen to Macron's magisterial address to the nation on the radio as we drive to a Hogmanay party. Grand gestures but no solutions. It looks like the *Gilets Jaunes* will continue until he steps down or until squabbles break out and it all fizzles away. The party is at Armando and Freek's lovely barn in Lalandusse with thirty people we do not know. A beautiful Russian opera singer sings '*O mio babbino caro*' and '*Ave Maria*'.

Bonne Année.

$\mathcal{S}$ixteen

BURNS, BABY, BURNS

Inviting sixteen guests to a Burns Night in January seemed such a good idea in the languorous heat of the summer; but now, in freezing conditions and no bedrooms in sight, somehow it has lost its appeal. Burns Night is a misnomer; the party will last four nights, encompassing two birthdays and Australia Day. No pressure. Never mind; one must crack on. We sharpen our pencils, rub our foreheads and write out the Scottish patter to stick under the plates for our guests to decipher.

Time to plunder the rich mine of Scottish vocabulary.

Bonny... douce... plastered... ginger... dug... shenanigans... malarkey... keich... squoosh... bairns... pan-bried... The Broons... glaikit... bowfin... beamer... black-affronted... manky... paralytic... brass neck... pie-eyed...

I wake up on the Ryanair flight as we land in Bergerac, covered from head to toe with tiny bits of prawn cocktail crisps. Who would have thought decompression would make my favourite savoury snack erupt? It is a fitting end to two flights to Glasgow in the space of a fortnight: one to Auntie Margaret's funeral and the other to replace the boiler in the house we had rented out. It had made growling, threatening noises and the tenants had decamped to a hotel. While I am away, two determined Jehovah's Witnesses in sharp, conservative suits, manage to navigate their way up the quagmire. They knock at the door, ready to convert Gerry. I think they are surprised to find this diminutive man covered head to foot in dust, as if emerging from an enormous bag of flour. They fail in their proselytising mission.

It has been a depressing start to the year. It is difficult to believe I will never see Auntie Margaret again. I have cried enough tears and drunk enough wine to fill a lake; from cobra to corpse position. I keep reminding myself of the South African saying I had seen on the wall of the women's prison in Johannesburg which had so moved me: 'The bitter heart eats his owner.' Graffiti on the pavement on Byres Road in Glasgow piques my curiosity. 'It won't always be like this.' It won't be since it is written in chalk. It lightens my mood a little.

On arrival at Bergerac airport (the size of both our barns), passengers are welcomed with the sign: 'Immigration controls reinforced at arrivals. Extended waiting time. Thank you for your understanding.' We stand outside in the cold and shiver. In the arrivals hall a big sign at the passport desk awaits us, 'ON AND ABOUT THE BREXIT' with a web address and a reminder: 'You have chosen to reside in the Dordogne, the 2nd department in France, after Paris, to welcome the largest number of British nationals.' It went on to describe, now that we have chosen to exit the comforts of the EU, just what it means. Ergo, outside in the cold, away from the party.

Welcome *Coutal Haut surrounded by sunflowers*

Coutal Haut in the early 1970s

Timeless. Villeréal night market

Gerry, Blanche and me

Ron, Gerry and Janet

With Étienne and Suzanne Gouget

A good start

Gerry and the Big Slipper

Old tools from barn

In Figeac with my mother and Douglas

Our life of glamour

Cooking on the old stove

The big barn

Joanna and Ziggy

Home alone for Christmas. Pass the bottle!

We have a floor!

Ant and Irena

Alex, Ant, Adam, Catriona, Cristina, me, Nina, David, Irena, Peter

In the Reichstag

Berlin. Michael Brawley and Christine Bovill

With Jen.
From Glasgow to Lascaux

Frolics in Bordeaux
with Bridget

Windows in

Giant Panda
needs a hug

Gerry in
Gdańsk

Me, Mhairi, Jim,
Kathryn, Karen, Gerry

Monflanquin
Gerry, Julie and Ron

Cedar up

Joining the Gilets Jaunes in Bordeaux

With Jennie

With Eunice and Sharon

Simon, Linda, Jill, me, Ian, Bill, Jo, Gerry and Anthea

Unsurprisingly, there has been a massive surge in applications for French residency.

A week before our very own party, four Spanish and Swedish friends from Barcelona pull out after a car accident. The lengths people will go to…

We stoically, but grimly, keep on sticking the patter under the plates:

Stoater… reeking… bampot… dreich… scunnered… peely-wally… drouthie… belter… havering… skelpt… unco foo… clout… kent… sleekit… banter… piece… galoshans… haud yer wheesht… keek…

Other unwelcome residents have appeared in our part of the world. The ducks are back and I can see them from the kitchen window. I have been handed a flyer for the 'Grand Loto' in Monflanquin. The sought-after prize is *canards avec foie* (ducks with liver) as the main draw. 'Just come round our way and take away the whole lot of them, the pesky varmints,' I mutter to myself.

In Sri Lanka, there are certain villages whose fields are attacked by elephants as they try to stoke up on the 150 kilogrammes of vegetables they need to survive daily. The resourceful villagers have surrounded their fields with lime trees since elephants are allergic to citrus fruits, and I am frantically trying to find what ducks find repugnant. I am still trying to look on the bright side. At least we do not live in Paris where, according to latest estimates, there are two rats to every inhabitant and there are 2.5 million people living in the Paris limits. They must be adequately nourished, rats and humans alike.

Friends from London cancel coming over for our Burns Supper with a tale of woe. Luckily, my daughter, Irena, and her partner, Ant, are still coming.

I am starting to feel truly *crabbit*. I know, it is easier if you know the vernacular. Now we are eight: four Scottish, one Australian, one Dutch, one Irish and one Paraguayan.

This is starting to sound like an Agatha Christie novel.

Now is the time and now is the hour.

The day has arrived and we pull ourselves together. There is nothing else for it. The LP 'The Songs of Robert Burns,' sung by William McAlpine, is popped on the turn table (our nod to retro chic); the throbbing beat of 'Clanadonia' blares out of the speakers and our log-burning stove in the kitchen is stuffed full of casseroles, haggis, neeps and tatties. The aroma is intoxicating, the fires are burning bright orange and a large bowl of cranachan is in the fridge. The casserole dish with stew is gently bubbling on the stove in the living room. The whisky glasses are at the ready. Ironically, neither of us is too fond of the amber nectar, but the occasion calls for it. We line up the whisky bottles: Laphroaig, Talisker, Bowmore, Highland Park and Lagavulin, like soldiers at the ready. Scottish whisky is far cheaper to buy here in France than in Scotland. In pride of place is the whisky I bought in the tourist shop in Lascaux, a new distillation in the Périgord. What if it were blended and rebranded, 'Glasgaux'?

Och wheesht and git oan wae it.

A cracking evening was had, full of banter in Scots, English, Italian, Polish and Dutch, a complete *swally*, with Burns, Tom Leonard, Liz Lochhead and other stalwarts recited and celebrated. Naoimh and Sharon are swaddled in tartan. Sharon sings 'Ae fond kiss' beautifully.

Whit a rammy, a kerry oan we had, laughing, *steamin'*, dancing the Canadian Barn Dance and Gay Gordons, *whirlin'* and *birlin'*.

Completely *wabbit* next day, but our spirits are high.

Burnst-oot.

A few days after our guests depart we attend a local Burns Supper in Castillonnès. We have had a surfeit of haggis by this time, but it would be *de trop* to let the side down. Besides, we joined the Scottish country dancing class a few weeks before to refresh our steps and nearly collapsed with exhaustion.

Congratulating myself on my organisational skills, I had stuffed the trailer with all things Scottish and driven it back to Coutal in October. There was enough haggis to feed eighteen people. In Glasgow I bought white heather, only to find it on sale in the local Saturday market in Villeréal! The evening was unexpectedly rousing and I came away remembering the hitherto unknown fact (to me) that Abraham Lincoln had been buried with a copy of Burns' poetry in his coffin.

I thanked one of the organisers and told her that, after all the fundraising events we had done in the past, we were acutely aware of how much time, tears and effort went into them. She replied that, in fact, it had been surprisingly easy given the disasters of the past, such as the chef who downed all the leftover whiskies and was so *stotious/paralytic/smashed* that the rest of the evening resembled a Basil Fawlty sketch as the dessert was scraped off the floor.

I have been meaning to go to a Folk Night in Lauzun since we arrived here. Gerry cries off, preferring to watch the Wales v France rugby match on TV. After chopping back some trees, especially the massive bay tree outside the door, we have repositioned the satellite dish and can now access British and French TV channels. The novelty has not worn off with French TV: all the dating programmes, dreadful soaps and home renovation extravaganzas that I just can't get enough of. The French are obsessed with *la dictée* – dictation – since their school days and there is always a version of *Apostrophes* (language programme) on the box.

I leave Gerry in charge of the big slipper, remote control and leftovers in the fridge and head out into the night. Battling the rain and creaky car, I eventually pin down the venue and beg to be allowed in thirty minutes late to hear a bearded man with a pot belly announce, 'Burns Night has just passed and we cannot have an evening without Burns tunes' as he proceeds to murder 'Auld Lang Syne' and 'A Man's a Man for a' That'. Rabbie needs to be put to bed forthwith.

It is the end of January and there are rumblings that Britain is begging for Brexit to be delayed. All sorts of other options are being pursued in haste. One such option is joining the EFTA (European Free Trade Association) with Norway, Switzerland, Iceland and Liechtenstein as members. EFTA is not in the EU but abides by many of its rules such as free movement of people across the bloc, and crucially accepts the rulings by the European Court of Justice.

I listened to an interview last month with Heidi Nordby Lunde, president of Norway's European Movement, and it is stunning, the extent to which Britain is not wanted in their club. Two comments are especially damning:

'I think you would mess it all up for us, the way you have messed it all up for yourselves.'

'It would be like inviting the rowdy uncle to a Christmas party, spiking the drinks and hoping that things go well. They would not.'

On the 21st of January 2019, Brittany Ferries announced that 10,000 passengers had their bookings modified or cancelled as the government commandeered the crossings to be used as freight for critical goods in the event of a no deal Brexit. This fast resembles a quasi-war scenario. We will soon have a new updated series of *Dad's Army* on TV. 'Don't panic!' The Japanese car company Nissan has just announced it is pulling out of Sunderland as a direct result of the uncertainty around Brexit.

I hear people evoking the nostalgic reverie of the Greatness of Britain. Let's not forget that the British Empire was not some project designed to bring enlightenment, joy and plenitude to ignorant masses of those oppressed, but, as many believe, it was a cynical exercise in exploitation.

Meanwhile the whole kerfuffle of the Irish backstop rumbles on, but as the Irish TV personality Dara Ó Briain points out: 'It's not the Irish border, it's the British border in Ireland. The Irish border is the beach.'

I have been reading a book called *Trigger Warning: Is the Fear of Being Offensive Killing Free Speech*? by Mick Hume. It is illuminating and thought-provoking. I had watched Piers Morgan (breakfast TV host) lambasting Ross Greer MSP, for calling Winston Churchill a white supremacist and mass murderer. A mite far-fetched, some people might argue, and a fiery debate ensued, which ended up with Morgan shouting at Greer that he had no right to be so offensive.

This is the whole premise of Hume's book, that in the interests of free speech, we all have the right to be offensive. Which words qualify as offensive or hate speech? Should we leave it to politicians to dictate what is unacceptable? After all, everybody has an agenda and interests of their own. I have been increasingly critical of politicians' attempts to silence debate. As it is frequently pointed out, they haven't yet managed to repair the potholes. I am reminded of the famous quote, wrongly attributed to Voltaire:

'I disapprove of what you say, but I will defend to the death your right to say it' (Evelyn Beatrice Hall).

I have just checked out the website of Reporters Without Borders. The UK still ranks as thirty-third in the World Press Freedom Index (2019).

To quote from their website:

'A continued heavy-handed approach towards the press (often in the name of national security) has resulted in the UK keeping its status as one of the worst-ranked Western European countries in the World Press Freedom Index. The government began to implement the Investigatory Powers Act – the most extreme surveillance legislation in UK history – with insufficient protection mechanisms for whistleblowers, journalists, and their sources. Home Secretary Amber Rudd repeatedly threatened to restrict encryption tools such as WhatsApp and announced plans to criminalise the repeated viewing of extremist content.' Who decides what is 'extremist content'?

Incidentally, France is thirty-two in the rankings.

What is worrying is that people are forgetting that words are just that: words. They are not actions and people should be free to say what they wish. I find myself censoring my language lest people don't understand exactly what I mean to say. One has to have clarity through argument and healthy debate. The important thing is to be able to listen, to debate, to think and come to one's own conclusions. And if they are different from others, then so be it.

It is so disheartening to find that organisations you think are morally robust, like Reporters Without Borders (or RSF in French – Reporters sans Frontières), are corrupt. On the 19th May 2019, RSF received the Dan David Prize in Tel Aviv for its 'Contribution in Defending Democracy'. Elsa Lefort, French human rights campaigner, said she was 'speechless in the face of such cynicism'. Lefort, the wife of Salah Hamouri, a Palestinian-French lawyer recently jailed by Israel for more than a year without charge or trial, added that her thoughts went out to 'Palestinian journalists killed in Gaza, and those who languish in the occupier's prisons'.

There is a statue of 'la Pasionara' on the banks of the River Clyde in Glasgow, with the republican heroine's famous words (translated from Spanish) 'Better to die on your feet than live forever on your knees.' The statue was commissioned to remember the Scottish volunteers who fought with the International Brigades in the 1936–1939 Spanish Civil War. It strikes me now in the febrile, paranoid atmosphere of today that volunteers such as these would be hauled away before they went off to fight for their foreign cause for 'thought crimes'.

Seventeen

NO SMOKE WITHOUT FIRE
February 2019

We have been eying up a fire engine parked in a neighbour's drive for a long time. It's the husband's toy; he had picked it up in the Gers region after seeing it advertised on the internet. It was then transported back on a trailer. It goes on occasional outings although we have never seen it around. These neighbours are now selling up and returning to Holland and we are curious to know what will happen to this giant toy. We fantasise about uniforms, helmets and hoses and our friends Ian and Linda, who live near the fire engine house, are now joining in our imaginary world.

The last time firemen came round was in December when they visited all the houses and farms to sell their calendars. I felt a frisson of hope; at last something akin to the titillating 'calendar girls' with a Gallic twist. *Mais non*! The frisson fizzled out as we flicked from one grey, boring page consisting of formal line-ups of fully clothed firemen to local worthies. *Pas de titillation.*

We indulge in our fantasies of our neighbour's fire engine. 'Do you think we could have a consortium and we could all take turns?' 'What about a pole in the middle of the barn?' we ask each other hopefully.

A fire engine would be quite a practical thing to have since it has been so unseasonably hot (twenty-six degrees today) that people are tanning on the beach in Biarritz and there have been massive fires in Corsica. As well as that, firemen have the job of killing wasps and I think I spot the tell-tale signs of a wasp nest in the shape of a giant white lantern hanging from a tree in the garden.

The other thing I have set my heart on, much less practical I concede, is a life-size metal elephant sculpture. We spotted it on the roadside on the way from Villeneuve and Agen and immediately swerved into the studio driveway. However, discovering that even teeny elephants on display were way out of our budget range (and there is the small matter of transportation) we have reluctantly talked ourselves out of its viability. Such a shame since it is clearly made for our barn; I can just visualise it hanging from the beams and I can hear the solemn conversation in my head: 'Please don't talk about the elephant in the room.' Sadly, no pole and no elephant.

Nevertheless, there has been a slight consolation in the acquisitions department. The spectre of Brexit has chased some Brits away, and we have scavenged their goods for a song; others have given away their unwanted items. The garage and trailer have had the addition of three bikes, a bed, mattress, nail gun, washing machine, dishwasher, pots, 'strimmer', mulching machine and a host of other things which probably won't work. All for the princely sum of €300.

We have been back to the building merchants with a vengeance picking up doors, a water heater and wood panelling. This gets me on the topic of French awkwardness. Noting that we have spent a fortune in one store, we were asked if we would consider a loyalty card. *Mais, oui, bien sûr,* we answered: 'Of course we would like a loyalty card.' One and a half hours later, we were still in the store, begging not to be given said card. The registration process did not recognise 'Glasgow, Ecosse'. The reception lady refused to accept defeat and resolutely ignored our pleas to let us leave.

I know that Thatcher's Britain dumped manufacture and turned to the financial services and arms industry, but mostly those in the service industry do just that – provide a service! Yes, I am aware this is a facile argument.

Last month, my friend Sharon travelled up from Bordeaux with other guests to Bergerac for our Burns event. She couldn't find the email reservation on her phone and was trying to tell the lady at the ticket desk that it was okay, she would buy another three tickets. Before she could do that, la petite Hitlère started to wag her finger in front of Sharon's face, shouting *Écoutez-moi! Écoutez-moi!* 'Listen to me! Listen to me!'

I had booked a table for the evening in a cosy restaurant in Issigeac for our guests. Our table was right next to the hearth which was belching smoke and ruining 'zee ambiance'. When we complained the waiter took the huff and poked at the fire thus burning his hand. For the rest of the evening he glared at us and treated us with disdain, which marred the beautifully prepared meal.

I have plastic bags full of loose change that I have been trying to convert into bigger denominations. *Hélas!* Whenever I go into a bank or supermarket I am given 'le short shrift'.

As it is so incredibly warm, I ask if the local swimming-pool is open. Of course, it is too early, but then I find that it will not open till July, regardless of the weather. The temperature hit forty degrees in June a few years ago.

Clearly, estate agents are not on commission. There is a glut of houses on the market here, which reflects the growing unease of Britain's slow suicidal quest. I cannot help but look at the photos of the houses for sale, purely for entertainment value. In many cases, there are unmade beds on show, dishes in the sink and washing hanging over the radiators. Why don't the estate agents point out that such sloppiness will surely affect potential sales?

Sometimes I am reminded of shopping in communist times in Poland: you order the product, get handed a chit, take it to one place to pay and then go to the back of the building and pick up the order. No one is ever in a hurry, and woe betide anyone if they miss the midday curfew; all is closed until lunch is well and truly over and retail life is grudgingly recommenced at 2pm.

While I am on a rant, let me talk about signposts, my *bête noire*. So many times we have driven past a turning, because the directions display the opposite direction. Signposts reflect their *commune*; if you come the 'wrong way' you will not be able to see the signs. Great in a wartime situation, but not if you are trying to find your way home in the dead of night from an unfamiliar part of the country. There are signs of progress, however; in the next few years all houses will be given a number which will help with GPS navigation. At last we will be located.

Gerry has been *hors de combat* for the last three weeks. He has now been assigned 'light duties' and painting *le lambris*, the panelling. A pretty osteopath jumps on his back and recommends that he walk a few hours each afternoon to joogle the vertebrae. He has a brief relapse when we are about to set off on a long-awaited trip with friends to the Lot Valley. After a leisurely breakfast we amble to the car to find – *horreur*! – that the tyre has a puncture so poor Gerry lies on the ground to change the wheel before we set off. 'Are you all right?' I ask anxiously. 'I'm fine,' he answers, wincing.

As for me, a filling falls out of one of my teeth and it takes a week to find a dentist to repair it. Meanwhile, my tongue has been fiendishly finding its way to the hollow, as an addict to his addiction.

Since Gerry has no alternative but to take things easy, I have been forced to up my game now: clearing the land of the thorny bushes and trees, painting, and moving stones to create a driveway. It has been so dry that the mud has hardened and the impetus to do the work has lessened somewhat. I have spent many mundane hours helping Gerry by pulling wires through narrow electrical conduits.

I have been promoted from junior zero-hours labourer to senior zero-hours labourer. I have tendonitis and my thumbs look deformed, but unless it is cold it doesn't hurt. One night I have a nightmare about work and wake up in a panic, with sweat running down my body, only to discover I have left the electric blanket on and I am being cooked alive.

It has taken some time to get over Auntie Margaret's death. I wish that I could somehow be injected with her self-containment and stoicism. Even a little dose. I try to keep occupied to keep morose thoughts at bay. The poem read out at her funeral offers some solace:

I am a thousand winds that blow.
I am the diamond glints on snow.
I am the sunlight on ripened grain.
I am the gentle autumn rain.
When you awaken in the morning's hush
I am the swift uplifting rush

Of quiet birds in circled flight.
I am the soft stars that shine at night.

Mary Elizabeth Frye.

In homage to Auntie Margaret, I stencil a door with her favourite saying, 'Musn't grumble.' She was averse to angels, but somehow an angel with skull and crossbones didn't seem quite right. She was also fond of the saying 'A cup of tea without a biscuit is too wet; a biscuit without a cup of tea is too dry.' But that was a bit too long, so I make do with 'Here Be Dragons.' I really miss her waspish humour and her encouragement. Auntie Margaret had a strong work ethic, and when I feel I am shirking from a task, I remind myself of how she described those who were work-shy, 'under-worked and over-slept'.

I think of her in her wicker coffin, looking like the Lady of Shalott. Auntie Margaret would probably have said to stop navel gazing and ditch the onion allusion. I cast my mind back to when we were on holiday in Japan. We visited an 'onsen' – a nature spa in the mountains – and she sat naked on a rock at the age of seventy-four, without inhibitions, looking like a zen-like sprite. I will have to be more stoical and accept that she lives on by her example of how to live life with dignity.

The car, apart from a puncture, has had its fair share of ailments too, owing to its advanced age, so it has gone in and out of the garage clinic for various kinds of tweaking.

We have managed a few outings. Rugby season is now in full swing, and, given the fact I am not an aficionada of rugby or beer, I am the perfect chauffeur for Gerry and friends. A new brewery has opened in Monpazier and we spend a satisfying day watching France trounce Scotland, and Wales defeat England.

Our grand day out is to Saint-Cirq-Lapopie, a beautiful medieval village perched on a cliff with the River Lot meandering below. The village is known as an artists' colony. André Breton, founder of the Surrealist movement, had a house there, and, from the 1950s, artists flocked to the area.

We are joined by our artist friends, Armando and Freek. Freek, who is Dutch, comments, 'Do you know that La Nouvelle-Aquitaine is bigger than the Netherlands?' Normally the place is stowed out with tourists, but on a Monday in February there is hardly anyone to be seen and we wander around the ancient alleyways in the bright sunshine as if in a film set. All the souvenir shops are closed and I hanker to buy a sign hanging in one of the closed shop windows saying '*Attention: chien susceptible.*'

How lucky to live in a region which has so many prehistoric cave paintings. There is something profoundly moving about looking at a 36,000-year-old painting; the artist from generations past sharing the same sensibilities as us. No doubt Pech Merle will one day follow the same way as Lascaux and a facsimile will be built beside it. But, for the moment, we can see the footprints of children, handprints on the cave walls, the face of a man, mammoths and other animals clearly depicted on the cave walls. There is a massive tree root that dangles all the way down, deep underground. The tree does not look like anything special above ground; its claim to fame is that it is the only tree around to survive the drought of 1949.

There is something contagious about French bolshiness. We stop at a café in an out of the way part of this region to find the *patron* who has a cigarette dangling from his lips. We look around to find five other workers smoking in what is a smoker's paradise. I stare at the *patron*. He shrugs and stretches out his hands. *Eh, alors?* Yes, indeed, what precisely am I going to do about it? It's his café and he can smoke if he wants to.

An edict was passed last year banning bonfires in the countryside. As if any farmer was going to take heed. '*C'est ridicule!*' exclaim my neighbours, pulling faces of annoyance and gesticulating wildly. Taking their lead, we have had a few bonfires to get rid of all the garden detritus. One morning, the bonfire looked quite dead except for the thinnest wreath of smoke. I popped a wheelbarrow of branches on it and wandered off. When I looked around ten minutes later, I was surprised to see a full-blown fire licking the air. *Bien sûr*, no smoke without fire. This is where a fire engine would be really handy.

27th February 2019.
Sud Ouest newspaper reports another defeat in the Brexit debacle in the House of Commons. Headline on the front cover: '*Theresa May mange son chapeau*', with the picture of a suitably woebegone Madame May underneath.

Sans chapeau.

GILETS JAUNES

When we heard someone's suggestion that stealing the local cinema takings was linked to the fecklessness of the *Gilets Jaunes* movement, we thought it was time to find out what it was all about. It's pointless trying to find out anything in the French news, since the protesters are depicted as lazy rascals disrupting the country. Civil servants are handsomely paid and railway workers can retire at fifty on a full pension; they and their family can travel on first-class rail. *Mon Dieu*, what are all these workers complaining about?

Bordeaux is the hotspot after Paris, and, as it happens, just down the road from us. The month of March is upon us and march we shall. We had, after all, been severely affected by the first week of protests in November, when we had to sleep in the car overnight in freezing conditions before setting off to Shanghai, because there was no hotel room to be had in the city. At that time we were told that it was a spontaneous protest about petrol hikes. Macron duly stopped the price rise and raised the minimum wage, yet still the unrest has continued, with workers manning main exits on roundabouts and slowing traffic. Shops are suffering the most; no one wants to head off to the city on a Saturday.

We are rather the worse for wear from the revelries of curry and drink at our neighbours' (Anthea and Bill) the night before, but soon perk up with the bright sunshine and the carnival atmosphere in Bordeaux. The protesters come from all walks of life: teachers, doctors, pensioners, students, parents with their children.

The strict maximum thirty-five-hour working week is a boon for some and a bind for others. Poorly paid workers, mostly in the caring professions, speak about how they cannot take on second jobs to augment their income of €900 a month. The self-employed are crippled by social charges.

The *Gilets Jaunes* view themselves as taking up where the 1968 riots left off. But those riots only lasted three weeks and there is no sign of the *Gilets Jaunes* losing steam in this, the sixteenth week of protest. As a sign of support, people display their yellow high-vis jackets on the car dashboards.

Not so long ago, the comedian Mark Thomas suggested that the best way to engage in civil disobedience is to don a high-vis jacket, since no one would notice you. *Au contraire.* This is no longer the case.

There is no obvious head of this unorganised movement and anyone can come up and exercise their democratic right to speak. The trade unions keep a distance despite the *Gilets Jaunes* calling for strike action. There are three main areas they are fighting for as a movement: social and ecologic progress, political change and a referendum to effect institutional change. It is a tall order.

We march with 5,000 other protesters through the quiet streets of Bordeaux from 2.30pm until just before 5pm. Some of the shops and banks are boarded up and for half the time the shops are shut. There is no sign of police.

Every week the *Gilets Jaunes* adopt a slight switch in tactics. This time they take over the train station for about fifteen minutes, marching in, banners high, before resuming the prearranged, but unauthorised, route. The clear message is to show who owns the streets. As the marchers are heading towards the final rallying point for a meeting, we notice a handful of young men joining in, slipping in from alleyways, their faces covered with balaclavas. We decide it is time for a sharp exit as the inevitable brouhaha breaks out.

Heading towards the car, I count twelve vans of CRS riot police coming to disperse the crowd which rushes out in all directions as tear gas hits the air and water cannons are deployed. We assume this has to do with the *agents provocateurs* who made an appearance right at the end of the march. Later, listening to reports through Twitter and elsewhere, there is no mention of this. A peaceful demonstration nearing its end is broken up by violent means. Police stop using rubber bullets after public protests.

There are signs of the movement mobilising to become a political party with the main objective being to keep on going until the elections in May, in order to kick Macron out of office. There is a banner doing the rounds, '*Macron nous a tous Trumpés*' (Macron has fooled us all), a clever play on Franglais. The political honeymoon with Macron is over and he is regarded as a bit of a chancer.

I don't quite understand their animosity towards Emmanuel Macron. I suppose it is a problem of perception: there is distrust towards a wealthy banker with neo-liberal views who styles himself as 'centrist'. He is nothing of the sort;

he is as right-wing as they come! Yet he is prepared to do a tour of the country, roll up his sleeves, sit right in the middle of crowds and answer their questions. I can't think of any British politician who would subject themselves to such a grilling from the populace. One of his more unpopular and drastic proposals is to amalgamate the *communes*. These *communes* were set up after the Revolution and they work so well with only a mayor who knows everything that is going on in his/her patch and a few staff. This cost-cutting measure is under the guise of 'efficiency' which is a false economy. There is so much opposition that it is unclear if the government will manage to push through this proposal.

Macron is an enigmatic figure, but one fascinating fact about him is that he married his former schoolteacher, Brigitte, who is twenty-five years older than him. His parents thought he was going out with Brigitte's daughter, who was at the same school, and were horrified to discover that the object of his affections was the mother, not the daughter.

Among the many gongs handed out to foreign leaders, Macron is a recipient of 'The Order of the Elephant' from Denmark. I could only aspire to such an accolade. For his university thesis he studied Hegel and Machiavelli, obvious prerequisites for presidential office... He has published a book laying out his vision of France, how he is going to pull it up from the dysfunctional social model and recapture its former *grandeur*. The title is fitting for the French Republic: *Revolution*. The French are excellent at revolting. The British with their tendency to be reticent and obedient should follow their neighbour's example of hitting the streets whenever riled. I wonder what the title of Theresa May's book would be: 'Carrying out the will of the people', 'Maybot in action', 'Sleepwalk with Terry'?

We look on in embarrassment as the British are depicted as the laughingstock of the world in their self-made Brexit chaos. A cartoon is doing the rounds of a cat going round a revolving door with the caption 'So are you staying in? Or are you going out?' I'm not sure where we are at the moment with one vote after another being defeated in the UK parliament. Even the Minister for Brexit abstained from voting in support of his leader. It looks like the 29th March 2019 leaving date has been now moved to June. This does not alleviate the unease among the British here. The clear manifestation of this is the stockpiling of British products in the supermarkets. 'What am I going to do without my Yorkshire Tea?' Yes, it boils down to that.

French presidents are good at pontificating, which is why a title such as *Revolution* is so apt for Macron's book. Macron has incurred the wrath of the 'lower classes' as his tone is often contemptuous, depicting them as freeloaders and slackers. We watch a clip on television where he is berating a young man for not being sufficiently deferential. 'Do you know who I am?' Macron asks him, condescendingly.

In his short time as president, he has revised the labour code, taxed capital investments and overhauled the education system. No one can dispute the fact that French bureaucracy is a nightmare.

Amélie, a family friend, put it like this:

'I have worked all my life as a respite carer, and my pension is a miserable €300 a month once I have paid my rent. Now that I have moved to a smaller flat I have €900 a month. There is a huge disparity between the civil servant salaries and those of the ordinary worker. But this is not Macron's fault. He is simply inheriting the problem of years of corrupt politicians. Yes, we have to do something to overhaul the system, but getting at poor people is not the way.'

Slightly more than half of the French population owns their own home, so, unlike in Britain, buying and selling property is not seen as a way of creating wealth. There is also a huge wealth gap between town and country. One tends to forget that France is a huge country, still mostly agricultural.

There have been troubling backlashes to the *Gilets Jaunes* movement. The government has sought various means to discredit them. Anarchists have attempted to hijack the movement, smashing windows, setting cars alight and graffitiing shop fronts. Even more troubling is that the *Gilets* have spread to Britain, but there the movement is right-wing and fascist! There are still many deeply conservative areas in France, very *bourgeois*, narrow-minded and xenophobic.

An acquaintance who had been brought up in Cahors, a small city nearly two hours from here, told us how much he hated the place, describing it as *bourgeois*. Incidentally, Peter the Great of Russia loved Cahors wine so much he bought vineyards in the area and there still exists a wine called *Kahorski* which is drunk in Russia today.

Lot-et-Garonne is not *bourgeois* at all. It was always a poor backwater and sparsely populated. Immigrants were therefore always welcome: the Italians after World War I and later the British and Dutch in the late twentieth century. The Portuguese are the new kids on the block. The *Gilets Jaunes* have only had a marginal effect on life here, thus far.

When we return home from Bordeaux we settle down to watch the film *Nae Pasaran!* about the Scottish Rolls-Royce workers in the 1970s who set out to sabotage the sending of Pinochet's military jets to Chile, after the dictator had overthrown the incumbent president, Allende. It shows how a small act of defiance has huge repercussions and the Scottish workers' action brought an end to Pinochet's brutal regime. It was a moving and poignant tale; maybe the small things we do will accumulate to change the situation in Palestine for the better. Maybe the grievances of the French people will be heard and hope will take the place of despair. Who knows what will happen?

This is week six of Gerry's inaction. Still *hors de combat* despite another visit to a specialist. It is so frustrating for someone like him who hates to keep still for any length of time.

Weirder still, in a local building yard they are selling BBQs called 'le Barbecue Glasgow'. Is this a joke? This is pushing global warming too far, but I guess Scotland can be viewed as the sunny South of Scandinavia.

We take a short trip to the Pyrenees with my mother and her partner, Douglas. Douglas remarks as we approach Lourdes that usually there are a few cars to be seen with crutches sticking out of the windows, waiting for the miracle. A billboard advertises 'Bernadette: The Musical.' As we pass the 'My Lord' disco, through the town to the grotto where Bernadette is reported to have heard the voice of the Virgin Mary, we can't help but notice how prosperous Lourdes is. The holy visitation came at the right time when the scourge of atheism was sweeping through the land. The miracle is that since the 1860s this sleepy backwater has been transformed into a thriving tourist industry with 350 hotels and a nice line in kitsch. I keep yearning to see a 'Dave Allen' (the late Irish comedian), dressed up as the Pope dancing and singing, 'My God is better than your God.'

We keep a lookout for neon-filled Mary figurines, or at least revolving ones, but no such luck. What cannot be denied are the sheer numbers this town attracts with pilgrims coming from all parts of the globe; a few cathedrals soak up the overspill. There is even an underground church that resembles a massive concrete bunker, which accommodates 3,000 people. Lourdes is twinned with Bethlehem and Częstochowa.

Częstochowa is a holy place in Poland, home to the religious painting 'The Black Madonna of Częstochowa'. Every year, millions of tourists come from all over the world to see it. My extremely religious paternal grandmother used to go there on pilgrimages, walking up the steep hill to the shrine, with stones in her shoes to experience the rapture of suffering. I didn't inherit any of her piety.

We head to the mountains and trudge in the snow, marvelling at the beauty of the Cirque de Gavarnie. Just over the mountain lies Spain. Despite a quick sprinkling of the holy water, no miracle occurs and Gerry is still the hunchback of Notre Dame.

Nineteen

THE POLISH CONNECTION

You can take the boy out of the shipyards but you can't take the shipyards out of the boy! Gerry, unfortunately, is not the shipyard electrician who won the Nobel Prize. Years after leaving the Yarrow Shipbuilders on the Clyde, Gerry paid a nostalgic visit to the Solidarity Museum in Gdańsk.

Of course a SOLIDARNOŚĆ mug is bought to commemorate the event. We were young during those heady times in 1980 when the spotlight of the world was on the Polish strikers whose first demand out of twenty-one was to recognise the workers' right to join Solidarność as an independent trade union. This was really the beginning of the end of communism and the powerful hold of the Soviet Union over the satellite states. The uprisings in Hungary and Czechoslovakia had been quashed, but this Polish uprising was different. What drove the miners to strike this time was not idealism or independence from the Soviet stranglehold. It was hunger, first and foremost; not having enough money in their pockets to feed their families. In the 1970s a similar strike was crushed in the Lenin Shipyard in Gdańsk and forty-five miners were killed by government forces. Their comrades raised the money for a monument. The stark steel structure stands outside the entrance to the shipyard.

The momentum in 1980 could not be stopped as the Nobel Prize for Literature was awarded to the exiled Polish poet Czesław Miłosz and Andrzej Wajda's film *Man of Iron* swept the awards at the Cannes Film Festival. To top the lot in Polish dominance, Karol Wojtyła became the Polish Pope. The Popemobile (the car that took many a prominent place in many a cavalcade) is one of the displays in the Solidarity Museum. Ten million Poles immediately signed up as members of the union.

Good things could not last and martial law was imposed in December 1981. These pesky Poles, like the French, are forever revolting. The strike leader, Lech Wałęsa, and other union officials were arrested. The Italian Communist Solidarity Union gave money to the Poles' fight against communism.

I remember the protest marches and meetings in Paris, the uncertainty, the migration of prominent Poles, like the actor Daniel Olbrychski, who lived around the corner from me near the Luxembourg Gardens. The haunting songs of Maciej Pietrzyk, '*Piosenka dla córki*' (Song to my daughter) and '*Boże Nasz*' (Our Lord), filled the airwaves. I vividly recall the concert by the poet and singer Jacek Kaczmarski and his rousing protest songs. Kaczmarski found himself in Paris at the time of martial law. It was an agonising decision for artists and other prominent Poles who spoke out against the Polish puppet government to remain in Poland (and languish in prison) or leave and join protesters abroad. As the world looked on, willing the Poles to take a stand against their oppressors, there was a palpable feeling of unbridled hope and optimism. I am listening to Kaczmarski's songs now while writing this. I didn't realise that he left Poland in 1989 for good as part of the Polish diaspora, disillusioned at the way Polish politics was going, and eventually died at the age of forty-seven in Gdańsk in 2004. The Polish miners are well educated and recited protest poetry and literature from a people whose country has been continuously plundered and destroyed by their neighbours. Polish literature is full of allegorical allusions since it has played a part in resistance and the fight for independence, and many Poles are well-versed in the more famous lines; a bit like a Scot reciting excerpts of Robert Burns.

The Polish government led by General Jaruzelski went into full propaganda mode, claiming that martial law had been imposed to maintain democracy. The Solidarity Museum displays the TV coverage of the time, constantly intent in blackening the image of Solidarność. One clip shows a farmer sending a pig to the government as thanks for saving the country on the brink of anarchy. Food that was scarce before and resulted in huge queues outside shops now miraculously appeared again.

But everyone knew the truth behind the lies. Solidarność supporters rallied underground. Printing presses were assembled made out of various parts, such as washing machines; clandestine TV and radio outlets challenged the government's version. The outcry and support from the West ensured that the struggle went on and therefore when the Berlin Wall fell in 1989, communism limped to an end and democracy was eventually restored. It goes to show that a fight without violence can be effective.

Jadą, jadą dzieci drogą
siostrzyczka i brat,
i nadziwić się nie mogą,
jaki piękny świat.

When I was about four years old, my Aunt Magda in Paris sent this popular song on a forty-five vinyl record to Glasgow as a present. The lyrics are about a sister and brother who are travelling down a road, marvelling at *jaki piękny świat* – how beautiful the world is. It is the happiest song I know. I sing this in Coutal on exceptionally sunny days, changing the ending to *kaky dak* (nonsense words) which have changed into *clucky duck*, for reasons which are abundantly obvious.

My Polish now is not so much rusty as corroded. I have rarely spoken Polish as an adult; all the words lie dormant in my head. As a consequence, I use many childish expressions and make huge grammatical errors. It does not help that Polish not only has the same cases as Latin (Nominative, Accusative, Genitive, Dative, and Ablative) – NAGDA for short – it also has Locative and Instrumental cases. Oh, I forgot Vocative. It means that you can move the words around with gay abandon because the specific ending of the word determines the meaning. It can do your head in. It does do my head in.

My *babcia* – paternal grandmother – sent us, her grandchildren, beautifully drawn comics every month. She had about seventeen grandchildren and never forgot their birthdays. This *babcia* was the same grandmother who made pilgrimages with stones in her shoes. Her religion, children and music meant everything to her. Babcia was a professional pianist and ran a music school, so we were exposed to all sorts of Polish songs, from the folklore tunes of *Mazowsze*, to the more classical songs of *Anna German*. In the Polish School in Glasgow we were taught Polish dances by the redoubtable

Mrs Indyk. 'Girls, you have to sway like wheat in the wind!' The elephant in me would have nothing to do with this. When I read Polish now I have to read it aloud in my head so I can understand it. 'Basia' is one of the most common names in Poland. I am constantly turning round in the street to see who is calling me.

Whenever I have gone to Poland it has mainly been to visit family who live either in Warsaw or in Krakow. Occasionally I venture to the Carpathian and Tatra Mountains. The closest Gerry and I have come to a holiday in Poland is a visit to my cousin in Szczecin who took us to the seaside and the Wild Bison Park. Bison grass vodka has always been a favourite tipple of mine and it is the grass that makes the taste so distinctive. It's fitting that the bison and I have this in common.

Gdańsk is a new pasture for both me and Gerry. We have less time there than planned. Once we board our flight in Bergerac we are informed that because of a French air traffic controllers' strike (*encore quelle surprise*) we can expect a two-hour delay before taking off. This means that on arrival in London we have to vault across the airport to catch our connecting flight. We nearly make it. Just as we get to the gate, we see the plane revving up and taking off without us. Unfortunately my tooth cracks again, as does Gerry's back.

After an unplanned night in London, where we seek refuge in my daughter's new flat, we set off once more in the morning and land in Lech Wałęsa Airport in Gdańsk without a hitch. The same day, I find myself in a dental surgery with other Brits, being given a form which asks if I am in Poland for dental tourism!

Gdańsk had the unique status of a free city state in the inter-war period. Danzig, as it was known then, had its own currency and stamps, and was of vital importance to both Germany and Poland as a thriving port on the Baltic. Most of the population then were German speaking, although they sided with the Poles during World War II. The city was devastated and took years to rebuild, but the old part is still extensive, attractive and worth a visit. A plaque on a door states that the house is the birthplace of Daniel Gabriel Fahrenheit, best known for inventing the mercury thermometer (1714) and the Fahrenheit temperature scale which is still commonly used in the United States.

All German names of streets, buildings, shipyards and districts, even names on tombstones, were changed to Polish names after the war.

By sheer chance we bump into my cousin Nicky and his wife Jen who have come over for a short break in March from Glasgow. What are the odds? Springtime in Gdańsk.

One of the attractions of Gdańsk is a visit to the World War II museum built a few years ago. We really do know how to amuse ourselves. The clunky alliterative literature describes it thus: 'the alliance between the two totalitarians, Soviet Communism and German Nazism, led to the outbreak of the most tragic conflict in global history – the Second World War.' The exhibition presents the Polish experience of the war within the wider European and global context: 'The Road to the War', 'The Horror of War' and 'The Long Shadow of the War'. The Poles have been under the jackboot of the Germans, Soviets and communism for so long that it is no wonder they have gallows humour.

One of my heroes is Marek Edelman, the only remaining leader of the Jewish Ghetto uprising to survive, who also took part in the Warsaw Uprising. His name is slowly being erased from history. Edelman said: 'The Bundists' (Jewish socialists in Poland) 'did not wait for the Messiah, nor did they plan to leave for Palestine. They believed that Poland was their country, and they fought for a just, socialist Poland in which each nationality would have its own cultural autonomy and in which minorities' rights would be guaranteed.'

There is a Polish word – *los* – which reflects the Polish condition. It is difficult to completely encapsulate the meaning in translation; the word signifies a mix of destiny, fate, death and chance with a dollop of nostalgia.

The current government in Poland is tightening its grip and hard-won freedoms are being stamped out. People are afraid to speak out. Votes are won by giving generous maternity allowances to women.

The West used to laud the 'brave Poles' during the Solidarity years. Now, in the Western press, there are constant disparaging articles about Poland.

In 2012, Barack Obama referred to the German concentration camps in Poland as 'Polish death camps'. For many Poles, Obama's statement is more than ignorance or an innocent gaffe: it is a grave distortion of the darkest chapter in Polish history. The former prime minister of Poland Donald Tusk replied in scathing terms: 'When someone says "Polish death camps", it's as if there were no Nazis, no German responsibility, as if there was no Hitler. That is why our Polish sensitivity in these situations is so much more than just simply a feeling of national pride.'

There is now a law to ban such misleading statements in Poland, but in the interests of free speech, I disagree with this.

Auschwitz was turned into a museum immediately after the war by the Soviets to highlight the atrocities of the Germans. What is never spoken about is that the Soviets kept another concentration camp going in Poland after the war called Majdanek, which moved from German control to Soviet control. Majdanek was filled with returning Poles who had fought with the Allies as well as other Poles the Soviets deemed 'undesirable'. The fact that the Polish government did not capitulate or collaborate, but instead went into exile, is also rarely commented on. What we need is more information and better education.

Obama is frequently depicted as a man of peace, fond of retelling Martin Luther King's famous quote: 'the arc of the moral universe is long, but it bends toward justice.' No it doesn't! And especially where Obama is concerned. He has been proven to be the most warmongering of all US presidents. Under Obama's watch, the drone global assassination campaign was deployed in 147 countries in 2015. This breaks new records in international terrorism. No justice here. Obama joins the ranks of Kissinger in the undeserving Nobel Peace Prize winners as far as I am concerned.

We meet our old family friend, Staś Pruszyński, who runs the Radio Café, which was once the headquarters of Radio Free Europe, in the centre of Warsaw. His café was the first to open up in the street after the fall of communism; now the whole area is bustling with swanky restaurants, cocktail restaurants and boutiques. We also meet up with my aunt Teresa and family who live in one of the few houses to survive the war. The house is now on the tourist trail and gaggles of tourists stand by the gate, trying to peer in, shining torches through the bathroom window!

The comparatively affluent Poland today is a far cry from the Communist Poland of my youth. No more *Polakoktas* sold in shops – the state version of Coca-Cola – which tasted cloyingly sweet and metallic. Just before the Iron Curtain was lifted, my mother's cousin Ewa took me to a Chinese restaurant in Warsaw centre. There were about twenty items on the menu and as we asked for a dish we were told time and time again, *nie ma* – we don't have it. Eventually we struck lucky and named the two dishes available. It would have been funny if it did not so poignantly strike a chord on the privations at the time. There was hardly anything to be bought anywhere.

We cross Poland from north to south to Katowice and meet my father's brother Wojtek and wife, Kazia. Here we eat and eat and eat pierogi (stuffed dumplings). This is the same aunt and uncle who saved me from the re-education facility in Poland many years before and visited us once in Coutal, just after my father had bought the house. Our two families used to meet up every summer in a different communist country. They were very fit and good-looking then, but now they appear very frail. My uncle is now the only one left out of a family of thirteen brothers and sisters.

'It's really difficult to get any help around here,' says my Aunt Kazia. 'All the Poles who have gone to the West to work in service industries are being replaced by the Ukrainians. There are now one million Ukrainians working in Poland.'

'We always go out together,' adds my Uncle Wojtek, smiling at his wife. 'Hand in hand. Just in case one of us falls.'

I meet up again with their son, my cousin Tomek, for the first time after ten years. He now lives in Switzerland. He reminds me to look after the work-life balance. For six months of the year he works as a doctor and for the rest of the year he sails round the Caribbean. I have a lot to learn from him. I am really enjoying speaking Polish again, although Gerry finds the lack of vowels a linguistic nightmare.

Tomek – like all the Poles I spoke to – is perplexed by Britain's decision to leave the rest of Europe and sees it as a foolhardy and reckless move, completely out of keeping with the normally pragmatic British stance. In Eastern Europe, Great Britain has always been regarded as a beacon of democracy and openness, and it is not by chance that nearly a million Poles have come to work in Britain in the last few years. Britain's demand to 'take back its sovereignty' is seen as madness. 'But you have always had sovereignty!' exclaims Tomek. 'The act of holding a referendum proves you have sovereignty, the ability to make your own decisions. Can you imagine what would have happened if any Eastern Bloc country demanded a referendum to leave the Warsaw Pact in the 1980s? They would have been utterly crushed by the USSR!'

Maybe my affinity to the Palestinian cause stems from my Polish background; oppression, dispossession and occupation permeate my family's narrative. There are distinct comparisons to be drawn between Poland and Palestine: the way that people and countries can be wiped off the map. Both have suffered from long periods of occupation and rapacious exploitation by others. Both countries have been looted, ravaged and reviled; their histories rewritten. Civil disobedience and the lesson to resist, resist, resist are what they have most in common; a powerful force to effect change.

Britain is complicit in breaking the promises to both peoples. Roosevelt, Stalin and Churchill carved up their spheres of influence at the Yalta Conference in 1945 and sacrificed the Poles to Soviet domination which lasted for forty years. The betrayal of the Poles was compounded by being excluded from the celebration at the end of the war in London in 1945, despite the sacrifices made by the Polish pilots. Likewise, the British walked away from the chaos wreaked in the Middle East under their watch and abandoned the Palestinians to the ethnic cleansing that ensued. What both Palestinians and Poles hang on to as their lifeline is their culture.

Countries contract and expand, borders disappear then reappear, but what remains are the people of the land itself.

Meanwhile back in Britain, Brexit has proved to be a damp squib. March 29th has come and gone and the negotiations are still limping on. The only certainty so far is uncertainty. Boris Johnson, all smartened up, has been propped up on the TV, with more statistical garbage. Has everyone forgotten his big lie emblazoned on the side of a red bus during the EU referendum of 2016? 'We send the EU £350 million a week, let's fund our NHS instead'. He is the King of Soundbites: 'Poppycock and balderdash' and 'A mutton-headed old mugwump' (referring to Jeremy Corbyn). We are also given the frequent commentary of Jacob Rees-Mogg, another right-wing throwback to the Victorian era. The French – and the Poles – have no idea what to make of all this mess and these weird people.

Earlier in the month, my mother gave two talks in the 'Hôtel de Cours de Thomazeau' in the *bastide* of Castillonnès. There was no emotion in her voice as she spoke about her early childhood in war-torn Poland and her scramble for survival. She only met up with her parents as an adult. My mother's voice sounds like Zsa Zsa Gabor. It was a full house; people were amazed and shocked in equal measure as my mother is very matter of fact and blunt. Dispassionate. Detached. Disassociated. How else was she going to tell the tale of a fractured childhood? I translated her talk into French. One of the motivating factors for her to speak out now is that she wants to warn people of the consequences of the rise of the right and extremism in world politics. She is one of the very few people still alive who witnessed the burning of the Warsaw Ghetto.

In Christchurch, New Zealand, fifty Muslims are killed in a mosque. The world contrasts the dignified, compassionate response of Jacinda Ardern, New Zealand's premier, with that of Donald Trump's crass comments and support of gun laws. Stephen Colbert, host of *The Late Show* in the US, makes this comment on the president:

'I'm just saying, if it walks like a duck and talks like a duck, then why does it keep goose-stepping?'

I think I am obsessed with ducks.

At last, back home in Coutal, the ducks have gone and now the shooting season is truly over. We make batches of soap with argan powder, lemon grass, orange blossom and bay leaves, handily picked from our massive bay tree outside the front door. Making soap was our grand plan for making money a few years ago in Scotland, and we spent nearly every weekend at local markets selling our wares while working in schools during the week. One thing led to another and we realised the soap by-product made excellent body oil. Next came body scrubs, shampoo bars and candles. The possibilities were endless, and we experimented with different combinations of rosemary, lavender, cinnamon, grapefruit, oud and vetivert. Bog myrtle (plentiful in Scotland) proved effective in deterring midges and mosquitoes. Part of the fun was to make an entirely natural product, but it took months for the soaps to harden without chemicals. We travelled to women's co-operatives in the arid parts of Morocco – the Argania – to buy argan powder and knew that we were being diddled when on one memorable occasion we were buying vast amounts of argan which was to be shipped over. 'And what is this place called again?' I asked, as I handed over the money. 'Amskroud,' she answered. And so we were.

On another occasion we travelled in the Argania during Ramadan and consequently there were no shops open. We survived on a diet of olives, nuts and water for a week. Once we were ripped off by a fraudster who posed as a Franciscan monk, and much of our stuff was ruined by a torrential thunderstorm during an outdoor festival. Thankfully, we have washed our hands of this particular business venture. We now have a far more challenging one.

I endlessly mow the grass. Who knew that grass has to be mowed so often? It would be another thing altogether if it were bison grass, but this is the common garden stuff that proliferates from every nook and cranny.

We watch our favourite French TV series (*Bienvenue chez Nous*) where bed and breakfast owners judge each other's businesses. We are completely hooked. At the St Patrick's Day dinner in Villeréal we are mistaken for token Irish. Not to disappoint anyone we adopt a clichéd Irish lilt. It was hilarious! The local dance group thud out 'Riverdance' with such force the floor almost gives way. My persistent cough persists. Gerry takes constant walks to ease his back pain. He is now more *hors de service* than *hors de combat*. He is adding to his photo montage of burnt out cars abandoned in the countryside. There is an affinity there.

The sun shines brightly; the days are longer. We get ready for the next batch of visitors.

Twenty

SHOW ME THE WAY, MONTAIGNE

Apple blossoms float down inside from the barn roof, skilfully sliding through the roof tiles. Last week, hailstones bounced off the table. Maybe one day the barn ceiling will be fully insulated, but for the moment nature is joining us indoors. We invite friends over for aperitifs and canapés. How sophisticated we feel. Arum lilies and blue irises line the ditches by the roadside. Even the wildflowers here are upmarket.

There is a tradition on May 1st to give *muguets* – lily of the valley – to friends and family, as a symbol of springtime and to wish them happiness. Little bunches of the flower are sold in markets. One of the villagers has a garden full of *muguets* and is devastated to find that thieves plundered his garden the night before and took every single white flower. 'What sort of happiness is this?' he asks, with an air of disbelief.

My Aunt Teresa's colourful Easter eggs made from clay are dusted down and take pride of place in a bowl in the centre of the refectory table. The few precious and fragile Easter eggs decorated by my Great-uncle Ergo are carefully placed around the larger ones. I boil up six eggs with onion skins until they are a satisfying deep brown colour. When they are cool, I paint them in bright colours and add them to the bowl. The long rope that binds past and present is tied together.

Most of the visitors have been here before and are amazed at the transformation. David has popped over from Bordeaux where he has been marking French PhDs in nuclear physics. He was last here with his wife Ann in July. David helps me take out an old fridge to the dump. We have had four fridges in the kitchen until recently, all of them with various degrees of functionality. My mother could never bear to throw anything out. I guess it's a wartime mentality. Ironically, the oldest fridge works quite well. When I was twelve I had saved up the ice-cream stickers called *Galak* and stuck them on the white fridge door. No more will I see a cartoon of a small boy riding a dolphin.

'Sarkozy did an interesting thing,' David tells us. 'He wanted to boost the French universities' standing to MIT status by pumping millions of euros into his project, and, to a certain extent, he has succeeded. What might make it unravel, of course, is the fact that rivalry between universities might undo all the academic excellence.'

I can't believe my eyes when I spot an enormous brass birdcage in the Sunday market at Issigeac. 'Look!' I said to Gerry. 'If we can't have an elephant suspended from the ceiling roof, let's have this birdcage instead!' The €1,500 price tag stops us in our tracks.

Our cultural highlight is a visit to Montaigne's tower near Castillon-la-Bataille, over an hour away, with David, Ann,

Terry and Fran. Fran and I had studied Montaigne's *Complete Essays* at university many moons before. Montaigne is the epitome of the Renaissance Man, living in the sixteenth century, asking himself questions about the human condition and writing about his travels. His personal experience led to his writing streams of consciousness, merging anecdotes from his own life with intellectual insight, trying to make sense of the world.

Que sais-je? (What do I know?), he asked.

He believed that the *l'art de vivre* – the art of living – should be based on wisdom, tolerance and common sense. His discourse on friendship and his tribute to his friend, the philosopher Étienne de la Boétie, as a kindred spirit is especially touching. Montaigne put it simply and beautifully, *parce que c'était lui, parce que c'était moi* – because it was him, because it was me. They were two sides of the same coin.

De la Boétie recognised the link between government oppression and the subservience of the masses, domination and obedience, and put forward a solution of simply refusing to support the tyrant. In a France of week twenty-two of *Gilet Jaunes* unrest it is good to remember de la Boétie was one of the earliest advocates of civil disobedience and nonviolent resistance. A man after my own heart.

The weather has cleared up and we arrive at Montaigne's tower just in time for a vintage car gathering, an added plus for the car enthusiasts among us. The last time I had visited the tower was well over thirty years before. It was left open to the public and anyone could just walk in. Now it has been scrubbed up for guided visits only. I had always imagined that here was Montaigne's refuge away from the troubles of the war-stricken world of the Middle Ages, where he shut himself away, lost in his thoughts, and scribbled away. But now the guide has illuminated us away from fancy notions.

'Montaigne was too mean to pay for windows so the tower was totally dark. His scribe wrote by candlelight while Montaigne paced the floor. Montaigne's wife had her own tower across the field, but they tended to avoid each other,' she said. The tower was Montaigne's refuge from the world and the guide showed us a place in the tower where Montaigne hid when he heard his name called.

He was an *homme particulier* she added, a singular man. He spoke Latin and Greek and only learnt Gascon, the local French dialect, when he was seventeen. At the age of three he was taken from home to a nurse, rather than the nurse working at the château, so he would be more grounded. His father instructed that minstrels should be at his bedside all night playing music so he would be lulled to sleep and woken in the morning by the gentle sound of music. 'I bet,' remarks Fran, 'as soon as they saw his eyes flicker and shut they would pack up the instruments and have a snooze themselves.'

Montaigne was the only Protestant nobleman around Catholics and yet he did not close the gates to his castle, reasoning that it would be better to welcome his enemies in and speak to them directly. It was a ruse that seemed to have worked and he was so widely respected and admired that he was elected twice as mayor of Bordeaux, much to his dismay.

It was sad to hear that his disgruntled daughter gave away or destroyed most of the books in his extensive library rather than give them to his young muse to whom they had been bequeathed.

We have the good fortune of being surrounded by wonderful wines and of course repair to the tasting of the Montaigne wine estates. The bottles are now slyly labelled 'Les Essais' and the marketing is admirable and sleekit: *La plus grande chose du monde, est de savoir être à soi.*

After the tastings, we meander back through the vineyards around Bergerac, soaking up the convivial atmosphere and the early evening sun, before embarking on a home-made feast at Coutal. Food, friends, fun, sun, wine and music: all the ingredients for happiness.

There are stern government warnings on the TV about the dangers of alcohol: *Pas plus de deux verres du vin par jour, et pas tous les jours.* No more than two glasses of wine a day, and not every day. 'What the hell,' I say, and imbibe a glorious glass of white Verdots.

'Do you remember,' I ask Gerry, 'years ago when we were in Cyprus, we saw a mosaic on the ground, celebrating Dionysus, the god of the grape-harvest, winemaking and wine, of fertility, ritual madness, religious ecstasy, and theatre in ancient Greek religion? At the same time warning us of over-drinking? What was it again?'

'I drink a little and I am like the bird. Tweet, tweet, tweet. I drink a little more and I am like the lion. Roarrrrr! I have a little more to drink and I am like the donkey. Ee-aw, ee-aw!' answers Gerry, the philosopher.

The latest Brexit date, 12th April, has come and gone and now has been reset for Hallowe'en. What ghouls and hobgoblins will come out then?

We tend to steer clear of political opinions on our ladies' Friday walking group, but it was interesting to overhear the chat this week as we walked around the beautiful hilltop village of Monségur. We passed by a stunning display of Judas trees, a profusion of pink flowers dazzling in the sun. The name sparked off a conversation about the recent elections and I was surprised to hear sympathy for the Palestinians being voiced. One of the group said:

'Years ago, I was working in Bahrain. Whenever we sent letters we had to stick on a normal stamp and a blue stamp as well. I didn't know why we had the blue stamp so one day I met the Emir of Bahrain and asked him.

'"Well," he answered, "the money raised by the blue stamps goes directly to the Palestinian cause. We don't publicise it but that is the reason for the stamps."

'"And what if I don't put on a blue stamp?" "Then your letter will not be sent," came his curt reply.'

'Come quickly!' yells Gerry, from the living room. We look in horror at the images on the television of Notre Dame de Paris in flames. Suddenly, the spire topples to the ground, a lit candle extinguished.

Macron has postponed his speech which has been eagerly awaited. He has spent weeks touring the country in *les grands débats* discussing the *Gilets Jaunes* crisis. Now with the icon of France in flames, there is a different sort of devastation hitting the country.

Twenty-One

THE SHOW MUST GO ON

We know that things are not right when the mechanic comes round the corner, scratches his head and asks his boss to have a look. Soon we are all staring at the undercarriage of our old car, our trusty workhorse. We have spent a small fortune in the last few months to keep it on the road.

'*C'est bien foutu,*' says the boss eloquently. 'It's completely fucked. I cannot let you leave this garage in this car. I must condemn the car.' We have already had one car condemned in France and now another one was up for the knackers yard. Looking at the corrosion and the rust, we can only agree with his prognosis. A feeling of hopelessness spreads over us.

The other day I had been foraging for wood at a friend's woodpile (I had sought permission, eventually), and on the way back home the car brakes started to go a bit wonky again. It's Wednesday and guests are due to arrive on Friday and we

THE SHOW MUST GO ON

179

have promised to pick up Ron and Janet from Bergerac airport the next morning. Twelve people are due to arrive for lunch on Saturday. This is not the moment for a completely fucked car. I was starting to panic. Luckily, I had stumbled out of the Leclerc hypermarket the day before, laden with supplies of food and wine, so we will not starve or dehydrate (in a French manner of speaking), but not having a car in La France Profonde is akin to bucolic madness.

'Any car for sale here?' we ask hopefully. In this way, we become the proud owners of a sixteen-year-old Citroën car, which has a tow-hook, I am assured. However, we cannot pick it up until it has a *contrôle technique* – a MOT – and a clean-up. Things are not looking so bleak. 'So when will do you think it will be ready?' we ask, ever hopeful. Not until Friday afternoon at the latest we are told. Hope abandoned. Our shoulders slump. We have promised our friends Ron and Julie that we will pick them up from Bordeaux airport on Friday. I met Julie at school when we were thirteen years old or thereabouts and ever since then she has been trying to come to Coutal. But invariably something gets in the way. Now at last the time has come to turn up.

Julie has lived all over the world, married Ron, a Tibetan scholar originally from California, and they settled in Canada after years of wandering. Her job as a linguistics professor involves travelling to Cree communities and documenting their language and grammar. I really want Julie to see the lovely blue and yellow patchwork counterpane she made which is now on my bed.

We don't want to let them down after all these years of planning. Arrangements are made for other friends to pick up Ron and Janet, our neighbours who live a ten-minute cycle ride away. They selflessly lend us their car and on Friday we arrive at the garage, with the optimism of the ingénue, waiting for the release of our newly acquired car. We bring our cheque book, passports and every piece of paper we can think will be of use. 'Ah,' says the lady at the desk. 'Do you have anything on paper to prove Gerry lives at this address?' I furnish a letter to this effect. 'Do you have three latest bills at your address?' I explain that everything is online so it is not possible to do that. I whip out the proof of ownership letter from the lawyer. So far, so good. We are proceeding to the payment stage. It is nearing the critical cut-off time of 12 o'clock, the all-important lunchtime where all negotiations will halt and resume after 2pm. This looks like a done deal. I bring out my credit card. '*Ah, non, pas de cartes de crédit.*' She shakes her head. The deal is off.

'But look at the sign on your desk!' I protest. 'It says you do not accept any cheque over €50. That's why I would like to pay by credit card!'

'This sign is meant to be ignored,' she responds sternly. She then takes pity on us. 'I will wait until you return with your cheque book, but you had better be quick.' We dash home then back to the garage, cheque book in hand. I ask where the tow-hook is. 'The old man who owned the car removed it and doesn't know where it is now.'

'But you promised us a tow-hook!' My face is turning an unattractive shade of puce. 'Could you get me a new tow-hook?' I ask, lowering my voice. I am pleading.

'Yes of course, but it will cost you another €500,' comes the answer.

Ron and Julie emerge from Bordeaux airport in brilliant spring sunshine. It's good to have them on their own to catch up and reminisce before other guests arrive. Julie manages to do a Skype conference in Hawaii – Hawaiian being another endangered language. Ron tells us that the Tibetans have very low entrances to their house to foil the 'ro-langs' – the zombies. As an American, Ron has a very interesting take on Trump's popularity. 'It was very risky, but he said the unsayable, how racism is acceptable, and the American public embraced the concept.'

I tell Ron and Julie what the French think of Trump. At first the French public are extremely perplexed by the French translation of his words. Trump's announcements do not seem to have the eloquence, the statesmanship that a person of his office should command. 'It is like a ten-year-old speaking with a very limited vocabulary,' they complain. They are astonished to be told that, *oui, c'est vrai*, this is a verbatim translation of the thoughts of the Great Leader. To counteract this incredulity, translators feel it incumbent upon themselves to give Trump's words a bit of finesse in translation, not to jar in the French ear.

I have known most of my best friends since childhood, so we can adopt a code – a shorthand – in conversations. Julie knows all about the 'Cone', the fearsome depute headteacher at secondary school (no need to go into details), and Sharon needs just to be told to get that down her with a frog-chaser (again, no need to go into details). When I tell Sharon that I have been 'working like Luba' she knows that I am talking about a friend's long-term live-in help in Poland who is a domestic whizz and does everything in the house: cooking, cleaning, baking and sewing. We all understand the context.

I love to hear Julie's tales about life in Newfoundland, especially all the place names which can compete with the French ones here for hilarity: the Irish Loop, Dildo (Upper and Lower), Come by chance, Little heart's content, Blow me down, Little heart's ease. The best one must surely be Bay despair, which has such depressing connotations in English, yet it comes from the French, Baie d'Espoir – the Bay of Hope – the opposite meaning!

Ron is thrilled to be taken to the square in Monflanquin, just up the road from us. His excitement mounts. 'I can't believe it! This is where the Black Prince assembled his troops! As a boy I watched the swashbuckling film about this starring Errol Flynn! I will never forget the immortal words he addressed to the soldiers to rally them into action.'

Ron pauses for effect, deepens his voice and declaims:

'Men of the Middle Ages! We are about to begin the Hundred Years' War!'

Ron is about to cry with mirth and bends over double, hugging his sides. 'Classic lines!' he wheezes.

Ron is also a bee lover (there are so many around these parts) and is impressed by the prodigious honey effusions of the French bees. We are regaled with many a bee story but the sting in the end is that the bees end up destroying each other and their queen.

I make up a spreadsheet of everyone's comings and goings, entertainment and accommodation. Hotel Coutal Haut must run like clockwork. 'Organisation is the key,' I grimly remind myself as I change beds, cook and clean up. Some recently encountered psycho-babble bubbles up in my brain. 'I choose to be an artist, of being, not doing.' I vaguely recall a quote from the incomparable Quentin Crisp: 'If I have any talent at all, it is not for doing but for being.'

Then a light-bulb moment pings. 'Hey man, I am doing *and* being!' It is so mad I can't help laughing, tears in my eyes, dustpan at hand.

I am often asked, 'Do you like gardening?' and the answer is, yes, in a limited way, but at the moment I can hardly control the grass and weeds that have sprouted like triffids with all the heat and rain. It takes an eight-hour session to do one cut with my petrol-filled mower.

As the gods of contrariness would have it, it's always a case of being in the wrong country when things go belly-up. At the same time as the car is being scrapped, the lovely tenants in Glasgow announce they are leaving and the neighbours above flood our flat.

Everyone arrives as we are in the middle of frantic phone calls to sort out the mess. To be fair, all our visitors are so helpful and generous, and this French farmhouse lends itself to entertaining. What's the point of all this if your loved ones cannot share it? Although it is still a lot of house with too few bedrooms…

Knowing Ron and Julie, Ron and Janet, and Ron and Jennie has led to a few mishaps in communication, especially in telephone messages. Gerry ends up delivering tools to the wrong R & J's.

Ron and Jennie have spent many years refurbishing and rebuilding their beloved *Monument Historique* in Castillonnès. After a chance conversation about putting on events with Jennie, I am more than happy to help out. As well as introducing my mother (who gave her talk in March) and then Ian Herbert who gave an entertaining talk on his life as an international theatre critic, the next event would be Christine Bovill's Paris Show at the end of the month. We last met Christine at her show in Berlin back in October. Earlier in the year we had a phone chat about the fact that, despite being known for her interpretation of *La Chanson Française*, she has never sung professionally in France. After all, a Glaswegian singing in French in France is not an easy concept to master. Maybe her 'Piaf' show should be renamed 'Pee-aff' to give it the full Glaswegian *je ne sais quoi*.

An anomaly that has to be righted, I decide, and *le grand salon* in Hôtel de Cours de Thomazeau is just the venue: a cosy setting with beautiful antique décor on the right side of *grandeur*. It will also be fun to have Christine come over to spend time with us. We manage to enlist the services of the talented pianist Stanley Hanks, who lives a baguette's throw from us. Even though time is tight with only three rehearsals scheduled, Stan, being the perfectionist he is, learns most of the repertoire before Christine's arrival.

Our old friends Ian and Susan decide to extend their visit to coincide with Christine's concert. It is an excuse to take a trip down memory lane. Susan and her three children, our good friend Sharon and her daughter, plus me and my two weans used to spend many summer holidays in Coutal; effectively 'glamping' and keeping ourselves far from the madding crowd.

Just as I did when I was a child, the kids found amusing ways to entertain themselves. We had no computers, television or phones and neither did they. Our kids spent hours chasing lizards and pulling off their tails. The boys baited Sharon's daughter, stealing her anatomically correct dolls, William and Outjie, and hanging them by the neck from the trees. As an added torment, they would sometimes take Polaroid pictures of the dolls with their heads down the toilet or in other compromising positions. Then they would wait patiently for the inevitable blood-curdling screams to rend the air. When they got bored, they would practise their 'keepie-uppie' football skills. The girls, impervious to all the boys' shenanigans, spent hours inventing dance routines on the terrace to Steps, the Spice Girls and other pop groups of the time.

It was very much a women's commune, with the three of us looking after the needs of our small brood. There is still a framed photograph of us all on the wall in the throughroom. We are squeezed into a small boat in the Gouffre de Padirac, the most famous cave in Europe with a subterranean river deep down in the bowels of the Earth. Utterly terrifying. 'Nick, knack Padirac, leave us all alone,' sang the children. 'Nick, knack Padirac, Show us the way home.' The glum expressions in the photograph say it all.

It wasn't easy to move around in such a big group. A highlight of the summer was the 'Coutal Games' where we would invite over neighbours and friends to preside as judges over the feats of baguette throwing, prune spitting, yodelling, jumping over the old toilet, and *boules*. It certainly sharpened the kids' competitive spirit as the judges got well inebriated during the course of the day.

My mother's friends would come to the event. John Holst-Friend's father was English, his mother Polish and he was born in Romania. He was brought up in Poland and kicked out when the Communists took over. His wife Mimi, born of Belgian parents, was brought up in Hong Kong. After a few years of diplomatic postings they ended up in a *gîte* outside of Villeréal. Mimi, of the deep, smoky Marlene Dietrich voice, was invaluable in helping our family navigate the legal complexities associated with Coutal Haut. John and Mimi are just one example of the hybrid international community Lot-et-Garonne attracts. They are also the only people I know whose house has been struck by lightning – twice.

Luckily, Ziggy, my son, is sorting out future tenants for the flat, so Gerry doesn't have to do a quick zip back to Glasgow. I am relieved because I still feel apprehensive about being here alone. I remember when Sharon was adamant that she saw the ghost of a woman sitting forlornly at the top of the stairs. I know it is rubbish, but it doesn't take much to feed my paranoia. The creaking of an old house in the middle of the night is enough to have me gripping the bedclothes.

Wine *dégustation* (we used to call it a 'disgusting' when we were kids) is an important part of life and we organise a wine tour and tasting at Château Feely, a vineyard specialising in organic and biodynamic wines, near Bergerac. The growth of all things *bio* or organic has been growing steadily. Ten years ago there were only 4% organic vineyards in France, now there are 10%. The official definition of biodynamic farming, according to the Biodynamic Farming and Gardening Association, is 'a spiritual-ethical-ecological approach to agriculture, gardens, food production and nutrition.' Biodynamic wine is made with a set of farming practices that views the farm or vineyard as one solid organism. However, controversially, it also uses agricultural practices based on the lunar calendar and astrological influences. I am not sure about how all this works, but not spraying lethal and toxic substances into the earth certainly seems like a good start.

'Mmmm,' says Ian, swirling his glass, watching the legs of the wine appear. 'This tastes of filet mignon.' '*Ah oui*,' I counter, 'this should be named Touché Feely.' A spate on variations of the Feely name ensues, lost on our charming guide.

Gerry, Ian, Susan and I walk over the back field to the Rolls-Royce Museum, a mere fifteen minutes from the house. 'The Spirit of Ecstasy', the bonnet ornament figurine on Rolls-Royce cars, is prominently displayed on each vehicle. It is in the form of a woman leaning forwards with her arms outstretched upwards. Billowing cloth runs from her arms, resembling wings. The owner points out that there is one car that is slightly different. The woman is to be found on her knees. The car had once been owned by a Saudi Arabian sheikh who could not countenance a woman being in a dominant role and customised the figurine accordingly. As we are the only visitors that day, our host is not going to let us go easily. It is an impressive collection, but nevertheless, vintage or not, it has the word 'car' in it which is a complete anathema to me and an involuntarily twitch starts to develop in my eye.

Work has effectively halted while we entertain. Californian Ron brings out his mobile and shows us icebergs floating past his home in Witless Bay in Newfoundland at that exact moment, and Susan shows us Ian's finished home renovations back in Scotland. They have pristine gravel surrounding their house. We have weeds sprouting wildly among the uneven stones of what will one day be our drive. I think about the line in one of John Betjeman's poems, which goes something like 'And here comes the Lagonda, crunching through private gravel.' At least I can derive comfort in plunging into a reverie.

As ever, guests provide the perfect excuse to visit the local chocolate factory, *vide-greniers*, markets, *brocantes*, artist friends' ateliers, walks, restaurants and cafés as well as the *bastide* villages. Frankly, we don't really need to have an excuse to down tools.

Christine is thrilled when we visit Josephine Baker's château, Les Milandes, which is only a forty-minute drive away. Baker, nicknamed the 'Black Venus', is a French icon even though she was a black American, coming from the Missouri slums. She wowed Paris in the 1920s with her daring singing and dancing stage shows and never looked back. She led an extravagant and over-the-top lifestyle with her menagerie of Ethel the chimpanzee, Chiquita the cheetah, Toot Toot the goat and Tomato the horse.

Les Milandes still feels like the home she lived in with her adopted twelve children, her own rainbow tribe. She was a complicated woman; despite being bi-sexual and having had loads of lovers, she nevertheless cut out one of her sons in her will when she discovered he was gay.

The banana skirt she wore in the 1926 Paris revue is on show and I love the opulent luxury of the Dior and Arpège bathrooms. La Baker was continually being cheated out of her cash by unscrupulous people. In the end, the château had to go when her money ran out. The saddest thing of all is the newspaper photo of her sitting alone on her kitchen steps, covered in a tartan shawl, refusing to budge for two days until she was carried off the premises. Then the bailiffs took over and Les Milandes was sold. Later, Grace, Princess of Monaco, came to her rescue and looked after her financially.

Christine is preparing a new show to be launched at the Edinburgh Fringe, based on songs in 1920s America and she sings one of Josephine Baker's numbers.

The heavens opened and the cold winds of the north swept in for the duration of our guests' stay. When Gerry's friend Liz heard that Christine was playing a concert nearby us, she flew over from Glasgow for a few days. Liz is full of surprises and anecdotes. She lived in Marseille many years ago and told us that she used to read Che Guevara in French since his work wasn't published in English at that time.

At the same time as our guests arrive, work starts on one of the habitable bedrooms in the barn. What did I say? A lot of house with fewer and fewer bedrooms.

Gerry and I move into the caravan. Christine is worried for us as she presses her face into the window, watching the fierce thunder and lightning storm light up the garden. She is sure we will be found fried in our tin can the next morning.

Christine's 'Paris' concert is a great success with a standing ovation at the end of her performance. Her mellifluous voice and warm presence infuse the room. '*Mais elle n'a pas d'accent!*' says the French contingent, clearly impressed. What they mean is she has a flawless French accent. The Mayor of Castillonnès is overwhelmed. A woman comes over to thank Christine at the end and then whispers into her ear, 'My husband has just left me after thirty-seven years.' Another person introduces himself with a title and it is only later we discover he has changed his name by deed poll so now his first name is 'Sir'.

Happy and relieved that the concert has gone so well, we tuck into a chilli con carne supper after the show.

We note that it is just over a year ago that we had our last fundraiser for Palestine with Christine in Glasgow: 'A Mediterranean evening with Afterburns', with fourteen different acts. It doesn't seem so long ago and yet so much has happened since then. Before leaving France, Christine sings a poignant duet with Ron Fairfax, '*Je t'attendrai*', the French version of 'We'll Meet Again'.

When the guests melt away, the sun comes out at last. Gerry and I go for an evening walk with the rays of the sun sweeping across the valley, green and lush after so much rain.

'You know,' says Gerry, 'the repertoire of the song thrush is completely different here. Far more melodious. In Glasgow they mimic fire and car alarms.'

And it's true; all we can hear is birdsong.

Twenty-Two

INACTION IS A WEAPON
OF MASS DESTRUCTION

Parce que les choses sont comme elles sont, les choses ne resteront pas comme elles sont.
Because things are the way they are, things will not stay the way they are.

Bertolt Brecht.

We could just as well be asking, in French, 'Hmm, I say, excuse me, where can we find The People's Front of Judea?' or indeed, 'The Judean People's Front' (campaigning for a Free Galilee) or maybe 'The Popular Judean People's Front?' Let's face it, any anti-imperialist group which reflects a divergence of interests in Judea's power base?

Earlier in the year, we had gone to Périgueux on a fruitless search for a Palestinian organisation and scoured the internet in vain for any sympathetic groups. It was starting to resemble a Monty Python sketch from *Life of Brian*. Many things about being a Palestinian activist resemble *Life of Brian*.

When we visited Palestine for the first time, Gerry decided to go incognito: dressed in full kilt regalia, setting off every electronic device known to the security services. Naively, we mentioned to the Israeli officials that we were going to Jenin to visit a school there. I explained that I had been asked by the school where I worked in Glasgow to form a partnership with a school in Jenin. This prompted three-and-a-half hours of intense questioning.

'Why Jenin? There is nothing to see there. A bus for Jerusalem is about to leave. Why don't you get on it?'

'You have another passport, don't you?'

'No, we don't.'

'You have been here before?'

'No, we haven't.'

'Ah, your name is Gordon. That is a Jewish name. Why do you have a Jewish name?'

Bizarrely, there are a lot of Cohens who have changed their names to Gordon and there is a Gordon Beach in Tel Aviv.

Gerry was asked where he was born and he answered 'Scotland.' 'Aha,' shouted the official in triumph. 'But you have a UK passport. So explain *that* then!'

In fact, there is a lot to see in Jenin. It has the fourth-oldest church in the world, called St George's Church in Burqin, where Jesus healed the lepers. Nevertheless, in Israeli eyes, Palestine does not exist; it is simply Samaria and Judea, part of Greater Israel.

And then all our Palestinian buses come at once. We discover that there is a shop in Villeneuve selling Palestinian products and that an active Palestinian group exists in the nearby city of Agen. Hallelujah! The annual Palestinian cultural evening with exhibition and dinner will take place in Villeneuve in May!

We set off to the event with hope in our hearts but few expectations. And so we are pleasantly surprised. Normally we do not expect a huge turnout for Palestine. One hundred and forty people from all backgrounds are gathered in the hall.

'*Bonsoir.*' The lady across the table beams and plants two fat kisses on my cheeks.

'*Je m'appelle Stéphanie et je suis Communiste.*' 'My name is Stephanie and I'm a communist.' You don't hear that much back in the UK, nor this: '*Nous, les intellectuels, pensent que*' 'we, the intellectuals think that...'

Seven hundred and ten resolutions of the UN General Assembly and eighty-six UN Security Council resolutions supporting Palestinian rights have been passed *and not a single one of them has been implemented*. It is clear that many people there are unaware of the occupation and the illegal settlements, and as they study the exhibition one can hear the gasps of *Mon Dieu* and *Ce n'est pas vrai!*

'How can this be acceptable?' they ask, horrified. 'It's bloody awful.'

It is the most moving and colourful evening with delicious food, a slide show and dancers and singers from Palestine. If only we could bring over PLLF (the Palestinian Laughter Liberation Front) from Jenin Freedom Theatre, whose actors mime today's satire. Of course, being France, copious amounts of aperitifs and wine are consumed. I had assumed, wrongly, that it would be a 'dry' affair.

One action begets another and we find ourselves in Bordeaux on May 18th for Acte 27, the weekly demonstration of the *Gilets Jaunes*. The demonstrations are now in their sixth month and there is no sign of them petering out, approaching the European elections. There has been a definite polarisation of the political right and left and little in between. Macron labels himself a 'progressive' but this is risible.

The tactics of the police have now changed from when we joined in a march in Bordeaux two months ago. Apparently, the mayor of Bordeaux has demanded that police find a way to stop the march, especially now that shoppers are no longer coming to Bordeaux on a Saturday and this is severely affecting tourism and the city coffers.

We recognise some of the protesters, but now the bikers and the young men in balaclavas are missing. The march has now gained the support of people from all walks of life united in disenchantment with government policy: the original *Gilets Jaunes*; those protesting against neo-liberalism; the Extinction Rebellion supporters; environmental supporters with anti-Monsanto slogans on their backs; parents with young children; people with disabilities; the working poor; the concerned, well-heeled and down-trodden; the elderly; pets on leads and young girls blowing bubbles.

A girl with a cigarette in her hand has written on her jacket:

'*Si on arrêtait acheter des choses inutiles et nuisibles?*'

'And what if we were to stop buying useless and harmful products?'

Another sign reads: '*Fin du monde. Fin du mois. Même combat*'

'The end of the world, the end of the month. Same battle'.

But the sign I like best is in a doorway:

'*Osteopathie Energique.*'

'Hervé BASTARD'.

I can just imagine Dr Bastard saying to one of his clients, 'Would sir like it harder?'

What is clear is that this is a peaceful protest. There is no sign of the *casseurs* (anarchist elements) highlighted earlier in news reports. A carnival atmosphere prevails with drummers, people singing; those inconvenienced in cars are smiling and waving.

This is in complete contrast to the vast numbers of riot police deployed, like huge black beetles in their twenty-first-century battle gear, against ordinary citizens marching together. It is completely out of all proportion. These are not even ordinary police; they are there, ready to intimidate and use tear gas, grenades and rubber bullets. Police are supposed to save and protect citizens, not threaten them.

According to the Minister of the Interior, eleven people have been killed in these protests, mostly trying to stop traffic at ad hoc roadblocks. According to police reports, 2,448 people have been injured on the marches so far. In addition, there have been 1,797 injuries to police officers. The police have arrested 10,718 people. Police have fired 13,905 rubber bullets (*balles de LDB*). Around twenty people have reported serious eye injuries from rubber bullets. In Marseille, an eighty-year-old woman has died of injuries from tear gas thrown by the police into her home as she was closing her windows for protection.

Last year, during a presidential visit to Louvain University, a Belgian student asked Macron: 'Why are you the only country that uses grenades against its own people?' (France is indeed the only European country that allows the armed forces to use TNT grenades against protesters.) At the time, Macron's response was: 'You're speaking nonsense.' It might be time someone asks him again. The public's confidence in the police, as well as the government, has plummeted.

The main shopping streets are now closed and one can feel the frustration of the crowd as they are stopped at the top of Cours Victor Hugo, trying to walk down the main shopping street, Rue Ste Catherine.

A woman turns to me and says angrily:

'This is outrageous. We have never seen anything like it. The French have a right to protest; it is in our nature. We protested against the proposed hike to the retirement age, and we won. We have had the French Revolution, the 1870 Commune of Paris (where revolutionaries took over the government after the Franco-Prussian War) and the riots of 1968. We will keep on going.'

And you do get the impression of being part of history.

I doubt if such a march would happen in Britain; we are too meek and mild. It annoys me to think that for years my daughter, Irena, worked on zero-hours contracts and unpaid internships. This would be unthinkable in France.

A few days later I chat to an acquaintance who works as a lawyer in Agen. She is highly contemptuous of the protesters.

'My secretary earns less than people on benefits! There they are, manning the roundabouts with their barbecues and red wine. It's become a social event, a way of meeting your friends, and now fifteen-year-olds are kept off school to join their parents! We need to cut their benefits and get them all back to work.'

Her assertion does not reflect the people we saw in Bordeaux as far as I am concerned.

'But how can you justify the scores of riot police on the streets? Isn't that highly unnecessary and intimidating?' I ask.

She shrugs her shoulders and assumes the French scrunched-up face of total disdain. '*On sait jamais quand ça va péter!*' (You never know when it's going to flare up!) *Péter* literally means to fart, but it's used all the time in various contexts.

While on the march we are following Ziggy's results in what will be his last football game, Hamilton Academicals v St Johnstone, back in Scotland. If they win it means there will be no play-offs and Ziggy, his fiancée, Joanna, and Rocco the dog will be free in a few days to visit us. Eleven minutes into the football match we are face to face with the riot police and Ziggy has scored a goal! He is a defender, so this is most unusual. The scowling faces of the riot police do not quite know how to react to this woman in front of them with a watermelon smile on her face. These black beetles cannot dampen my joy.

'*Et si je passe, tu me suis?*' (If I get through, will you follow me?) says the man beside me in a barely audible voice, urging me to try to sneak past the riot police. But people are now wary of the strong-armed response of the riot police. The only solution is to march around the core shopping centre, back to the original starting point, where the police 'kettle' the protesters between the traffic and the road – a complete impasse which could also be used as a metaphor to describe the situation of the *Gilets Jaunes* and government today.

Hamilton Academicals win the match 2-0. There is a roar from two members of the crowd waving wildly, far, far away.

That same evening, we attend a talk in Agen, by Dominique Vidal, a French journalist. This is his seventieth appearance on a promotional book tour. He is extremely informative and has incredible recall for statistics and data. As someone who frequently forgets all passwords, I am impressed. However, he also possesses formidable stamina and speaks for nearly three hours. Non-stop. After a full day protesting after a night of revelry, our heads are hanging off their stalks.

He is here to promote his book *Antisionisme = Antisémitisme?* The debate, the confusion of the two terms, was sparked off by Macron inviting Netanyahu to Paris in July 2017 to commemorate the ignoble event of France's Jews being rounded up and deported to death camps in World War

II. After an impassioned speech, Macron slipped in the lexical grenade:

'*Nous ne céderons rien à l'antisionisme, car il est la forme réinventée de l'antisémitisme.*' (We will never give way to anti-Zionism, because it is a reinvention of anti-Semitism.) Macron supporters and right-wingers have attempted to smear all *Gilets Jaunes* supporters as anti-Semites. Again, there is the deliberate conflation of anti-Zionism with anti-Semitism.

This has profound implications for French Jews like Vidal, who are now perversely, like Tony Greenstein in Britain, being accused of anti-Semitism by non-Jews. In Britain there are countless accusations of anti-Semitism in political life. The rhetoric is turning nasty. I like Tony Greenstein's analogy about whether there is anti-Semitism in the Labour Party in Britain.

'There may well be anti-Semites in the Labour Party just as there are zebras in Norway. Of course, there are zebras in Norway (zoos etc) but Norway is not known for its zebras.' I suppose this is true of all political parties.

Dominique Vidal's book exposes the absurdity of this conflation of anti-Zionism and anti-Semitism. He also discusses the impossibility of a two-state solution since Palestine is now so fragmented. Meanwhile, BDS (Boycott, Divestment and Sanctions) is in the forefront of the news as the Eurovision song contest will be held in Tel Aviv and the songbird, Madonna, crooned, 'Music should bring people together.' Tell that to the snipers in Gaza, Madge.

While in France, Gerry continues to run the Twitter account for the SPSC.

The day after Dominique Vidal's talk, Gerry was interviewed about Israeli cyber warfare exports to rogue regimes around the world. Over a thousand people viewed the podcast in the first day, so obviously this has touched a nerve. It is political overdrive of late.

> *Celui qui combat peut perdre, mais celui qui ne combat pas a déjà perdu.*
> He who fights can lose, but he who does not fight has already lost.
>
> Bertolt Brecht.

Or maybe another way of putting it is: if you do nothing, nothing happens.

Twenty-Three

BUILDING A HOME

Welcome to our inchoate home. Feng shui is desperately required; we walk through one room to the next but there is no flow here. Lack of money has dictated a slapdash approach throughout the years. My mother never refused anything that was offered. Consequently, the attic is full of broken bikes, chairs, mattresses, beds, three old lawnmowers and bits and bobs. Oh, to be able to rip it up and start again. This is just a minor complaint. My Aunt Magda from Paris made me promise that I would buy some outside furniture. 'Please, just a couple of benches. It would make all the difference.' And lo, it came to pass. Not a lot to ask of my superpowers.

From the outside this is a handsome house, a long house, with limestone shining white in the sunlight. A window in the middle room (dining room) of the old farmhouse gives an uninterrupted view to the two barns so it doesn't feel that we are in two distinct properties. Gerry has also looked to the future by installing an electric charge car post outside.

This has been the month where no one has distracted us with their company, and we have had a push on the house building. The moment when I felt we had turned a corner was back in September when the concrete lorry came and poured the beautiful liquid in the two barns under the supervision of Monsieur Menuet, our stonemason. We didn't have enough confidence to do it ourselves since it is a skilful job that can't be done twice. As far as possible we have used French artisans and, although they are expensive, we have never been let down. As they say, *À l'oeuvre on connaît l'ouvrier*, one judges a man by his work. One of the concrete laying men was recognisable at once as the man who was in Monsieur Pajot's shit-sucking business back in August. Now here he was back in our house pouring in the concrete. From shit sucker to concrete pourer. If there were enough funds available we would have installed underfloor heating or even had a polished concrete finish, but the area to cover is so vast we cannot even contemplate this.

Having a real, flat floor is transformative. It is spacious and strangely luxurious. It seems almost sacrilegious to place any objects in the barn. The beauty is its zen-like emptiness. What we do have is something cathedral-like. The windows with 'Rennie Mackintosh' strong black frames change the vibe. Although there is plenty of space, there is no question of putting another floor in. Even the exposed stone walls are objects of beauty.

When we fill the barn with music our spirits soar. My favourite tracks are Zazie's 'Speed' (constantly on the French airwaves), the madness of Gong's 'Camembert Electrique' and Trevor Morrison's ethereal 'Lost Songs of St Kilda'. Nothing sounds more uplifting than a blast of Pink Floyd's 'Shine on

You Crazy Diamond', a song which has a special place in our hearts.

Before leaving Glasgow in June 2018 we attended the Roger Waters (former member of Pink Floyd) concert at the Hydro. Good old Roger, asking everyone to support BDS even though he had been hassled recently in Berlin. BDS is officially banned in France. He never usually appears in Glasgow, but we think it was a way of acknowledging the Celtic football fans for their support for Palestine, although when he mentioned this, the Rangers football fans started booing. Roger had not quite twigged the rivalry between the Old Firm. He is obviously not a Trump fan as highlighted by the big neon sign projected behind him: TRUMP IS A BAWBAG.

I wonder what my father would have thought of all the changes we are making to Coutal Haut. He is a shadowy presence in this house. There are so many questions I would have liked to ask him. When he lived as an engineer student in London he went out with Jackie Collins (the novelist) and complained that her pesky sister, Joan, would always be hanging around. Apart from his love of gardening, he was also a keen amateur photographer and developed his own photos. He took photos of the Queen's coronation in London in 1953, and later one of his first jobs when he moved to Scotland was to put up telegraph poles in the Western Isles. He was one of the last to photograph the black houses with old ladies dressed in sombre clothes outside their homes chatting in Gaelic. Most of these photographs have now been lost.

I did not know this father: a charming and debonair man, surrounded by pretty women. I had only glimpses of the man he once was. He made me a kite and a stool, took me out mushrooming and listened intently to his collection of classical records on the stereo. I wonder if he thought about his mother, a classical pianist, when he listened to the music. There were no goodbyes, no deep conversations, no probing, no explanations. Children will never truly know the secret lives of their parents.

Usually, when he returned home after work, he would quickly get changed into casual clothes (or *szmaty* as we called them, rags in Polish) and head out to his beloved garden for an hour or two before dinner. One day I asked him, 'Tatuś,' (daddy) 'how old are you?' He was in the middle of digging and the spade momentarily hovered in the air. 'Forty-seven,' he answered and then immediately burst out laughing when he saw the look of horror in my face. 'I bet you think that's ancient!' And I did.

An eagerly awaited event of an evening was the setting up of the camera and projector. My father loved filming us on holiday on Super 8 (before Coutal) but after he bought the house he was too busy working on the renovation and too tired to bother; there was no time for frivolity.

I last saw him three weeks before he died in hospital. I was shocked at his wizened state. 'Do you like oranges?' he asked falteringly. I was starting to say that I liked all citrus fruit when he interrupted with impatience. 'I asked you if you are religious!' I didn't even get that one right. Both my parents had been staunch atheists when I was a child.

In a box somewhere – probably in the attic – are the last letters he sent to me, full of love and concern. 'I wonder what you are going to do in your life?'

I cannot bear to see them or re-read them.

There is still so much that I want to do in my life.

My most coveted possessions in Coutal Haut are the framed photos of the children when they were young and our pictures. For once, our personal, eclectic bibelots are carefully selected to ensure a Scandi-chic feel in stark contrast to the traditional, heavy oak furniture in the main farmhouse. It is an outlet for our creativity. I am beginning to sound like a pretentious twit.

We have plundered *brocantes* and *vide-greniers* for, inter alia, an antique wine rack, complete with labels (Monbazillac 1983) hanging from each shelf, a wicker table and an old wooden cupboard which now houses our plates and glasses. A spanking new Italian cooker takes pride of place in the *coin cuisine* – the kitchenette – in the corner of the barn. No longer will we have to hold in the button for the whole of the recitation of the Lord's Prayer in Polish before the gas lights in the oven.

I have become a dab hand with power tools (a complete macho invention) and built kitchen and bathroom units. Gerry has found a new lease of life issuing instructions, as I balance precariously on ladders doing the electric cabling. The builder's yard is like a second home to us: they know us so well as we stock up materials for the bedrooms.

I paint the utility room and wield my trusty brush at any stick of furniture I can find: tables, chairs and beds, usually brilliant white or a fetching shade of bunker green. I am overcome with emulsion.

I have attacked the garden with gusto and planted wisteria ready to climb up the walls. Unfortunately, all the roses and vines proliferating on the outside walls of the house had to be pulled down to make way for the new windows. War has been waged on the pesky moles that have been hard at work creating mountains from their hills or maybe motorways and tunnels underground. All I know is that a ton of soil is deposited on my freshly mown lawn every morning. 'Move over, Nelson Mandela,' I think grimly as I move the stones around the driveway.

'What are you doing today?' asks Gerry and, most of the time, I shrug my shoulders and answer, 'You know, the usual – stones.' And out I go, head bent. Gerry, the old hippie, picks up his books nonchalantly and ploughs through the French subjunctive and a thick copy of the book *Papillon*. I should really not be so amazed at the improvement in his French. It's a long way from '*Château-du-lait*' – Castlemilk – the high flats where he was brought up in Glasgow. Castlemilk is a peripheral housing scheme built in the 1960s with access to the green belt. The planners made a huge mistake and forgot to include pubs and shops. People used to say to Gerry that he must have enjoyed looking at the amazing view over the city, but that was not the case at all. You could only see the view if you stood up and peered out the window. The high flats – and the primary school Gerry attended – were blown up with explosives a few years ago, the event captured spectacularly on television screens. It was a failed social experiment. 'Not only that,' complained Gerry, 'they even demolished the flat where I was born in the Gorbals and the secondary school I went to.' It all seems highly suspicious to me. 'You bring a trail of destruction in your wake,' I warn Gerry, 'so please don't burn the house down.'

When he is not educating himself, Gerry sticks plugs into his lugs so as better not to hear me. Perfect peace.

We have called in a friend to do some of the building work and tiling. Gerry is now an armchair supervisor. Occasionally he dons his slipper, hat and pipe as he trots out his *badinage* – banter.

All this manic activity, combined with all my allergies (hay fever, cat, asthma and dust) swirling into a noxious mix, results in a dash to the *Urgences* (Accident and Emergency) in Villeneuve as my throat swells up and I struggle to breathe. Luckily, the doctors manage to avoid a tracheotomy as my face starts to turn blue and I spend a few blissful hours with an oxygen mask on. I discover later that an atmospheric change has caused a lot of respiratory problems for many people this month.

Gerry regards all this as attention-seeking since his back gives him a *lot* of pain. The only thing that helps is taking long walks in the afternoon. He has been in and out of doctors' surgeries but X-rays have been inconclusive. He calls me his *aide-de-camp* and sometimes his *compagnonne-de-campagne*. In an ideal world I would be his *compagnonne-de-champagne*. Together we have stacked up a cocktail of drugs we have to take throughout the day.

Every five years the French Health Service gives older people a whole body check-up that takes up most of the day – a complete MOT. This is what we really require as we are rapidly crumbling. I cannot praise the system highly enough; even though the French pay insurance towards it, it is still heavily subsidised by the state. There is a tendency towards preventative measures because the individual still pays something towards their health care. I was a student in Paris many moons ago and I was slightly bemused when told by a fellow student that she was feeling slightly sluggish. Her self-diagnosis was zinc deficiency. 'Zinc!' I thought. How on earth would she know? Every student's bathroom cabinet bulges with all sorts of medicines for every ailment known to man.

'*If you go out to the woods today, you'd better go in disguise*
If you go out to the woods today, you're in for a big surprise.'

From 'The Teddy Bears' Picnic'

On the National French Hunting site is the following advice in stilted English: 'Do not forget when hunting... if you go hunting with your dog or with your ferret, which must be identified and vaccinated against rage.' I take it they mean rabies. There are quite a few fatalities during hunting season in France. We tend to avoid going into the woods on hunting days: either Sunday or Wednesday depending on the time of year.

Last year, signs popped up beside the roads saying *Sauvez la planète; mangez végane.* (Save the planet, eat vegan.) Someone had gone round graffitiing the sign, inserting *un* between *mangez* and *végane* so it now reads 'Save the planet, eat a vegan'. Hunters – of which there are many – tend to be macho and right-wing. It has been a long time since we have seen any prowling in the woods but shooting season will start up again in September – with a vengeance. The chomping of meat and hunting is deeply ingrained in the French psyche.

The former French president François Mitterrand died in 1996. He is still the longest-serving statesman in French political life. His last meal consisted of a rare – and illegal – dish of *ortolan*, a songbird. Mitterrand came from Jarnac in the south-west of France, and it is a dish that is revered in these parts. The songbird is plucked, roasted and served in a ritualistic manner in 'secret' societies. A white napkin is draped over the head and face of the diner so as to better trap the aromas and tastes of the succulent meat. Traditionally people ate beneath the cloth napkin because they didn't want to have God see them eating these little songbirds. Normally, the whole of the bird is eaten – *tête inclus* – head included. The hunters believe the *ortolan* to be the zenith of French cuisine. There is a reason why birdsong is so muted here.

We haven't heard a quack from the ducks either; it has been suspiciously quiet on the canard front.

'Never eat more than you can lift,' said Miss Piggy. Sound advice at a Chasse (Hunter's) meal, where we wolf down nine courses, mostly venison (no ortolan as far as I can make out), and liberally quaff the local wine. Seven hours later we roll down the hill from our nearby village, clutching our stomachs. It is a Rabelaisian feast. Enjoying the scrumptious food and drink here is one of life's joys, but nothing is consumed quickly. We invite some friends for an *aperitif* (a pair of teeth as we call it) at 5pm and they leave just before midnight, blootered but replete and happy. Buying *les BIBs* – five litres of excellent wine for €11 – has improved our consumption rate and contributed to our 'five a day'. I used to think that BIB had something to do with the word 'imbibe' but in fact it stands for the plain English 'bag in a box'.

In Villeréal, as a way of marking the village's 750th anniversary, the *commune* has called everyone together for a photograph. It is taken in exactly the same spot where the last group photo was taken in 1906. The place is more or less the same; the styles are different. The sun actually pokes its head out for a few minutes; we all look up, dazzled, the shutter clicks and our faces will be part of Villeréal's history.

I have been assiduously putting evidence together over the year for my CPD – Continual Professional Development – for work. This is important because every five years it is scrutinised by the GTC – General Teaching Council – and this is the year where my teaching credentials are being verified. I am feeling quite smug; after all, here I am, a French teacher, living in France from my own savings, reading *Le Monde* and watching France 24 every day, writing about the *bastides*, translating twenty-eight pages of my mother's talk into French, dealing endlessly with French bureaucracy and being fully immersed in all things *français*. I could write a dissertation on French building terms.

I phoned up the person in charge who listened carefully to all I had to say and then asked: 'But have you done any certificated courses in French?' *Mais non, pas du tout!* What use would that be to me here? She was having none of it. 'Then, I'm sorry, it's not enough. You will have to defer your CPD for a year because there is nothing to prove that you are doing what you say you are doing.' 'But I am here, in France, speaking French all the time, for God's sake!' I reply, with a Gallic flourish. I am starting to sound a tad shrill. There is nothing set to drive me more demented than when someone says, 'I'm sorry if you feel...' – which means I am not sorry at all – and 'with all due respect...' – which means I am now going to say something terribly insulting. All my arguments are dismissed. '*Non*' or rather an emphatic 'No' is the jobsworth reply. *Quel cornichon*! What a nitwit! I should have said that I was a consultant/ambassador/CEO of some international twinning project, but I have always been somewhat deficient in Eduspeak. I put down the phone and use my most choice French words to express the frustration I feel. I could have given her a mission statement that would be unforgettable. It makes me feel *slightly* better.

What's a new month without a new car? Ron and Janet ask us if we can help them buy a car and we buy a Renault Espace converted into a campervan for ourselves instead. We had bought the Citroën in desperation, but it has in fact turned out to be a fine car. However, what we really need just now is a British car with a tow-hook. Again, the Renault does not answer all our criteria as we don't need a campervan, but we need the right car for the right country which we can sell on our return to Britain. We were initially concerned about the plumes of smoke belching from behind but were reassured that this is a common fault in diesel cars. It was a bit disconcerting to have a car stop and the driver tell us how worried he was at the state of our engine. I have a déjà vu moment when I see ourselves stranded on a motorway, yet again. Our back field is rapidly turning into a parking lot with the caravan, trailer, campervan, car and bikes. I have been inexpertly winding the lawnmower round an obstacle course and smash one of the rear lights.

There are three national holidays in France in the month of May. As a reasonable woman said to me, *'C'est normale; c'est loin jusqu'à août'* – 'It's normal, it's a long time till August'.

To cut a long story short, friends cannot take the holiday they had arranged in Arcachon on the Atlantic coast (but which we had paid for), so we end up booking in their stead for the middle of May. The weather is to be stormy and rainy, but no matter; we are looking forward to just being beside the seaside. We pack up the house, empty the fridge, put our bags in the car and head south. After five minutes I decide to head back as I have forgotten to pack my socks and take an umbrella. As soon as I enter the house, the telephone rings. It is the owner of the hotel. She has completely forgotten we are coming and is on holiday in Portugal! *'C'est un peu ma faute,'* she says ('it's partly my fault') and so we arrange another date for June. *'Mais non!'* I think, as I unpack the car again. It *is* completely and utterly her fault. We end up with a beer and plate of peanuts in an empty café in Pujols for the evening as the rain pelts down.

We vote by proxy in the European elections. It is heartening to see the SNP sweep the board in Scotland but the trend to the right and success of the Brexit party in England is worrying. Here, in France, Marine Le Pen and her right-wing party just manage to pip Macron to the post with the final count of 23.3% to 22.4%. The Greens do surprisingly well (13.4%) in an otherwise depressing state of affairs. Meanwhile the *Gilets Jaunes* candidates score just 0.54% of the vote, below the Animalist party which poll 2.17 %. The *Frexit* party, with essentially the same aspirations as the Brexiteers, have a dismal result. It has been suggested that many *Gilets Jaunes* voted right-wing, but it is difficult to know as there are many conflicting reports.

Emmanuelle Reungoat, Lecturer at Montpellier University, made an interesting observation. 'When we talk about the *Gilets Jaunes*, we tend to consider them as a whole. But what makes the movement unique is the fact that every member is very different from the other.'

Back in Britain, Theresa May has finally had enough, spat the dummy out and walked out in tears. 'She looks like Margaret Thatcher's *Spitting Image* puppet,' remarks Gerry, and I think he is right.

I like the journalist Owen Jones' comment: 'Had this weird dream. Theresa May humiliated herself in snap election and clung to power with homophobic fundamentalist terrorist sympathisers.'

Ziggy has signed up to the Bucharest football team 'Dinamo Bucharest' and we expect him here any day, before he goes off to pastures new. This has posed a Rocco the Dog dilemma and we have tried to find ways of getting him over. We really miss having him here, sniffing around, barking *oauf, oauf* (woof, woof). Occasionally, I find dog toys lying around. Rocco is not the cleverest of dogs and his face is usually one unclouded by thought, but we were most impressed when one day the chickens were clucking loudly in the farmyard across the field, and I said, 'Listen, Rocco, chickens!' Rocco cocked his head to one side and looked at me quizzically and then went into the house. A few minutes later he brought out his favourite badly mauled toy chicken and dropped it at my feet as if to say,

'What are you talking about? Now *that's* what I call a chicken!'
Apparently there is a St Rocco, the patron saint of plagues.
To be very precise, St Rocco is the patron saint of epidemics,
plagues, skin diseases, dogs, invalids, falsely accused people,
bachelors, cholera, knee problems, surgeons and pilgrims. It
just recently dawned on me that St Rocco is the patron saint
against plagues, which makes more sense. Even better, St
Rocco is the patron saint of dogs!

Airlines will not transport animals if it is minus zero
degrees centigrade or more than twenty-nine degrees
centigrade. After a slew of emails and phone calls we thought
everything was sorted until we got the final quote of £1,200.
Rocco will just have to wait.

I love this old joke. A dog goes into the post office to
send a telegram. (Some readers might not know what this is.)
He goes up to the counter and says to the clerk, 'Here is my
message: Woof. Woof. Woof. Woof. Woof. Woof. Woof. Woof.
Woof.' The clerk looks at the dog and says, 'You know you can
have another woof in there because ten words cost the same
as nine.' The dog is scathing: 'But that just wouldn't make any
sense!'

'Walkies!' I bark at Gerry, my Rocco substitute, and off we
trot, singing that famous French ballad, '*Non, no baguettes!
Non, we will have no baguettes!*'

Twenty-Four

SWITCHING SUMMER ON & OFF

Snakes are slumbering on the roadside and Gerry accidently drives over one. It loops up in the air, a perfect '0'. They are not venomous here, no need to fear the African boomslang. It is as if a switch has been flicked – the temperatures are soaring, skies are cloudless, windows and doors are open and the shorts are on. When we sit under the lime tree just outside the house, the noise of the bees overhead is deafening. The lilies beside the door are a dazzling orange colour. The cherry trees are so overgrown we cannot reach the boughs heavy with deep-red fruit, tantalisingly too high for us. One day there will have to be an almighty coppicing. Summer season is around the corner and we meet up with friends for gossip at the weekly evening barbecue in Lac de Lougratte, ten minutes' drive away. We have had to wait for Chas and Jen to return to their holiday house as they are the only ones who can organise us properly. They are the sheepdogs to us, their sheep. We need to be rounded up and pointed in the right direction.

The flypaper is back in the kitchen and suddenly the buzzards are back, circling round the duck farm. When I hear the scarecrow gun go off again, I know for sure the ducks have reappeared, although I cannot smell them yet. Only when we go up close to the fence can we hear them cluck. In French the duck's noise-making is described as *coin coin* – or in the local accent they *cwang cwang*. The verb to cluck is *cancaner* but it can also mean to gossip, which I am sure they do, *le canard cancane*. Onomatopoeia for animal sounds in different languages is delightful for linguists. In French the snake whistles, *le serpent siffle* – *siff, sssssss*. *Cocorico* is the early morning sound of the cocks from the neighbouring farms. It is a cacophony here in the morning, the chicks go *piou-piou*, the frogs *croac croac*, the bees *bourdonnent* – bzzzzz. The guinea fowls *glougloutent* – *glou glou glou glou…* all the way home. And the crickets chirp, *les grillons chantent*. They sing. And in the evening the noise is deafening.

I dutifully hand in a gold ring studded with diamonds that I find outside the post office and promptly drop the memory stick I was holding at the time. There was no trace of it when I went back to forensically check the pavement. A wee bit of karma would go a long way.

We visit the Cramptons who have just had sixty tons of gravel delivered and spread around their property and we are in a state of driveway envy.

There are quite a few half-finished properties around here for sale. It's sad to see the evidence of a dream that has crumbled and is now abandoned. Property is still cheap to buy with outhouses and swimming-pools, but it is the cost of the renovations that can be eye-watering. Nothing, however, compares to the cost of buying in Paris or the main cities. A studio (thirty-three square metres) in an edgy part of Paris sells for over €400,000.

We are all working like the clappers to get the bathroom and bedroom ready but, like someone once said, we can hear the whooshing of deadlines come and go and they are still not quite finished. When I look up from my bed I see cables dangling from the ceiling.

One morning, in the middle of cleaning the barn, I look out and notice that the multi-coloured hammock gently swaying between the trees is beckoning me over like a siren. 'Come on over, bring a book, have a wee siesta, you know you want to...' I hesitate. 'Swing low, sweet chariot...' I can see Gerry in the last barn, visor on, sawing metal. Sparks are flying. He will never notice.

'*Viens ici*... It's lovely and warm, I'll wrap you in my cocoon, the ants can't get you up here...'

I immediately cave into temptation, grab my book and a glass of lemonade, and tip-toe to the door. My hand is on the handle when I hear Gerry shout, 'Basia!' I freeze, in a classic Pink Panther pose. I can just pretend I have not heard him. '*Basia, come here and help me lift a beam!*'

Fuck a duck. I cave in, not to temptation, put book and glass down and regretfully wave the hammock goodbye.

The toilet has been lying on the table for a week, rather like a take on Marcel Duchamp's artwork 'Fontain'. I know, we are surrounded by art and culture. We move all the tiles into the house from the garage and I spend a morning scrubbing the tiles with caustic soda, trying to remove the unidentifiable marks on them.

The reek of mouse droppings in the garage is overwhelming. I open a drawer and a mouse pops out its head. Anything fabric has been eaten to bits.

When we go for our evening walk, the *Blondes d'Aquitaine* – the cows native to the region – amble over to say hello. Or rather they say *meuh* to us. The verb *mugir* (to moo) is also used to describe the wailing of sirens. This is not a sound we hear often in these parts but reminds me sadly of the lost possibility of buying the fire engine up the road.

It is only when we have visitors eating in the barn that the resident *loir* – dormouse – with their huge eyes and stripy body – makes an appearance. He/she is friendly and curious and sits on the wall, observing the scene below.

After a ten-year absence, Ziggy comes to Coutal with his fiancée, Joanna. It is ironic that while we have been in France, they have both been living in Glasgow. Ziggy returned for a year to play for his old team, Hamilton Academicals, and write a football column for a tabloid, while Joanna studied for a post-graduate law degree at Glasgow University.

It seems that all these years of driving Ziggy after school to various stadia, usually in dreich weather, has paid off. Usually I would be sitting on the benches, marking a pile of jotters, and look up when the whistle blows and ask, 'Who won?'

I am still clueless about football, although I did pick up a certificate once for Ziggy which said that he had mastered the off-side rule. The poor man who gave me the certificate thought, mistakenly, that I was the deserving recipient of the award and said that it was good to see grown women involved with the sport. I hasten to add I love going to football matches and watching Ziggy play the beautiful game and I am the first to listen to the football commentary – 'On the ball, gie's a call' – if Ziggy's team has been playing. Auntie Margaret would often phone up to tell me that Ziggy had been mentioned. She followed his career avidly. I admire his skill and dexterity. He certainly did not inherit his coordination and sporting prowess from me.

Ziggy is so excited to see Coutal again but keeps bumping his head on the low beams. 'It used to be so much bigger; the garden went on forever!' exclaims the strapping footballer, no longer the red mop-headed young boy of yesteryear. However, he is right to say that the sink is too low in the kitchen; much of this house is only suitable for midgets, like me and Gerry, who is gradually turning into Rumpelstiltskin.

It is a sweltering thirty-six degrees as we make our way to Le Moderne bar in the centre of Villeréal to watch the European Champions League. Liverpool wins 2-0 against Tottenham.

After initial enquiries at the *Mairie* where they are issued with the booklet *Guide des Futurs Époux* (Guide for bride and groom to be), Ziggy and Joanna decide to abandon their wedding plans in France and have it in Białystok, Poland, next year instead. 'And besides,' I ask them, 'why would you say your wedding vows in a language you don't understand?'

Joanna comes from the town of Białystok in eastern Poland near the Byelorussian border and, coincidentally, Ziggy played with the football team in the Premier League a few years back. My mother is delighted that her grandson is going to marry a Polish girl with the same name as her; serendipity. Białystok is famous for being the birthplace of Esperanto, invented by one Ludwig Lejzer Zamenhof. I once tried to learn Esperanto years ago, and, for a language invented so that all people can communicate easily with one another, I couldn't believe it was so difficult. It has *cases* for God's sake! But what I found really funny was that an Esperinto refers to someone who used to be hopeful, but no longer is. It's a word that surely must sum up neatly the mood of all Esperanto speakers.

A day after Ziggy and Joanna arrive, they receive devastating news. The manager of the Romanian team, Dinamo Bucharest, who had waited six months for Ziggy to be released from his Scottish contract, had suddenly resigned after an argument with the chairman. Ziggy is on the phone constantly for the next few days to find out if they will honour the contract; they won't. And he doesn't know if another team will sign him. It still has to be settled, so all of a sudden, they are homeless and jobless. We try not to let it ruin our time together but obviously the uncertainty casts a cloud.

Ziggy is keen to see the neighbours and we go round to Madame Gouget who is now in hospital. She has been so unwell of late and to make matters worse her phone was out of order last month and she would wake us up at 7am by banging her stick against the window so she could use our phone to contact the doctor.

Her daughter shows us around the property. The farmstead is exactly as Ziggy remembers it, and we stroke the newborn lambs. One hen had inadvertently sat on a duck's eggs, so now the ducklings are following around their mother hen, who looks puzzled (in a puzzled hen way) when her 'little ones' plunge and swim in the pond. The duck has been sitting on goose eggs so there will be a big surprise when they eventually hatch. Lately, nature has been a bit topsy-turvy.

'I think you have been sold a lemon,' drawls Gary, our Californian friend. He's right; we have been sold a lemon: a pup, a turkey, all rolled into one fruity animal mess. We were holding off driving the Renault campervan until we had new tyres fitted. We had ordered them online and they were delivered to a nearby garage, but when we went to pick them up the garage was closed. Of course, yet another holiday has befallen France, *Ascension* or Pentecost – and instead of one day off, the garage is closed for a week. Everything is a waiting game here and one just has to be patient. The smoke problem has not completely disappeared and we decide to take the car into another garage to get the engine checked over. The next day the garage hands us a long list of things to be repaired which add up to €1,700. Granted, we had paid only €1,500 because it is a British car with a MOT soon to expire and two tyres needing to be replaced. Nevertheless, this seems excessive. We return home to ruminate. We decide we do not want to pay one more euro for the car as we have lost confidence in it. When we return to pick it up we promptly receive a bill for €198 – for the honour of checking it over. We are *tout baba*, utterly flabbergasted, so we drive over to another garage and explain what has just happened and they are equally outraged on our behalf. They promise to phone some British clients to see if they are interested in buying the lemon/pup/turkey for a song, as we have decided to cut our losses and get rid of it.

As fate would have it, that very same evening, we go to a quiz attended mostly by the British community around here. We spy the architect of our woes, an Englishman previously unknown to us. He looks horrified, truly gobsmaquéd, as Gerry marches up to him, waving the bill and the list of repairs in his face. 'You must have known all the things wrong with the car!' The man protests his innocence, claiming that he sold the car in good faith and that it had been working perfectly. But even the first garage said he must have known it was deeply faulty. His wife slinks past us, head down, at the queue for food. It is such a stupid thing to do, because inevitably we will bump into people who know them both. We have hardly driven the beast and had only owned it for a month.

Gerry has a plan. It is a mad plan. If no one shows any interest, he will drive it slowly, for thirty-five hours up to the North of Scotland and deliver to it to his mechanic nephew to check over and sell on. After all, campervans are very popular in the Highlands. Luckily, after a week of nail-biting, a friend has found a potential buyer and we happily celebrate, only writing off €1,300 at the end. When we go to pick up the car it won't start initially, so we have to go to get the jump leads. It is now parked on our driveway. This tale is far from over.

The 'waterman' has recently come to check that our septic tank conforms to all the recent legislation. I used to dread this yearly visit, since a tank in the barn is a problem. Now I rejoice in this visitation. I smugly produce all our paperwork. The tank was moved from the barn to the field outside for the princely sum of €12k. Coutal is built on bedrock, which means that it will never suffer from subsidence. We can rejoice in this fact, but unfortunately we had to enlist the services of a rock-blaster to re-site the septic tank. I thought the official-looking letter in the post box was the bill from the hospital and so I had avoided opening it for a few days, but once I had relented I realised it was from the water board to say we had passed the inspection.

The arrival of visitors prompts me to get the broom out and sweep away the cobwebs from the beams. Luckily, there is no marble mantelpiece carved with seraphim to get in the way of a deep clean.

I have not seen our Californian friends, Gary and Barbara, since 2006. I met Barbara when we were teenagers working in Paris and we have kept in touch ever since. Our lives have followed very different paths. Way back last year we had promised them an en-suite bathroom. I privately view en-suites as passion killers (too close to the bedroom, with the possibility of pong), but it is true, I did say at the time, '*Bien sûr, pas de problème.*'

'You shouldn't have promised them something you could not deliver,' says Gerry, grumpily. His back is still no better. I feel really desperate. However, with a stroke of genius, I clean up the caravan toilet and park it on the terrace outside the living-room door. The living room has been turned into a makeshift bedroom. Gary and Barbara take it all with good grace. I am so relieved.

I have been running a kosher kitchen for a week. They know about our Palestinian allegiance, but we try not to speak about the elephant in the room.

The weather has suddenly turned dismal: cold and raining. Most of Europe is under the same cloud and two people have been killed in storms in Bavaria. We are told the weather in California is forty degrees. We drag out the heaters and winter clothes again. We somehow manage to have one sunny evening outside for cocktails with friends, but otherwise we coorie in and play parlour games in the kitchen. No one feels much like going out and Gary, an accountant, works every day on his computer. Barbara wraps herself in blankets and rips through a mountain of books.

We still manage to have a few laughs. When Gary asks what I have been up to I reply nonchalantly, 'Oh you know, the usual. I'm busy radicalising the neighbourhood, sowing seeds of dissent and spouting hate speech.' Then I mutter under my breath, 'And right after that I'm out all night to a drug-fuelled orgy in the backstreets of Villeréal, but don't worry, I'll be back in time to make your breakfast.'

Barbara and Gary teach us about 'manifest destiny', the belief of the US settlers in the mid-19th century that they were pre-ordained by God to colonise America and they had the right to be there rather than the natives. (Barbara and Gary do not share this view, I hasten to add.) Sounds a familiar scenario, I think, but my lips are firmly sealed. We teach them the English verb 'to trump' meaning 'to fart' and the hitherto unused word in the States which I have been flinging around with gay abandon, 'wanker'. Maybe we should rename the en-suite toilet 'Trump quarters'. One prize fact nugget is that Trump once dated a Norwegian socialite called Celina Midelfart and it is such a shame that they didn't get married and join surnames.

I still manage to do my two outings a week. The first is to my Pilates class (ABC as our teacher keeps on reminding us – Agility, Balance and Coordination). She used to be a ballet dancer and we dutifully practise our pliés and arabesques.

On Friday morning I am back to walking at least ten kilometres with the ladies' walking group and discover the area and its unknown footpaths into the bargain. I counter all this fitness by eating an excess of cheese and ice-cream so I have not lost any weight.

The ducks, for all the initial promise of utter misery, have failed to materialise. Who knows what Mr Duckman is up to?

The first sunflower I planted in autumn has revealed its bright and sunny face. I gather all the grass with a pitchfork and build my first haystack. For the first time since I was a teenager I climb up to the top of the cherry tree, beating off the bird competition for the reddest, most succulent fruit.

'Basia, where are you? shouts Gerry. Caught again. 'I'm at the top of the tree. Why?'

'It's just that I don't understand this sentence, something about Scottish broad beans. I mean what are they doing importing broad beans from Scotland?' He looks pensive and puzzled. This is a very hard look to master. 'It really does not make sense.' I sigh. I carefully clamber down the branches and look at the sentence. 'Nothing to do with Scottish broad beans,' I explain impatiently to my pupil. God, sometimes he is so earnest. '*Fèves à écosser* means to shell broad beans, *écosser* means to shell.' Then the conversation turns to *éplucher – to peel* and *dénoyauter – to take the stones out* as in *dénoyauter les pruneaux*. It strikes me suddenly that we would never have had a conversation like this even last year.

One glorious evening we join about 160 others on a *Marche Gourmande* organised by the *commune* of Laurès near Monflanquin. We had no idea it would be so much fun. Start times are staggered from 6.30pm till 8.30pm. The wine à gogo ensures there is a lot of staggering back at the end. *Je suis pompette*, – 'I am tipsy'– slurred a chap beside me. We are issued with chits to pay for the various courses. We walk from one farmhouse to another where a feast has been prepared, each one more lavish than the last, all accompanied by the 'correct' colour of wine. This is not the place for a teetotaller, as one of the ladies serving says cheerily, 'I always cook with wine; sometimes I put it into my food.'

After nearly ten kilometres of walking, eating and drinking, we end up meandering back under the bright moonlit sky to the *Salle de Fêtes* – the community hall – in Laurès where an accordion player strikes up a medley of Cuban classics. The joy of such walks is that there are few tourists around, just the locals. Our friends remind us that while one can say *une lune pleine* – a full moon – one should never say *je suis pleine* which means 'I am pregnant' rather than 'I am full' for which one would use *J'en ai mangé assez*. It's the little things that catch you out.

Who goes trip-trap over my bridge? What would Chicken-Licken do? The sky has fallen in on us. In the morning we awake with a humdinger of *la gueule de bois* – hangover.

The weather has been so wet followed by searing heat which is perfect for mushrooms to flourish. There is an abundance of girolles which bizarrely translate into English as 'chanterelles' and *morilles* – the mushrooms which are spongy with a long stalk, called 'morels' in English. My mother is a connoisseur of mushrooms and it would have been a pleasure for her to be here to pick them. I also discover that there are two ways of saying 'to lisp' in French, *zézayer* and *zozoter* which is wonderful madness, since the two words must put fear in the hearts of all lispers.

Twenty-Five

THE OPPOSITE OF HOSPITABLE
June 2019

Inhospitable. This is the first thing I think when I clap eyes on Madame Lily for the first time. She is the female equivalent of Basil Fawlty. In fact, she could give Basil a run for his money.

We tentatively turn up in Arcachon on the Atlantic coast in the fervent hope that we can cool down now that the temperature is hitting mid-forties degrees. The full *canicule* – heatwave. Three people have died so far in this area; the fire service report that this is due to 'thermic shock' – going from full heat into the sea to swim and the difference in temperature being too great for the body to tolerate. Madame Lily proves too difficult for us to tolerate.

The last time we had arranged to turn up at this B&B back in May, the delectable Madame Lily had forgotten about us and popped off to Portugal for her own holidays. Instead of the four days she owed us, she could only book us in for three nights because her B&B was now full. The summer season was about to start. 'That's alright,' I answered on the phone, 'you can just give us the cash for the one night you owe us.' There was a short intake of breath: '*Non, je ne peux pas faire ça,*' she answered. 'I cannot do that.' I sighed and realised maybe this was a battle to be fought face to face. I was soon to find that Madame Lily never took responsibility for anything she did, never said sorry, obfuscated frequently and was quite, quite barking mad.

We turn up on a Sunday afternoon at 4pm on the dot, the agreed time of arrival. We are determined that Madame Lily cannot reproach us for anything. On the booking form it reads 'Free Parking', but there is no trace of this at the narrow entrance to her abode, around the corner from the beach. I decide to ring the doorbell and ask where the parking is while Gerry drives around the streets, trying to squeeze into a parking place. I ring the bell. No reply. I ring again, and again no response. Puzzled, I go back onto the street and find Gerry, who has found a parking space not far away. We go for a walk into the centre of town for half an hour and go back to track down the elusive Madame Lily, who answers the door this time.

'*Vous êtes arrivés, enfin!*'

I explain that we actually had turned up before but she wasn't in.

'*Mais si, j'étais là!*' (I was there.) She frowns.

'Okay, maybe you were, but you didn't answer the door.' I persist.

Her face brightens up a little. She explains that she was ironing, and possibly didn't hear us when she did 'Psssht, pssht' with the iron spray, but anyway, it was our fault, she countered, because why didn't we phone immediately? I am too tired to bother saying that the phone was in the car and I had just hopped out without my handbag. 'So where is the free parking?' we ask.

'It is street parking and it is free, but don't worry, the day-trippers will be going home soon and you will find a place.'

To be fair to Madame Lily, the B&B was *nickel* – spotless.

That evening we make the mistake of going to Cap Ferret, thinking that we would meander along country roads with beautiful coastal vistas revealing themselves at every bend. We have been spoilt living on the West Coast of Scotland. A French acquaintance told us that she had been to Scotland recently and stayed in a rainy place called *Moules*. I couldn't work out where this mussels place was until it dawned on me that she meant the Isle of Mull.

The three-hour round trip to the headland was mundane and undramatic, passing through miles of flat roads with fenced-off housing on either side, although the village of Cap Ferret was pretty enough.

Arcachon itself is a prosperous, attractive town with red-tiled villas built in the nineteenth century for the burgeoning bourgeoisie. At the far end of the beach you can see the impressive site of the Pilat Dune. We were last there in September with Keith and Bridget.

The phone rings and we learn of Ziggy's imminent move to the Central Coast Mariners, an A League football team in the north of Sydney. Over a plate of *moules* (mussels) we excitedly hatch plans to go over and visit him in Australia. By the time we walk to the beach I can feel the mussels having a swally in my stomach.

'We have to go back to the B&B *tout de suite*! This is an emergency!' I shout at Gerry, with alarm.

I just manage to get to the toilet in time for the revenge of the shellfish explosions to take place. To my dismay, when I flush the toilet, the water level rises. I flush again and now the whole putrid mess is about to spill over to the floor. There is nothing for it but to alert Madame Lily. She looks in disgust. 'How much toilet paper did you put down? Now I will have to find a plumber!' A few minutes later she comes back. 'I have just phoned the plumber; he can come tomorrow.'

'But what do we do now?' I wail.

Madame Lily has the perfect solution. She comes back with a saucepan, bucket and rubber gloves. 'There! You will have to empty the toilet yourself!'

I find myself gagging as I slop out. It is the *Heart of Darkness* moment: the horror, the horror. Soon after, the plumber does in fact turn up, so we skedaddle to the beach for a long walk. My legs feel like jelly, but we keep on walking for hours. I text Madame to ask if it is safe to come back. '*Non*,' is the emphatic response. 'The plumber has to find another part. The shop is closed now so he will get it tomorrow. My husband, who is not a plumber, will see what he can do and we will keep you informed.'

'What now?' I ask Gerry. 'Shall we ask for a *commode*?'

I just wanted us to pick up our bags and go home, but our friend Maura is due to arrive at Bordeaux airport in two days' time so it makes sense to stick around. After an hour I text Madame Lily again to find out about the toilet situation and the reply comes back that the toilet has now been fixed.

'Please, Gerry, you flush it this time,' I whisper. The toilet is not repaired and water seeps out all over the floor. I am in despair and knock at Madame Lily the Torturer's door. She is not in and I leave a note under the door. When we return late at night all is quiet on the Arcachon front and the toilet seems to function. I am exhausted and fall into a comatose sleep.

In the morning I decide to confront Madame Lily.

'Madame,' I begin, 'do not worry, we will not come back for a fourth night but we would like you to give the money back instead.'

She looks perplexed. Her eyebrows shoot up. 'What do you mean? You are only booked in for three nights!'

'That is because you did not have room at the inn for a fourth night!' This is becoming farcical.

'And,' I add for good measure, 'we were supposed to be here in May but you had gone to Portugal on your holidays.'

She checks her book. '*C'est vrai.*' She looks momentarily downcast, then perks up triumphantly. 'But now you owe me more than €500 for the repair of the toilet!'

'What?' I stare at her dumbfounded. 'What are you talking about?'

She crosses her arms. 'Do you have toilet insurance?' asks the cheeky cow.

This is a step too far. 'I would like our money tomorrow morning,' I say, firmly.

Madame changes tack and looks slightly crestfallen. 'Do you have a bank account here? Can I give you a cheque?'

We spend our last day on the beach, lying in the sun, picnicking and swimming in the sea, trying to put all the unpleasantness to one side. The sting in the tail comes at the moment of departure.

Madame regains her combative posture. She insists that we owe her €150 for the toilet (the day before it had been €500). After all, she had been kind enough to let us rebook our initial stay. 'I only owe you 50% of the total,' she says, and the cheque will be sent to us directly by her accountant. We will never see the cheque but, thankfully, pigs will fly, hell will freeze over and the devil will go skiing before we see the dour demeanour and hard, pitiless eyes of Madame Lily ever again.

We meet an elderly couple at breakfast who had just returned from the seventy-fifth commemoration of the Normandy landings. They visited a village where a paratrooper had landed on the village church spire. He dangled there for some time before he was spotted. When the church bells started to ring, the noise was so unbearable that he went completely deaf.

Recently there has been a whiff of *merde* in the air. On the way to Arcachon we stop briefly at a friend's house. She is holding a garden fête on her immaculate lawn. Out of the corner of my eye, I catch sight of a well-heeled young woman walking a miniature dog that stops and releases a mound of poo. The woman looks around and then walks on without picking up the mess. I go absolutely ballistic and corner her: 'What do you think you are doing? How inconsiderate! How would you feel if you stepped in it?' She shrugs: *'Je ne comprends pas.'* So I give her it all again, this time in French, with a few expletives thrown in. I am in *aucune doute* that now she understands my ire completely. Only later do I realise she is doing a favour for a friend of mine. Actually, this doesn't matter. What matters is that I have become short-tempered of late. Here, in this quintessentially English setting, I suddenly feel like an outsider, as I so often did as a child, not quite comfortable in my own skin. I feel clumsy and careless, misinterpreting events, not able to pick up on social cues. I cannot blame anyone for my discomfiture. I have been sorely tempted to tell someone who has been pestering me for a while: 'Piss off. You look like a stuffed cabbage and you are really getting on my tits.' Of course I don't say that. A friend who follows Buddhist teachings told me once, 'If being angry with someone could hurt them, arguably it might be worth staying angry at them. But the only person it hurts is you.'

Another pearl of wisdom I find useful is: 'Forgiveness is not just an expression of altruism; it is an act of self-interest.'

Maura (whom we pick up from Bordeaux airport on the way back from Arcachon) is a mindfulness expert and psychiatrist, a true voice of reason. She tells me about Brené Brown's phrase: 'What is the most generous interpretation I can make here without being naive?'

I resolve to keep all these phrases in mind, before I speak without thinking.

We visit Barbara and Gary's rented holiday home in the Dordogne with Maura for two nights. They left Coutal in grey weather and rudimentary comfort to this immaculate *gîte*. It is absolute luxury and I must not be jealous. I must not be jealous. I must not be jealous. The house and swimming-pool are bloody gorgeous. There are bathrooms galore. I must master Zen. God, it's all too difficult. My wine glass needs a top-up.

Good living and wine make the conversation flow effortlessly. Barbara stops on the steps of the kitchen and brings out an apricot tart as the finale to a beautiful meal. 'Ta da!' she sings, then trips, and the tart tips onto the gravel. We laugh as we spend the rest of the evening salvaging dessert from bits of stone.

We have been meaning to go to the Musée d'Aquitaine in Bordeaux for a long time, not just to see Montaigne's sarcophagus but to marvel at the extent of Bordeaux's Roman heritage. What a magnificent city it must have been 2,000 years ago, and now it has completely integrated the past and modernised itself. Cars are discouraged and we go into the city centre by tram.

In the spirit of sustainable living, we pay a visit to the architect Le Corbusier's futuristic workers' homes in Pessac, just beside the airport. Le Corbusier meticulously designed not only the exterior of the houses, but the interiors as well.

He believed that man, machine, and nature should coexist in a state of equilibrium. The spacious houses were built for sawmill workers with running water, heating, septic tanks, garages and big windows looking out over gardens. Each house is slightly different and painted in vibrant colours.

This experimental estate, unique in its time and mostly built in concrete, was the brainchild of Henri Frugès, a Bordeaux industrialist and lover of modern architecture. Compare his vision to the brown pebbledash identical houses built all over Britain in the late twentieth century. Gerry's architect friend, John, described the houses in his native Outer Hebrides as a 'meanness'. Frugès' motivation was philanthropic: he wanted to provide everyone with housing, with a dash of individuality, regardless of their financial situation. Fifty houses (about half the number envisaged) were built in 1929. It is an astonishing, ambitious project and was listed as a UNESCO Heritage site in 2016.

Twenty-Six

WALNUT WINE IS SWEET AND HEADY

'Cats!' I yell at Gerry as I swerve out the drive. Gerry looks confused. I stop the car and stick my head out of the window and shout louder, pointing at the garage. 'Cats! There, in the garage!' Or rather, to be precise, kittens. Two poke their heads around the garage doors. Upon further inspection we find four feral kittens, fearful and trembling. Gerry feeds them water and tinned tuna and we debate what to do with them. Living in the middle of a field, as we do, we are always looking for ways of dissuading the rodent population from coming into the house, and cats are the perfect solution. But of course, we will soon be gone and there will be no one to look after them – and in any case my cat allergy precludes welcoming them into our lives.

The doctor prescribed copious supplies of medication after my dash to the hospital last month. I am so drugged up that my tubes are perfectly clear and even the huge dust clouds of hay and pollen thrown up by the recent harvesting have not affected me one jot.

Luckily, the mother cat eventually returns for her brood and takes them to a safer place.

Our friends Simon and Jill have supplied a temporary dog fix and lent us their two Jack Russell terriers, Ruby and Arnie, for the weekend. They spend their time birling around the house and trying to dig up moles.

We note two absences of things that usually test our patience: ducks and mosquitoes. We don't know what is going on.

Shit happens, to me more than others it would seem lately. Only a few years ago we were chucking out fossilised poo from the barn and it seems to be the shovelful that keeps on giving. We have lunch in the beautiful main square in Toulouse in front of the Capitole and pigeon shit lands from high on our food, wine and tablecloth.

'I was wondering why there was avocado on the plate,' says Maura dolefully, as she scrapes the green gunge from the porcelain. We deposit Maura at Toulouse airport and spend an afternoon as boulevardiers or *flâneurs* to be more accurate, as we meander through alleys and back streets. The pink city glows in the sun.

It is a hot Sunday afternoon and the shops are closed. Siesta time is in full snooze mode. We have the place to ourselves. In Moissac on the way back home, we decide to stop off for a drink but my *vide-grenier* antennae are on full alert and within seconds I buy a table and four chairs that will be perfect for the top terrace. Somehow we manage to jam them all into the car. It is a bit ironic as we have a trailer and a converted campervan at home. Not quite true, we have managed to sell the latter for €600 (a massive loss), but at least it gives us ready cash till the end of the month.

We return to the Citroën garage to collect the long-awaited tow-hook (*crochet de remorque*) for the Citroën. It still hasn't materialised. We do, however, get a bill for €298 for the *carte grise* (registration document) and new plates, mandatory when you buy a car in France. We are again, 'gobsmaquéd'. When we do go back to the garage to collect said hook I am very anxious about the bill. It takes three hours and three mechanics to fit it and I am about to have kittens myself. 'We will be eating baguettes, *sans fromage*, for a few weeks,' I balefully mutter to Gerry. However, miracle of miracles, our faith in garages and cars and mechanics is restored. 'That will be €100,' says the mechanic solemnly. 'I promised you a *crochet de remorque* with the car, and a *crochet de remorque* you will have.' *Le devoir avant tout*. Duty first. I would like to say he clicked his heels and saluted, but that would be going a step too far.

We are still waiting for the destruction papers for our old British car we had brought over originally. After two breakdowns and a shed load of money thrown at it for repairs, it is now going to the car knacker's yard. We had a momentary feeling of panic when we took the Citroën and the trailer for a spin and when we came back we couldn't get the tow-hook off. We had forgotten that the Citroën slowly deflates when the engine is turned off, so it wasn't sinking to the ground as we had thought. Disaster averted.

The fans and hammocks are out to combat the intense heat, but we are back on the chain gang: masticking, sanding, plastering and painting the bedroom and bathroom. Our friends' daughter Rachel comes in for a morning painting session before demolishing me at tennis, but I reason that this is absolutely normal because there is a thirty-eight-year age difference between us.

Gerry's back is suddenly much better and he is making up for lost time. He is wearing a thick black belt which resembles a whalebone corset and has the added effect of holding in his stomach. 'You look almost svelte,' I tell him, encouragingly.

We now have a functioning kitchen in the barn with hot and cold running water.

The *ramoneur* appears, a slim man suited to being a chimney sweep, and for the very first time, the chimney is swept. We only recently discovered that the house insurance is null and void if you cannot produce a *certificat de ramonage*: all the money paid since 1973 could well have gone up in smoke.

Madame Gouget calls me up. 'It's time for you to make walnut wine,' she informs me imperiously. The optimum time for vinification is between the name days of St Jean and St Pierre: it is the only window of opportunity. I turn up in her kitchen *tout de suite* and she ceremoniously passes on her secret recipe (it involves nuts, sugar, eau-de-vie, vanilla, rosé wine) and a ten-litre plastic bottle. I spend a morning happily smashing walnuts with a hammer and my hands and nails are once again stained nicotine brown. I faithfully roll my plastic barrel every morning. The winemaking process goes on for a few months but one thing is certain; it has mind-blowing properties.

I feel I have passed a neighbour test. There has been a tradition for generations of a 'hooch' still being passed from one farm to the other and this practice continues to this day. After all, this was always a wine-growing area until the hazelnut and plum trees and sunflower fields took over. Studies are constantly trotted out 'proving' that a few glasses of red wine a day can significantly reduce mortality due to its high level of antioxidants, which can prevent cancer and heart attacks.

When there was a spate of bad weather in summer twenty years ago, I turned the kitchen into a microdistillery for gin. The children were tasked with picking the juniper berries aplenty on nearby hedges. I bought at least twenty bottles of cheap gin and spent many happy evenings mixing the heady concoction with the precision of a chemist. It has now all evaporated/disappeared down throats. But it did taste delicious!

Concoctions must be a family trait. As a child in Scotland, I used to help my father make *sok malinowy* – raspberry cordial in Polish. We children spent a whole day picking raspberries in Kilcreggan (a place in Argyll). Once home, we washed our bounty and then our father pressed the berries through a muslin sieve before bottling the sweet, thick liquid. It was the ultimate healthy drink. My father died so many years ago and yet I can still hear his voice in my brain, as I can hear Auntie Margaret's. Sustenance of a different kind.

Belvès is a *bastide* thirty minutes' drive from here, famed for its troglodyte dwellings. These date from the 13th century onwards and provide a fascinating glimpse into life as it was in the medieval town. It's a perfect place to go on a hot day. The caves include ancient doorways and ladders, walls carved from the stone and items of furniture. Babies were swaddled and hung up on hooks on the backs of doors and the grandmother was given the job of guarding the precious salt chest, sitting on it all day long.

The first I ever heard of phylloxera was during a tour of the caves in Belvès. The town used to be surrounded by vines. Phylloxera is a blight that destroys vine roots, and from the late 1860s it left a devastating trail of destruction, wiping out vineyard after vineyard.

Originally, Spanish vines were brought over to California but in the 1830s better vines from Bordeaux – Cabernet and Sauvignon Blanc – were imported to produce better quality wines. The problem started when wine merchants began to import American vines *back* into France, the epicentre of viticulture. Competition for growing the best new wine grapes grew. Nobody at the time knew much about plant diseases and eventually a louse, an American stowaway, called phylloxera, proved disastrous for the French vines. By the 1890s, the French wine industry and vineyards across Europe were effectively wiped out by the blight. Then the French vineyard owners hit upon an ingenious solution. They began to plant phylloxera-resistant American grape vines and developed hybrid, or grafted, vines that could thrive in French soils, resist phylloxera and still make great wine. It took many years for the French wine industry to recover. Today nearly all French wine, including expensive French wine, comes from vines grafted onto American roots. French wine begat American wine begat French wine.

I emerge from the underground and blink in the bright sunlight. There is something I find unnerving about being underground or in caves – I hate basements and spelunking (exploring caves), but I love how the word rolls off the tongue. Spelunking. Spellllluuuuunking.

But I would always rather be on top – on a hill, mountain, house – looking down.

The countryside is awash with colour. The lavender and sunflowers we planted at the bottom of the garden are now a profusion of blue and yellow. The smell is quite heady. There are so many apples but they are far too high for me to reach, so they fall to the ground and rot. Dandelions are happily sprouting between the stones of my recently laid driveway. There are two words for the yellow weed in French: *dent-de-lion* (the lion's tooth), so called because of the serrated look of the yellow petals, and *pissenlit* which means 'pee in the bed'. Is that what munching dandelions does to you? It's just a *pensée*, a thought. *Pensée* is the French word for a pansy. The heat is starting to get to me. Every day I try to find somewhere – a pool, a lake – to immerse myself in cool water.

We have had a flurry of invitations which we have turned down in a bid to finish off the building work and any remaining business before our return to Glasgow, once described as the rambunctious underbelly of the north. We go to CPAM, the French medical insurance place in Villeneuve-sur-Lot, to deposit all the hospital and doctors' bills we have incurred in our year here, in the hope that with the European insurance card (EHIC) we will get some of our money back. I just cannot contemplate that we will be out of Europe soon…

Gerry and I are reading the most depressing books. One is about the Gaia theory by James Lovelock and the other is by Noam Chomsky, *Optimism Over Despair* – but it looks like despair is winning in both books. The conclusion seems to be: 'We are all completely fucking fucked, mate. Big Time.'

The hot weather makes me feel drowsy. A siesta is a necessity not a luxury.

For light relief we watch a film with my favourite French actor, Omar Sy, *un chaud lapin* – one hot bunny – and *Je suis un célébrité, sortez-moi de là* (the French version of *I'm a Celebrity… Get Me Out of Here!*). The Academie Française has lost the fight to retain the purity of the language. English words abound, for example, 'Must Haves' or rather, 'le moost av' and 'Old School'.

Blanche, our neighbour, has decided to go into the local old folks' home in Villeréal. She is the oldest of all the inmates – she will be a century old in December – but she has all her wits about her. Marbles and mobility, as they say, are the things we have to hang on to. We sit and chat in her bright room with a balcony looking over chickens and a courtyard. 'Would you like us to take you back to visit your house?' we ask her. For the first time, we see sadness in her eyes. This is the house where her parents lived and where Blanche has spent most of her life. 'No.' She shakes her head sadly. 'I will never go back there. It's too painful. The days were fine, but I couldn't be alone at night any longer – I was scared I would fall over. I don't want to die alone.' She has only been in the old folks' home for a few weeks so it is still raw for her as she adjusts to this new reality.

Friends of friends ask if we could do them a favour and take a present back to Glasgow for friends of theirs. It's a ring of friendship here. They are delighted when we say yes and hand us a very well-wrapped urn. 'But what's inside it – not ashes?' I ask, suspiciously. 'No, good God, no!' replies the lady, all too quickly. 'Ashes! Ashes! Of course not! What an outlandish idea!'

'It's just an urn she bought here because she liked it. She tried to take it on the flight but the airline would not allow it.'

No more questions asked.

Twenty-Seven

LES RIBAMBELLES D'AMIS
(THE SWARM OF FRIENDS)

Summer frolics are in full swing: the night markets are thronging in every village, the heat dial is turned up to the maximum and the valley resounds with the sound of gentle snoring every afternoon. 'It's taps aff' to use the vernacular, to describe the unveiling of vestments. Fiesta is in the air *toute la journée jusqu'à minuit* or, rather, all of the day and all of the night. After a few days of baking heat, an electric storm cracks lightning in the sky and thunder growls and shudders, sending a frisson of excitement. When the torrential rain abates, the air is fresh and sparkling, the sky peels back the clouds to let the Wedgwood blue seep back in.

I do realise how very fortunate we are, living in this beautiful place. As Mads Gilbert (my hero, a surgeon who works in Norway and Gaza) says, here in the West we live such stinking rich lives.

We have had a revolving door of visitors coming and going, all joining in the fun and games.

Charlie and Vicky, erstwhile Palestinian comrades, arrive for only two days, with boxes of tea and gossip like they were supplying Red Cross emergencies.

Once they leave, other friends text us to say that they are on holiday in a *gîte* in the area and are we nearby? We catch up with Jim and Karen, again fellow Palestinian supporters, before the appearance of Kathryn and Mhairi, who have travelled through from Toulouse. They are grateful for the fitful night's sleep since they were teargassed the night before on Bastille night by the French riot police.

Bastille Day (14th July) for us was a pleasant, local affair with close friends at the village nearby. We tucked into platefuls of *moules frites* and a muted display of fireworks. For a bit of *ooh là là*, the dancing girls came on for hours on end, flashing their well-toned pins in energetic can-can and Irish dancing.

It was a surreal moment. Life carries on while another is abruptly ended. Gerry's stepson died the night before, suddenly, without warning. Gerry is in a state of shock. We only have sketchy details but, in any case, Gerry has to fly back to Glasgow as soon as possible. The next day I drop Gerry off for his flight from Bordeaux and immediately pick up sisters Eunice and Sharon, who arrive on the incoming flight from Glasgow, and bring them back to Coutal. Sharon was here for Burns Night in freezing January and I had last seen Eunice in Shanghai in November. The girls have brought over the prerequisite requisition of Tunnock's Caramel Wafers. I yearn for Tunnock's Teacakes to complete my incipient greed. They are allowed through the portals once they hand over the ransom.

When I wake up in the morning, I can see Eunice from my bedroom window, practising her 'Tai Chi' moves in the garden, slowly with great concentration and deliberation.

We three ladies wander around all week like comatose, semi-clad sylvan nymphs, lightly sleep-deprived because of the imminent 'Strike back of the *Loirs*' – the dormice – and the ever-running tap of wine from the BIBS. Our favourite local tipple, Amblard, cannot be exported because it is a wine with no sulphates and consequently no hangover. It is a case of Beauty and the BIB. Or beauties and the BIBs. There is some justification in sticking to wine because we have to filter the water to get rid of the chalky taste, but there is always a soupçon remaining.

The harvest has chucked out the rodents from the fields and some have headed into the house. On her first night here, Eunice wakes up to find a *loir* – dormouse – sitting on top of her suitcase, studying her intently. On the second night, she goes to the toilet and there is the very same dormouse (or maybe a sibling) studying Eunice intently as she sits on the pan. We strike back and buy a product fittingly called 'Decamp'. Plates of poison are left in every room. Just as well Rocco is not here. The next night Sharon – the most rodent phobic person I know – is woken up by frantic scurrying coming from the attic immediately above her bed. Then the noise moves down the chimney and into the same room where Sharon is lying trembling on the bed, goggle-eyed, shrieking for help, simultaneously texting and phoning us. Still no reply. Eunice has her eye-mask and headphones on and I am blissfully in my slumbers at the other side of the house. Sharon is bursting for the toilet but too scared to run towards the door lest she collide with the dormouse, so, in a fit of mad panic, she jumps out the window and luckily relieves herself in the field without breaking her neck.

In the morning, her nerves are shattered and I take Eunice – who is far more sanguine in these matters – and Sharon round to friends Jill and Simon for some chat and laughter.

'You know,' says Sharon philosophically, 'sometimes all you long for is a cup of tea and Hobnob.'

'Did you say a hot-knob?' enquires Jill and we all crack up.

It's the first time Eunice has been to Lot-et-Garonne (she had last been in France thirty years before), and we visit all the usual haunts including Josephine Baker's château in the Dordogne. No one is keen to wander too far and we spend our days eating fresh produce from the markets or bringing out the raclette paraphernalia and watching the cheese melt and bubble. Thirty million fresh baguettes are sold in France every day, hence the many *boulangeries* in the country. A nod to modern times is found with the installation of *baguette distributeur* machines in most villages. Not only baguettes, but croissants, pain aux chocolats and pain aux raisins. Occasionally I cycle down to the village and return with a quiver of baguettes in my backpack.

Sharon brings out the photos of the children when they (and we) were so much younger. It is a nostalgic trip, but this place weaves the past and the present for us. We try on berets in a shop and all these years later discover that there exists a museum exclusively for berets in the Pyrenees. So many things for us still to discover!

We catch up with other friends for a gourmand evening around Monflanquin, stopping in forest clearings with well laid-out tables for aperitifs, starter, main course and dessert. The air is sparkling after the torpor of the day. When Sharon asks one of the organisers what is in the *apéritif* she is told, '*Piss de l'âne.*' Sharon looks at her quizzically. '*Piss de l'âne?*' The lady obligingly falls to the ground on all fours, cocks up her leg and makes an ee-aw (*hi han*) sound. Ah, we nod sagely, the piss of the donkey: the drink that will knock you off your hind legs.

After a week of overindulgence, our brains are full of mush. Luckily, the girls have brought over some brainless reading material with articles about Victoria Beckham eating watermelon cake for her birthday and my favourite, out of an interior decoration magazine, 'You must try Poisonous Medicine, a collection of ten paint shades named after a Buddhist concept and based on a Renaissance artwork'.

I rouse myself into action.

'Right, girls, now is the time to get the gargoyles out!' Eunice and Sharon steady the ladders as I clean out years of accumulated mouse droppings and nesting material from the stone ledges cut into the barn walls. In place of the keich, I pop in two repulsive creatures made of clay, scratching their noses.

Robert Crampton gives a talk on his life as a *Times* journalist in the 'Hôtel de Cours de Thomazeau' in Castillonnès. His career started in the early 1990s in the fag end of Fleet Street and he is one of the few journalists still to be published in print media. This is my last involvement with events here this year. We were relieved it was a sell-out, although some of the questions seemed a bit odd: 'Why does the press treat Cliff Richard so badly?'

I feel guilty about my sybaritic lifestyle of late, while Gerry is far away dealing with sadness and bereavement. He looks grey and shell-shocked when I collect him from Marmande station, but revives in the company of Eunice and Sharon. Gerry has had his share of misery in his life but he reminds us that it is not the bad things happening to you, it's simply how you deal with *la merde*.

Then the girls are gone and in their place Christina – a physics teacher from work – and her boyfriend John appear for a day and a night, travelling from their holiday place in Tours.

We watch the night sky from the top terrace and marvel at the pirouette of star manoeuvres in the dark; star, not spell, bound. Gerry is a keen amateur astronomer and can name many of the constellations as I squint and try to make out the most obvious ones. Christina and John tell us the tale of their recent visit to an observatory in Tours where they discover that the French have their own French version of constellations, as in the 'Giraffe'. This is the first we have heard of it. Later I read about it in an article about astronomy in the local paper. The constellation is called 'Camelopardalis' – a Greek word combining the words for camel and leopard – but meaning the word 'giraffe' in Latin. What other surprises are there in the firmament?

23rd July 2019

Today's announcement that Boris Johnson has become the prime minister is no surprise. Would that it were an 'inverted pyramid of piffle'. We watch the TV glumly with Nicola and Rachel. He tries the strategy to win the youth vote by mentioning the word 'DUDE' which is an acronym for the following: 'Deliver Brexit, Unite the country, Defeat Jeremy Corbyn and Energise.' However, the most convoluted statement Boris emits is 'manage the jostling sets of instincts in the human heart.' What madness are we going back to?

Twenty-Eight

THE BEST YEAR OF MY LIFE

---

*An autobiography is obituary in serial form with the last instalment
missing.*

Quentin Crisp.

Gerry has had a belated new lease of life, wielding power tools
and hammers. At this moment he is reassembling church pews,
bought originally in the East End of Glasgow, using twenty
BIBs of Amblard wine as ballast, weighing down one side as he
works on the other. Amblard is truly our elixir of choice. The
wine boxes will soon be joining other choice items which will be
accompanying us back in the trailer. Occasionally I use the BIBs
instead of dumbbells to tone my arms. Wine is truly multipurpose.
Some of the wine has been ordered by friends, *bien sûr*.

I have been declared redundant on the construction front
and my tools have been whipped from me. Who's complaining?

It's my time to loll around and read books. I disturb Gerry while he is doing his many chores and phone him from the top terrace to ask him to bring me up some light refreshments. He duly staggers up with a tray of glasses full of crisps and a bowl of wine. 'Anything else, m'lady?' he asks with a mischievous wink and gives a bow.

At last there are electric sockets in the walls, lights appearing all over the place; the sparkie has reignited. It is a case of trying to do as much as we can in the week we have left, tying up loose ends.

After the furnace it has been the downpour – *le deluge* – so I make a stab at pulling out the weeds in the back terrace, which have sprouted like glamorous desert creatures.

Last year we bought six original yellowing posters from the French Revolution with notes from officials written on the back. It was a time of hope and huge social change, which inevitably caused much suffering in its wake. After the French Revolution, the country was originally divided into eighty-two departments (now ninety-six) and named after the rivers in the area. Naming the departments after rivers brought a conformity and equality to France. This is why our corner of France, Lot-et-Garonne, named after the two rivers that run through it, has a rough-sounding edge to it! The Lot River merges into the Garonne which meets the Dordogne and this now mighty and wide river empties into the Atlantic Ocean.

Agen is still the capital, but in 2016 the regions were redrawn to amalgamate the three regions Aquitaine, Limousin and Poitou-Charente into one super-state, renamed Nouvelle-Aquitaine. The new name is hardly original but glides easily off the tongue, like runny honey, and is far more attractive than 'Lot-et-Garonne'. At last we have been redeemed in the name stakes!

Nouvelle-Aquitaine is the largest administrative region in France, spanning the west and southwest of the mainland. Our revolutionary posters declared a bold, new French Republic. The past was ripped up and a new order set into motion: Year 1 started from the first year after the Revolution. A new decimal calendar (ten months instead of twelve) was introduced; time was also 'reinvented', ten hours to the day rather than twelve, although this was quickly rescinded when it became too problematic. I have now got round to framing the posters (with help from my young assistant), ready to take pride of place on the barn walls. They will go well with the Polish folklore cut-outs made by my Aunt Teresa who had died in Glasgow just as we were about to set off last July.

One burning hot afternoon, I decide to stay indoors all day. I tackle the huge bundle of newspapers that has lain in the cupboard all year, spread them out on the refectory table and cut out articles of Ziggy's burgeoning career from 2011 until 2014. This was supposed to be a winter job, but inevitably I hadn't got round to it. I stopped collecting press cuttings once he was no longer a teenager and the articles became more numerous and then the internet took over. In one article, a columnist names her dream dinner party guests and Ziggy pops up as 'eye candy'. I appear in articles as the MOF, Mother of Footballer. It has been a roller-coaster career and I realise how arbitrary life is; we try to make our own luck but all we can do is to push our boundaries, love and be loved, and hope for the best. Keep things in perspective – remember the good times in the bad and that fear is the thief of hope. Platitudes abound and I am challenging myself epithetically here.

I am so glad both children and their partners managed to come to see us over the year. Irena's partner, Ant, is also from Sydney (although he has a Hungarian passport through his father) and I fret that both she and Ziggy will end up living in the Antipodes. They love the more relaxed way of living. I do not fancy twenty-odd hours and a numb bum in an aeroplane to see them.

The Gougets, our neighbours, come round to say goodbye, with tidings of great joy. The ducks are back and there is a faint whiff of eau de canard in the air, but this will only be for the short term. Mr Duckman, apparently, will retire in a few years' time and the land will be bought by Mr Sunflowerman. We will one day be completely surrounded by fields of sunflowers! Madame Gouget tells us that in order to stall off boredom in retirement she slaughtered fifteen ducks a week; gutted, plucked and prepared them and sold them to a local restaurant. 'I was always receiving compliments about my tasty ducks,' she says proudly.

We are regaled with the local gossip. The old folks' centre (one of the three *salles de fêtes* – local community halls) is down the road, but the Gougets don't frequent it, although they are in their nineties. They dismiss it as too much Lotto and playing cards and only fit for 'oldies'. Last week, the caretaker closed up the centre, not realising that one ninety-year-old man had gone to the toilet as he was locking up and therefore was still on the premises. The poor chap couldn't get out. He, too, did 'a Sharon' and in desperation jumped out of the window and broke both his knees.

We join Linda, Ian, Jill and Simon for a local *moules-frites* in one of the *salle de fêtes* in the village. We eat for four hours solid until our cheeks resemble those of hamsters or *loirs*. At midnight, the raffle winners are announced. The numbers keep coming as big chunks of meat from the hunters' booty are dispersed. To my delight, I am handed a huge hunk of *gigot* – leg of lamb – and now have the perfect substitute for my air guitar.

We had thought we would be here through Brexit, but instead have watched the debacle limp on and a new prime minister come on the scene. The newspapers in France have been scathing about Boris; the headlines of *Libération* state simply: *Boris Johnson, futur bouffon de la reine* – Boris Johnson, the Queen's future jester. He is a satirist's dream and a realist's nightmare. Hardly a recondite proposition. The French use the English term 'bromance' to describe the love-in between Boris and Trump. Meanwhile, Trump has got stuck into Emmanuel Macron and castigated him on his 'foolishness'. The current row is linked to a law passed by the French parliament this month on taxing digital companies for income even if their headquarters are elsewhere. This would aim directly at US-based global giants. In retaliation, Trump threatens to impose an additional tax on French wine, saying that American wine is far better. When it was pointed out that he doesn't drink alcohol anyway so how would he know, he retorted, 'That's true, I don't drink wine. I just like the way it looks.'

The *Gilets Jaunes* movement has run out of steam, but there are many still simmering with dissatisfaction. I only recently heard about the *Gilets Noirs*, mostly immigrants, *les sans papiers*, from Africa who live and work in France illegally. They have recently demonstrated en masse outside the Panthéon in Paris, one of the most illustrious French buildings, where all the great and the good are buried. The *Gilets Noirs* seek legal status and recognition for their contribution to society and this desperate act will see many deported. What will happen now? Everything is so unpredictable; there is a feeling of uneasiness in the air.

It is the final count-down. We will be heading back to Glasgow soon. Our time here is nearing the end and I face the ineluctable return to work on the chalkface/interactive screen and fiscal probity. When will I next pootle along country roads in my bikini singing Ivor Cutler's 'A Bubble or Two' at the top of my lungs?

The Tour de France has just been won by a Columbian, Egan Bernal. I haven't been on my bike for months. The reason, I decide, is that it has just been too hot. The thought of going back to a place where the weather can't make its mind up is not appealing. Too many days with a leaky sky.

I can't believe how much stuff I brought out with me – perhaps secretly I thought that this was it, no going back; this would be my life forever.

We have had forty-five visitors staying in the house throughout the year, notwithstanding those who have dined and partied with us.

Selection and omission: that is the nature of memoir. Memories rise to the surface, shouting, 'Pick me, pick me!' to the detriment of others, slumbering in the shallows, not insignificant but discarded for the moment. Everything is true, nothing is fabricated. Pruning the personal is not an easy exercise. I often think that my brain has been fashioned by 'the Numskulls', from the popular cartoon strip in the DC Thomson stable of comics: *The Beezer*, *The Dandy* and latterly *The Beano*. The Numskulls control all aspects of your mind and body. Brainy controls the brain, Blinky controls sight, Radar (originally Luggy) controls hearing, Snitch controls smell and Cruncher controls taste. Although I imagine I am at the mercy of the machinations of the Numskulls, I still have free will and my own personality. (This is not a Cartesian treatise, you may have noticed.) No offence to alcohol, but I cannot blame all the stupid things I have done in my life on drinking to excess.

I look back and see what we have achieved and if our experience has changed us. It has not been character forming because our characters are fully formed but maybe some rough edges have been knocked off. Gravity and levity propel me along. I still try to multitask and frequently find myself in a guddle. I am still a proper feartie and hate being alone in the house in the dark. I still love all that is quirky and ridiculous.

Has it all been worth it? Sometimes I feel overwhelmed by it all. I feel far less sentimental than I did at the beginning of our adventure. Bette Davis said that old age wasn't for wimps, and the same can be said about surviving winter in a freezing stone farmhouse. Even typing on the computer was a challenge when a cold draught clamped on my fingers.

More than capturing a year in Coutal Haut with all the rhythms of life, I have attempted to pin down the timeless essence of the place I love.

The peripherals of Brexit, the *Gilets Jaunes*, Macron and Johnson – all will come to some sort of conclusion, unknown to us as yet, as will the situation in Israel and Palestine. The world will keep on turning.

Sheryl Sandberg wrote 'better done than perfect' and at least we are seeing the fruit of some of our labour.

I will never believe the renovation programmes on television when they say how much things cost. I would simply double, even treble, the amount. It is also an eye-opener when people miraculously 'find' the extra money required, usually from some benevolent relative. Although the main big works are now completed, our project is far from finished and the debts are mounting; the only option we have is to keep the momentum going and keep chipping away.

However, there has been no existential breakdown. As Sartre said, 'Man is grasped in his becoming.' The party is not over yet. Taking time out to do this was the right thing to do. We have had difficult situations and heartbreak, but the overriding sentiment is one of joy. We have not succumbed to chasing each other round the house wielding axes or resorted to a trepanning session, although we have resurrected the rusty scythe of yesteryear. To amuse ourselves in the depths of winter, Gerry would kneel in front of me and I would lightly tap the scythe on both shoulders and intone, 'Arise, Sir Gerry!'

It would seem that Gerry and I can live together in harmony. Proximity has deepened our relationship and not harmed it. In short, the boy has not yet been handed his jotters. Or rather, he has not said *je rends mon tablier*, he has not quit. *C'est top*!

We celebrate on the top deck with a bottle of Pécharmant (a vineyard near Bergerac), a present from our Californian friends Gary and Barbara.

We hand over the house to our friends Jo and Grant, which sneakily saves us from cleaning it up and closing it down. The last time they were here a year ago the attack of the giant wasps occurred in their bedroom, so we couldn't let their arrival pass without incident. Just on cue, early in the wee small hours, there is a water mains explosion in the village and a fountain of water erupts. This means we have no running water so we decide, as everyone is suitably unwashed and filthy (Grant's mum used to say you had to wash the three Fs: Face, Feet and Fanny, although she didn't mention Farmpit), that we would visit the Cahors vineyard 'Clos de Coutale' and stock up on necessary supplies to take back in the trailer. We also buy the glasses to go with our red nectar with vineyard's name etched on the glass, and I am sorely tempted to scratch off the redundant 'e'. Breakfast sorted. We clink glasses and sing three

verses (because I can only remember three) of my favourite
French drinking song with all the actions:

Chevaliers de la Table Ronde,
Goûtons voir si le vin est bon.
Chevaliers de la Table Ronde,
Goûtons voir si le vin est bon.

Goûtons voir, oui, oui, oui,
Goûtons voir, non, non, non,
Goûtons voir si le vin est bon.

Quand je meurs, je veux qu'on m'enterre
Dans une cave où il y a du bon vin.
Quand je meurs, je veux qu'on m'enterre
Dans une cave où il y a du bon vin.

Dans une cave, oui, oui, oui,
Dans une cave, non, non, non,
Dans une cave où il y a du bon vin.

Les deux pieds contre la muraille
Et la tête sous le robinet.
Les deux pieds contre la muraille
Et la tête sous le robinet.

Et la tête, oui, oui, oui,
Et la tête, non, non, non,
Et la tête sous le robinet.

Knights of the Round Table
Knights of the Round Table,
Let's taste to see if the wine is good.

Knights of the Round Table,
Let's taste to see if the wine is good.

Let's taste, yes, yes, yes,
Let's taste, no, no, no,
Let's taste to see if the wine is good.

When I die, I want to be buried
In a cellar where there's good wine.
When I die, I want to be buried,
In a cellar where there's good wine.

In a cellar, yes, yes, yes,
In a cellar, no, no, no,
In a cellar where there's good wine.

My two feet against the wall
And my head under the tap
My two feet against the wall
And my head under the tap.

And my head, yes, yes, yes,
And my head, no, no, no,
And my head under the tap.

Apropos, if you can remember more than three verses then you are not adequately plastered.

Our friends Linda, Ian, Jill and Simon have organised a goodbye party for us. Maybe this is just to ensure that we are really leaving. It is a tearful moment to see all our friends together, corny Scottish music blasting over the valley, Saltires gently flapping in the breeze. The warmth of our friendships and the sense of belonging in our small community is palpable.

Linda is a turbocharged Olga Korbut, rushing in and out of the kitchen, as she tells us, 'My metabolism is like an elite sports athlete, hardly any pulse at all.' The feast is an epicurean delight. The humour flows effortlessly.

It reminds me of the joke where Putin tracks down Stalin, who is miraculously still alive in the Siberian Steppes. Putin goes to visit him and tries to persuade him that his people still need him and he should return with him to Moscow. 'Okay,' says Stalin. 'You have convinced me, but this time, no more Mr Nice Guy!'

We threaten our friends that we will be back sooner than they think.

Off to the lake tonight for a final swim and farewell, then *Allez Hop*!

Bonne continuation, as they say.

SCOTTISH GLOSSARY

bairn	n. a child of any age
bahookie	n. backside
bampot	n. col. An idiot, fool or nutcase
banter	to rebuke, scold, drive away by scolding
bawbag	col. the scrotum. An annoying or irritating person
beamer	a red face
belter	n. something great
birlin	hirling, twisting, dancing, hurrying
black-affrontit	thoroughly ashamed
blootered	adj. drunk, having been hit or kicked hard
boggin	col. adj. smelly, stinking
bonnie	adv. adj. beautifully, prettily, fairly,

	handsomely
bowfin	barking, smelly
brass neck	audacious
chancer	opportunist
clapped-oot	to be tired out
coorie in	to snuggle up to
crabbit	adj. in a bad temper, out of humour
dive	wretched, filthy place
douce	adj. sedate, sober, quiet, respectable, often with a connotation of circumspection or cautiousness. Pleasant, kindly, gentle, lovable. Neat, tidy, comfortable
dour	hard, implacable
dreich	adj. tedious, dull, protracted, dreary, hard to bear. Of time or journeys, etc.: long, wearisome, tedious, monotonous. Of speeches or sermons, etc.: long-winded, interminable, dull, dry, uninteresting. Of people: dull, gloomy, doleful. Of weather or scenery, etc.: dreary, cheerless, bleak.
drouthie	adj. thirsty. Addicted to drink. Of the weather: dry
dug	n. dog
feartie	col. a coward
foostie	adj. in a decayed state or smell
galoshans	going out for Hallowe'en in Greenock
ginger	fizzy drink
gie it laldy	to sing or do proudly; with great gusto
git oan wae it	best foot forward; assume your

	responsibilities
glaikit	adj. stupid, foolish, thoughtless
guddle	n. a mess, muddle, confusion. Toilsome, dirty or messy work
haiverin	babbling chatter. Nonsensical gossiping
haud yer wheesht	to call for silence
hooley	wild and windy weather n. as in blawn a hooley
jobbie	n. stool; turd
joogle	v. to juggle. To use sleight of hand
jotters	school notebook
(to get your) jotters	to be sacked
keek	n. a peep, a stolen glance
keich	n. ordure, excrement, filth or dirt of any kind. An exclamation of disgust, a warning to a child not to touch something dirty or undesirable.
kent	adj. known, recognisable
kerfuffle	n. disorder, mess, rumpling, creasing. A disagreement, quarrel. A state of excitement or agitation. v. To disarrange, throw into confusion, to disorder, to tumble, to crease.
kerry oan	something happening – pejorative
lugs	n. lugs; plural – a person's ears.
malarkey	up to something
manky	adj. inferior, worthless. Dirty and unpleasant
midden	a domestic ashpit or dusthold, a dirty place
numpty	an idiot

pan bried	dead
paralytic	drunk
peek	to have a sly look at something
peelie-wallie	sickly, feeble, pallid, delicate
piece	sandwich
plastered	drunk
plook	spot, blemish
ramy	fight
scorchio	hot weather
scunnered	tired out, fed up
shenanigans	pl. trickery, foolery, mischief, nonsense
short shrift	tight-lipped, curt treatment
skedaddle	to rush away
skeeter	to skid
skelf	very thin
skelp (past: skelpt)	to strike or hit with the palm of the hand, etc., to slap, smack
sleekit	adj. sly, hypocritical, smooth
smashed	drunk
squoosh	a dollop
steamin'	drunk
stoater	good-looking
stotious	drunk
stoushie	n. an uproar, hubbub, disturbance, commotion, turmoil, quarrel, brawl, row, frolic, banter
swally	drinking session
to swither	to be indecisive
take the huff	to be annoyed
taps aff	removal of outer vestments
The Broons	popular publication by Thomson comics

unco fou	drunk
wabbit	exhausted, tired out, played out, feeble, without energy
weans	children
wee	small
winching	necking, kissing

PERMISSIONS

Advice sought from copyright sources for permission to quote, where appropriate. I acknowledge and thank them for inspiring me.

Guidelines from 'The Copyright and Rights in Performances (Quotation and Parody) Regulations 2014' www.legislation.gov.uk

REFERENCES AND QUOTATIONS

Preface: Jimmy Reid. *Inaugural speech as Rector of Glasgow University. 28th April 1972.*

Ch.2: Shir Hever, *The Privatisation of Israel's Security.*

Ch.4: Quentin Crisp, *The Naked Civil Servant.* Craig Murray. On *Twitter.*

Ch.5: Christine de Védrines, *Nous n'étions pas armés.* Ghislaine de Védrines, *Diabolique.*

Ch.6: Unknown sources. Letters to newspapers 2004.

Henry Wadsworth Longfellow

Adapted. *There was a little girl,*
Who had a little curl,
Right in the middle of her forehead.
When she was good,
She was very, very good,
But when she was bad, she was horrid.

Ch.8: Mairi Hedderwick, *Katie Morag*. Stephen King. Excerpt, *On Writing*.

Ch.10: Robert Graves, *Goodbye to All That*.

Ch.11: Ksawery Pruszyński, *Polish Invasion*.

Ch.12: Hans Rosling, *Factfulness*.

Ch.12: ABBA, Andersson/Ulvaeus, excerpt from *Super Trouper*

Ch.13: Daniel Defoe, quote from *The Education of Women*.

Ch.15: Paul Verlaine, excerpt from poem, *Il pleure dans mon Coeur. Romances sans Paroles*. Louis MacNeice, line from poem, '*Circe*'.

R. Ortyl, Winter edition of *Lo Tambourinaïre* 2018–2019.

2018 aura été marquée par le mouvement des Gilets Jaunes, reflet d'un malaise, d'un mal-être grandissant depuis un trentaine d'années. Effectivement, on a l'impression de vivre dans un pays bicéphale, où on a oublié, ignoré, la France rurale et péri-urbaine.

Souhaitons que ce movement permettre à certains d'ouvrir les yeux, d'entendre, afin que tout le monde puisse vivre dans la dignité.

Eric Boswell, excerpt from the Christmas carol '*Little Donkey*'.

Ch.16: Mick Hume, *Trigger Warning: Is the Fear of Being Offensive Killing Free Speech?* Evelyn Beatrice Hall, *quote*. RSF Reporters sans Frontières. Reporters Without Borders, *quote*.

Ch.17: Mary Elizabeth Frye, excerpt from poem, 'Do not stand at my grave and weep'.

Ch.29: Maria Konopnicka, *Jadą, jadą dzieci drogą*.

Ch.20: Michel Montaigne, *Les Essais*.

Ch.22: Bertolt Brecht, *two quotes*. Tony Greenstein, *quote*.

Dominique Vidal, *Antisionisme = Antisémitisme?*

Ch.23: John Walter Bratton & Jimmy Kennedy, '*The Teddy Bears' Picnic*'.

Ch.28: DC Thomson, *The Beano*, *The Numskulls* comic strip.
Sheryl Sandberg, *Lean In*.
Wace (Norman poet), *Chevaliers de la Table Ronde*.
Epilogue: Philip Pullman, *on Twitter*.

EPILOGUE

It's all got to change. If we come out of this crisis with all the rickety, flyblown, worm-eaten old structures still intact, the same vain and indolent public schoolboys still in charge, the same hedge fund managers stuffing their overloaded pockets with greasy fingers, our descendants will not forgive us. Nor should they. We must burn out the old corruption and establish a better way of living together.

Philip Pullman.

This memoir started life as 'Bunnies can and will go to France', a nod to the line Jeremy Thorpe famously wrote to his erstwhile lover. It then became 'A Year in Aquitaine. Allez hop!' followed by 'Fanny Coiffure and the Year in Aquitaine' before settling on the less than snappy 'From the River to the Sea: Aquitaine, A Place for Me'. Decisiveness has never been one of my strong points. I could have given it the even less snappy title of 'Pre-COVID 19 Aquitaine', which lends a scholarly air, one that would fire up palaeontologists.

I am writing this in week five of COVID-19 lockdown in Glasgow. Our life in Aquitaine feels like a cocoon suspended in a past life. We long to get back there. Gerry and I have both had a mild dose of the virus and now have recovered. Rocco the dog has proved to be gold dust as he gives us the perfect excuse to go for a walk. Everything has been cancelled or postponed; our Easter in France and Ziggy's wedding plans have fallen by the wayside. Shoplifters and burglars are grumbling about lack of opportunities to ply their trade and the methadone queue is getting longer outside the chemist. 'Ridiculous,' I hear one say. 'If the sign says the shop opens at 9am then it should be open at that time.' He crosses his arms in indignation.

Boarded-up shops still promote Mother's Day and others are 'closed due to flooding'. That's what is called a double whammy. There are no planes in the sky, few cars on the ground; businesses are going ping and bust; Boris Johnson exhorts us to shake hands with everyone and promptly ends up in intensive care. Parks are full to the brim with people out for their one-hour ration of exercise; police are moving in on old ladies who have been resting too long on benches, although most people observe the two-metre social distancing rule. Trump has been encouraging Americans to ingest bleach; billionaires with their wealth in tax havens seek government bailouts – where is that magic money tree when you want it? Every evening we are hooked on the television screens, clocking up the daily death toll. A woman of 108 dies of COVID-19; her sister died of Spanish flu in 1918.

Nature has regenerated itself – the foxes screech and cavort at night; the cherry blossoms have taken over from the daffodil display. I have actually been forced to buy suntan lotion as it is the hottest April for the last forty years; I am starting to burn, for God's sake! There is an eerie calm; we keep ourselves to ourselves with virtual get-togethers with friends on the internet a few evenings a week and on Thursday night at 8pm the whole neighbourhood comes out to clap for the NHS and a bagpiper strikes up a tune. We are tentatively going back to work; remotely, as they say. Brexit, what's that? Theresa May, who is she? Wild hair is de rigueur, and I am cultivating an Indira Gandhi grey streak; none too fetching. A drunk man throws himself into the canal in front of us – but that is another story.

ACKNOWLEDGEMENTS

As George Michael said 'You gotta have faith'. I owe so much to those people who not only had faith in my ability to put words on paper in an interesting pattern, but kept on reading the drafts, offering invaluable suggestions and gentle nudges when I strayed off the path. Thanks to my first critics, Ian Herbert and Kathryn Potter; Annette McGarill for proof-reading; Alison Hill (luminous lone wolf); my fellow schemies, Jennifer Smith (honest, I will learn to punctuate, properly, one day) and Fran Cunningham (if only tortoises could read); Bryony Small and Alasdair Smith (who helped me find the right title), stalwarts Liana Marletta and Ann Fairfull and the ever-wise, ever-helpful Vicky McGraw.

Thanks to Heather Nevay for the gift of the beautiful cover illustration.

Thanks as always to Gerry Coutts; you can put away that scythe.

Thanks to the brilliant team at Matador/Troubador.

Thanks to Sharon Lancaster, Christine Bovill, Julie Brittain and Yvonne Blair for their constant encouragement. 'Stop swithering, get off your backside and write,' Muriel Gray told me, many years ago. Well, I have now.

 **Matador**